D1246356

Rand McNally
Pocket Atlas

Rand McNally & Company
Chicago • New York • San Francisco

CONTENTS

© 1980 Rand McNally & Company
All rights reserved.
Printed in the United States of America
Library of Congress Catalog Card Number: 80-83201
Second Printing

4/THE SOLAR SYSTEM

Our solar system is a tiny part of one of the millions of galaxies that make up the universe. The diameter of the solar system is about four light years, while that of its galaxy is an estimated 100,000 light years. The solar system consists of planets, moons, asteroids, comets, meteorites, dust and gases, and a central star, the Sun, around which the other bodies revolve.

The Sun is composed mainly of hydrogen and helium, and its energy comes from thermo-nuclear reactions which convert hydrogen to helium. It has a surface temperature around 6,000°C.

The solar system is about 4,600 million years old. Nearest the Sun are four relatively small, solid planets— Mercury, Venus, Earth, and Mars. Beyond Mars is a belt of minor planets called asteroids, and then four huge, low-density planets—Jupiter, Saturn, Uranus, and Neptune. Pluto, the outermost planet, is smaller than the other outer region planets. Seven planets—Earth, Mars, Jupiter, Saturn, Uranus, Neptune and Pluto—have satellites, or moons, in orbit around them.

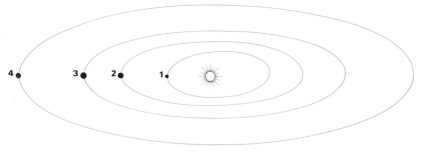

Above The orbits of the planets around the Sun. All planets travel in the same direction around the Sun, and most move in the same plane. Their paths are not perfect circles, and the nearer a planet is to the Sun the faster it moves.

Inner region planets
1 Mercury
2 Venus
3 Earth
4 Mars

1 Mercury
2 Venus
3 Earth
4 Mars
5 Jupiter
6 Saturn
7 Uranus

Above The relative distance of the planets from the Sun.

	Equatorial diameter (Earth = 1 or 7,926.4 ms)	Mass (Earth = 1)	Mean density (Water = 1) *Varies greatly with depth	Number of satellites	Mean distance from Sun (Earth = 1 or 92,957,000 ms)	Sidereal period of revolution around Sun	Mean orbital velocity (X miles/second)	Sidereal period of rotation on axis **25 days at Equator 33 days at 75° Latitude	Inclination of equator
Sun	109.2	333,000	1.5*	—	—	—	—	25.0 days**	7°
Mercury	0.38	0.06	5.42	0	0.39	88.0 days	29.7	58.6 days	‹7°
Venus	0.95	0.82	5.27	0	0.72	224.7 days	21.7	243.1 days	175°
Earth	1	1	5.52	1	1	1.00 yrs	18.5	23h 56m 04s	23°45
Mars	0.53	0.11	4.05	2	1.52	1.88 yrs	15.0	24h 37m 23s	24°9
Jupiter	11.19	318	1.33	14	5.20	11.86 yrs	8.1	09h 55m 30s	3°1
Saturn	9.47	95.2	0.69	11	9.54	29.46 yrs	6.0	10h 40m	26°7
Uranus	4.11	14.6	1.17	5	19.18	84.02 yrs	4.2	12h 48m	97°9
Neptune	3.50	17.2	1.66	2	30.06	164.8 yrs	3.4	15h 48m	28°8
Pluto	.24	.002	1	1	39.44	247.7 yrs	2.9	6d 09h 17m	?

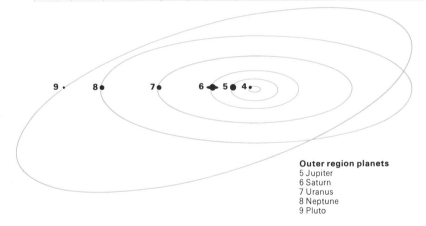

Outer region planets
5 Jupiter
6 Saturn
7 Uranus
8 Neptune
9 Pluto

8 Neptune   9 Pluto

Below The size of the Sun relative to Earth : the Sun's diameter is 109.2 times greater.

6/THE PLANETS

All the planets were probably formed at much the same time from the same great dust cloud. Despite this, they differ from each other in many ways.

1 Mercury is the smallest known planet and is thought to be mostly metals. If it has an atmosphere, this is probably of heavy inert gases such as krypton and xenon. Its year lasts 88 days. Mercury rotates on its axis once every 58.6 days. This long day and the planet's nearness to the Sun give Mercury a mid-day temperature around 350°C.

2 Venus is almost the same size as Earth and is probably similar in structure. It is, however, too hot to support similar life. The atmosphere of carbon dioxide is so dense and opaque that we can see the planet's surface only by radar. Venus spins on its own axis once every 243 Earth days. Its year lasts 224.7 Earth days, and so is slightly shorter than its day. Venus has no moons.

3 Earth is the largest of the inner planets. It has a dense iron-rich core, surrounded by layers of silicate rock. The thin outer layer, the crust, is seven-tenths covered with water. This water and the atmosphere containing oxygen and nitrogen make life possible. Surface temperatures vary between —90°C and +60°C. Earth rotates on its axis once every 23 hours 56 minutes 4 seconds. It is thought that

the Earth and Moon might be a double-planet system.

4 Mars is smaller than Earth. Its surface is cratered like the Moon and is a distinctive red. The thin atmosphere of carbon dioxide condenses at the poles to form 'ice' caps. There is as yet no firm evidence of life on Mars. Its day is almost the same length as that of Earth, but its year is almost twice as long. Mars has two moons.

The Asteroids are many thousands of small bodies, with diameters ranging from less than one mile to several hundred miles. They orbit the Sun mainly between Mars and Jupiter, though some have eccentric orbits that bring them within

500,000 miles of Earth.

5 Jupiter is the largest planet of the solar system. Its thick atmosphere contains hydrogen and helium. There are distinctive cloud belts and spots, of which the 'Great Red Spot' is apparently semi-permanent. Jupiter spins very rapidly, and its day is only 9 hours 55 minutes 30 seconds long. There are fourteen known satellites, with approximate diameters ranging from 10 miles to 3,240 miles.

6 Saturn is almost as large as Jupiter. It consists mainly of hydrogen and helium, and its density is so low that a typical sample would float on water. The rings around the planet are accumulations of ice-covered fragments.

Saturn's day is 10 hours 40 minutes long. There are eleven known satellites, with diameters between 130 miles and 3,000 miles.

7 Uranus, unlike all the other planets, rotates on its side. Its day lasts about 12 hours 50 minutes. Surface temperatures are very low, approximately —180°C. Methane in the atmosphere makes this planet appear green. Uranus has five satellites.

8 Neptune is similar to Uranus and it, too, has methane in its atmosphere and so looks green. Neptune's day is about 15 hours 50 minutes long. There are two satellites— one large and one very small.

9 Pluto was discovered only in 1930, and as yet little is known about this remotest planet. Pluto is much smaller than Neptune, and has a diameter probably about one quarter that of Earth. The orbit of Pluto is extremely elliptical, and the day is some 6.387 hours long. There is probably no atmosphere and there is one known moon.

8/THE MOON

The Moon travels around the Earth every 27.3 days at a mean distance of 238,860 miles. It has no atmosphere, no weather, and no wind. There is a thick dust covering and no evidence to suggest that the Moon has ever supported life. The dark areas of comparatively smooth low ground are called 'maria', or seas. The brightly reflecting, rugged mountains are called 'terrae'. The surface of the Moon is in all regions pitted with circular craters, of which the largest measure as much as 125 miles in diameter.

Right Man goes to the Moon—the landing sites of the US Apollo program.

Apollo 11 Sea of Tranquility (0°41'N, 23°26'E)

Apollo 12 Ocean of Storms (2°41'S, 23°34'W)

Apollo 14 Fra Mauro (3°40'S, 17°28'W)

Apollo 15 Hadly Rill (26°5'N, 3°40'E)

Apollo 16 Descartes (8°45'S, 15°30'E)

Apollo 17 Sea of Serenity (20°10'N, 30°45'E)

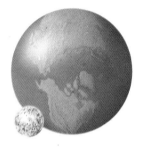

Above The diameter of the Moon is 2,160 miles, almost a quarter that of the Earth. Its mass is 1/81 that of the Earth.

Right The phases of the Moon. Since the Moon goes around the Earth in the same time that it takes to spin on its own axis, it always presents the same face to Earth. It is only the amount of the Moon visible from Earth that changes.

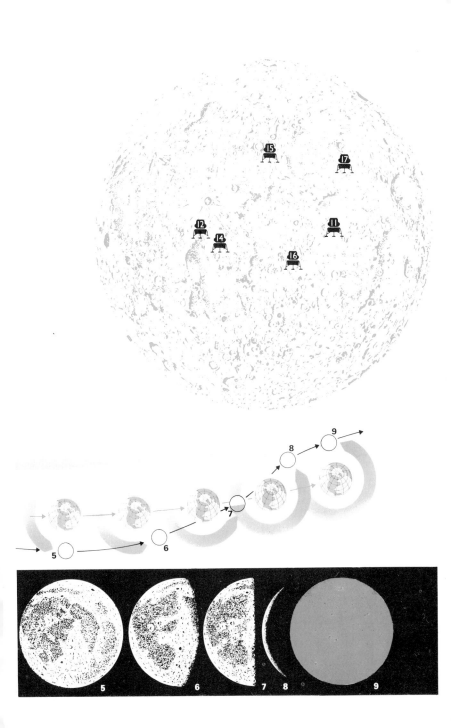

Capitals	Time Zones
Accra	12
Addis Ababa	15
Amsterdam	13
Ankara	15
Athens	14
Baghdad	15
Bangkok	19
Beirut	14
Belgrade	13
Berlin	13
Bern	13
Bogotá	7
Bon	13
Brasília	9
Brazzaville	13
Brussels	13
Bucharest	14
Budapest	13
Buenos Aires	9
Cairo	14
Caracas	8
Canberra	22
Colombo	17½
Copenhagen	13
Dacca	18
Dar-es-Salaam	15
Dublin	12
Hanoi	19
Jakarta	19
Kampala	15
Khartoum	14
Kuala Lumpur	19½
Lagos	13
Lisbon	12
London	12
Lusaka	14
Madrid	13
Manila	20
Mexico City	6
Moscow	15
Nairobi	15
New Delhi	17½
Oslo	13
Ottawa	7
Paris	13
Peking	20
Prague	13
Pretoria	14
Rabat	12
Reykjavik	12
Rome	13
Santiago	8
Seoul	21
Sofia	14
Stockholm	13
Tehran	15½
Tel Aviv	14
Tōkyō	21
Tunis	13
Vienna	13
Warsaw	13
Washington	7
Wellington	24

The world is divided into 24 time zones, each comprising about 15 degrees of longitude. This division is based on the mean solar time of the meridian of Greenwich, England (0° longitude), which is used as the prime basis of Standard Time throughout most of the world. Each country or section of a country within a time zone adopts the Standard Time most convenient to it. In summer, some countries adopt Daylight Saving Time, which is one hour ahead of Standard Time. Another demarcation is the International Date Line, which follows generally 180° longitude. Countries west of this line are one day ahead of those east of it.

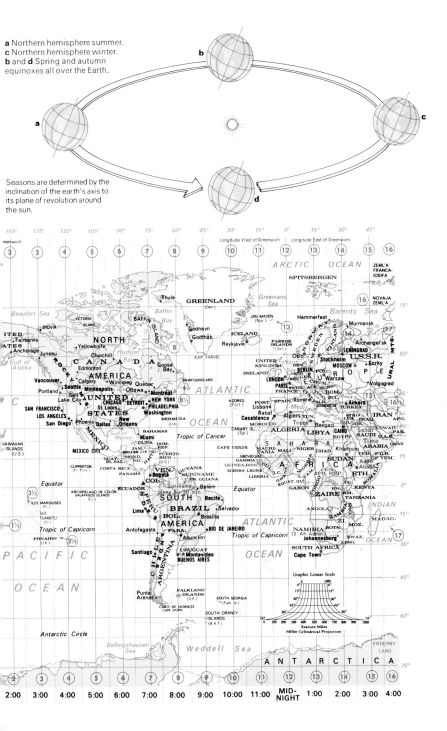

a Northern hemisphere summer.
c Northern hemisphere winter.
b and **d** Spring and autumn
equinoxes all over the Earth.

Seasons are determined by the
inclination of the earth's axis to
its plane of revolution around
the sun.

Great Circle distances between principal cities in statute miles and kilometres	Berlin, Germany	Bombay, India	Cape Town, South Africa	Darwin, Australia	Honolulu, Hawaii, U.S.	London, United Kingdom	Los Angeles, U.S.	Cuidad de México (Mexico City), Mexico	Moskva (Moscow), U.S.S.R.
Berlin, Germany		3910 6256	5977 9563	8036 12858	7305 11688	574 918	5782 9251	6037 9659	996 1594
Bombay, India	3910 6256		5134 8214	4503 7205	8020 12832	4462 7139	8701 13922	9722 15555	3131 5010
Cape Town, South Africa	5977 9563	5134 8214		6947 11115	11532 18451	6005 9608	9969 15950	8511 13618	6294 10070
Darwin, Australia	8036 12858	4303 7205	6947 11115		5355 8568	8598 13757	7835 12536	9081 14530	7046 11274
Honolulu, Hawaii, U.S.	7305 11688	8020 12832	11532 18451	5355 8568		7226 11562	2557 4091	3781 6050	7033 11253
London, United Kingdom	574 918	4462 7139	6005 9608	8598 13757	7226 11562		5439 8702	5541 8866	1549 2478
Los Angeles, U.S.	5782 9251	8701 13922	9969 15950	7835 12536	2557 4091	5439 8762		1542 2467	6068 9709
Cuidad de México (Mexico City), Mexico	6037 9659	9722 15555	8511 13618	9081 14530	3781 6050	5541 8866	1542 2467		6688 10700
Moskva (Moscow), U.S.S.R	996 1594	3131 5010	6294 10070	7046 11274	7033 11253	1549 2478	6068 9709	6688 10700	
New York, U.S.	3961 6338	7794 12470	7801 12482	9959 15934	4959 7934	3459 5534	2451 3922	2085 3336	4662 7459
Nome, Alaska, U.S.	4342 6947	5901 9442	10107 16171	6235 9976	3004 4806	4381 7010	2876 4602	4309 6894	4036 6458
Paris, France	542 867	4359 6974	5841 9346	8575 13720	7434 11894	213 341	5601 8962	5706 9130	1541 2466
Beijing (Peking), China	4567 7307	2964 4742	8045 12872	3728 5965	5067 8107	5054 8086	5054 8086	7733 12373	3597 5755
Būr Sāīd (Port Sudan), Egypt	1747 2795	2659 4254	4590 7344	7159 11454	8738 13981	2154 3446	7528 12045	7671 12274	1710 2736
Québec, Canada	3583 5733	7371 11794	7857 12571	9724 15558	5000 8000	3101 4962	2579 4126	2454 3926	4242 6787
Rio de Janeiro, Brazil	6144 9830	8257 13211	3769 6030	9960 15936	8190 13104	5772 9235	6296 10074	4770 7632	7179 11486
Roma (Rome), Italy	734 1174	3843 6149	5249 8398	8190 13104	8022 12835	887 1419	6326 10122	6353 10165	1474 2358
Singapore	6166 9866	2429 3886	6016 9626	2075 3320	6710 10736	6744 10790	8767 14027	10307 16491	5238 8381
Tōkyō, Japan	5538 8861	4188 6701	9071 14514	3367 5387	3850 6160	5938 9501	5470 8752	7035 11256	4650 7440
Wellington, New Zealand	11265 18024	7677 12283	7019 11230	3310 5296	4708 7532	11682 18691	6714 10742	6899 11038	10279 16446
Winnipeg, Canada	4286 6858	7644 12230	9054 14486	8684 13894	3806 6090	3918 6269	1525 2440	2097 3355	4687 7499
Zanzibar, Tanzania	4309 6894	2855 4568	2346 3754	6409 10254	10869 17390	4604 7366	10021 16034	9484 15174	4270 6832

New York, U.S.	Nome, Alaska, U.S.	Paris, France	Beijing (Peking), China	Būr Sāid (Port Sudan), Egypt	Québec, Canada	Rio de Janeiro, Brazil	Roma (Rome), Italy	Singapore	Tōkyō, Japan	Wellington, New Zealand	Winnipeg, Canada	Zanzibar, Tanzania
3961 / 6338	4342 / 6947	542 / 867	4567 / 7307	1747 / 2795	3583 / 5733	6144 / 9830	734 / 1174	6166 / 9866	5538 / 8861	11265 / 18024	4286 / 6858	4309 / 6894
7794 / 12470	5901 / 9442	4359 / 6974	2964 / 4742	2659 / 4254	7371 / 11794	8257 / 13211	3843 / 6149	2429 / 3886	4188 / 6701	7677 / 12283	7644 / 12230	2855 / 4568
7801 / 12482	10107 / 16171	5841 / 9346	8045 / 12872	4590 / 7344	7857 / 12571	3769 / 6030	5249 / 8398	6016 / 9626	9071 / 14514	7019 / 11230	9054 / 14486	2346 / 3754
9959 / 15934	6235 / 9976	8575 / 13720	3728 / 5965	7159 / 11454	9724 / 15558	9960 / 15936	8190 / 13104	2075 / 3320	3367 / 5387	3310 / 5296	8684 / 13894	6409 / 10254
4959 / 7934	3004 / 4806	7434 / 11894	5067 / 8107	8738 / 13981	5000 / 8000	8190 / 13104	8022 / 12835	6710 / 10736	3850 / 6160	4708 / 7532	3806 / 6090	10869 / 17390
3459 / 5534	4381 / 7010	213 / 341	5054 / 8086	2154 / 3446	3101 / 4962	5772 / 9235	887 / 1419	6744 / 10790	5938 / 9501	11682 / 18691	3918 / 6269	4604 / 7366
2451 / 3922	2876 / 4602	5601 / 8962	6250 / 10000	7528 / 12045	2579 / 4126	6296 / 10074	6326 / 10122	8767 / 14027	5470 / 8752	6714 / 10742	1525 / 2440	10021 / 16034
2085 / 3336	4309 / 6894	5706 / 9130	7733 / 12373	7671 / 12274	2454 / 3926	4770 / 7632	6353 / 10165	10307 / 16491	7035 / 11256	6899 / 11038	2097 / 3355	9484 / 15174
4662 / 7459	4036 / 6458	1541 / 2466	3597 / 5755	1710 / 2736	4242 / 6787	7179 / 11486	1474 / 2358	5238 / 8381	4650 / 7440	10279 / 16446	4687 / 7499	4270 / 6832
	3769 / 6030	3622 / 5795	6823 / 10917	5590 / 8944	439 / 702	4820 / 7712	4273 / 6837	9630 / 15408	6735 / 10776	8946 / 14314	1281 / 2050	7698 / 12317
3769 / 6030		4574 / 7318	3428 / 5483	5745 / 9192	3489 / 5582	8586 / 13738	5082 / 8131	6148 / 9837	2983 / 4773	7383 / 11813	2599 / 4158	8209 / 13134
3622 / 5795	4574 / 7318		5101 / 8162	1975 / 3160	3235 / 5176	5703 / 9125	682 / 1091	6671 / 10674	6033 / 9653	11791 / 18866	4118 / 6589	4396 / 7034
6823 / 10917	3428 / 5483	5101 / 8162		4584 / 7334	6423 / 10277	10768 / 17229	5047 / 8075	2774 / 4438	1307 / 2091	6698 / 10717	5907 / 9451	5803 / 9285
5590 / 8944	5745 / 9192	1975 / 3160	4584 / 7334		5250 / 8400	6244 / 9990	1317 / 2107	5088 / 8141	5842 / 9347	10249 / 16398	6032 / 9651	2729 / 4366
439 / 702	3489 / 5582	3255 / 5176	6423 / 10277	5250 / 8400		5125 / 8200	3943 / 6309	9097 / 14555	6417 / 10267	9228 / 14765	1199 / 1918	7443 / 11909
4820 / 7712	8586 / 13788	5703 / 8125	10768 / 17229	6244 / 9990	5125 / 8200		5684 / 9094	9774 / 15638	11535 / 18456	7349 / 11758	6010 / 9616	5589 / 8942
4273 / 6837	5082 / 8131	682 / 1091	5047 / 8075	1317 / 2107	3943 / 6309	5684 / 9094		6232 / 9971	6124 / 9798	11524 / 18438	4803 / 7685	3712 / 5939
9630 / 15408	6148 / 9837	6671 / 10674	2774 / 4438	5088 / 8141	9097 / 14555	9774 / 15638	6232 / 9971		3304 / 5286	5292 / 8467	8685 / 13896	4480 / 7168
6735 / 10776	2983 / 4773	6033 / 9653	1307 / 2091	5842 / 9347	6417 / 10267	11535 / 18456	6124 / 9798	3304 / 5286		5760 / 9216	5575 / 8920	7040 / 11264
8946 / 14314	7383 / 11813	11791 / 18866	6698 / 10717	10249 / 16398	9228 / 14765	7349 / 11758	11524 / 18438	5292 / 8467	5760 / 9216		8230 / 13168	8122 / 12995
1281 / 2050	2599 / 4158	4118 / 6589	5907 / 9451	6032 / 9651	1199 / 1918	6010 / 9616	4803 / 7685	8685 / 13896	5575 / 8920	8230 / 13168		8416 / 13465
7698 / 12317	8209 / 13134	4396 / 7434	5803 / 9285	2729 / 4366	7443 / 11909	5589 / 8942	3712 / 5939	4480 / 7168	7040 / 11264	8122 / 12995	8416 / 13465	

14/INFORMATION TABLE OF NATIONS

Nation	Area in sq. miles	Population 1/1/80 (est.)	Pop. per sq. mile	Form of government
Afghanistan	250,000	15,670,000	63	Republic
Albania	11,100	2,785,000	251	People's Republic
Algeria	919,595	19,415,000	21	Republic
Andorra	175	36,000	206	Principality
Angola	481,353	7,875,000	16	People's Republic
Argentina	1,068,301	26,885,000	25	Federal Republic
Australia	2,967,909	14,510,000	5	Monarchy (Federal)*
Austria	32,374	7,505,000	232	Federal Republic
Bahamas	5,380	235,000	44	Parliamentary State*
Bahrain	240	305,000	1,271	Emirate
Bangladesh	55,597	87,560,000	1,575	Republic*
Barbados	166	260,000	1,566	Parliamentary State*
Belgium	11,781	9,890,000	839	Monarchy
Benin	43,484	3,510,000	81	Republic
Bolivia	424,164	7,370,000	17	Republic
Botswana	231,805	750,000	3	Republic*
Brazil	3,286,488	120,400,000	37	Federal Republic
Bulgaria	42,823	8,865,000	207	People's Republic
Burma	261,218	33,255,000	127	Federal Republic
Burundi (Urundi)	10,747	4.435,000	413	Republic
Cameroon	183,569	8,310,000	45	Federal Republic
Canada	3,851,809	23,845,000	6	Monarchy (Federal)*
Cape Verde	1,557	320,000	206	Republic
Central African Republic	240,535	2,010,000	8	Republic
Chad	495,755	4,455,000	9	Republic
Chile	292,258	11,170,000	38	Republic
China (excl. Taiwan)	3,705,407	933,070,000	252	People's Republic
Colombia	439,737	26,710,000	61	Republic
Comoros	719	390,000	542	Republic
Congo	132,046	1,505,000	11	Republic
Costa Rica	19,575	2,185,000	112	Republic
Cuba	44,218	9,930,000	225	Republic
Cyprus	3,572	620,000	174	Republic*
Czechoslovakia	49,370	15,310,000	310	People's Republic
Denmark	16,629	5,120,000	308	Monarchy

Capital city	Currency	Predominant languages
Kābul	Afghāni	Dari, Pushtu
Tiranë	Lek	Albanian
Algiers (Alger)	Dinar	Arabic, French, Berber
Andorra	French franc, Spanish peseta	Catalan, Spanish, French
Luanda	Escudo	Bantu languages, Portuguese
Buenos Aires	Peso	Spanish
Canberra	Dollar	English
Vienna (Wien)	Schilling	German
Nassau	Dollar	English
Al-Manāmah	Dinar	Arabic
Dacca	Taka	Bangla, English
Bridgetown	Dollar	English
Brussels (Bruxelles)	Franc	Dutch, French
Porto-Novo	Franc	French, native languages
Sucre and La Paz	Peso	Spanish, Quechua, Aymará
Gaborone	Pula	Bechuana, other Bantu languages, English
Brasília	Cruzeiro	Portuguese
Sofia (Sofija)	Leva	Bulgarian
Rangoon	Kyat	Burmese, English
Bujumbura	Franc	Bantu and Hamitic languages, English
Yaoundé	CFA franc	French, English, native languages
Ottawa	Dollar	English, French
Praia	Escudo	Portuguese
Bangui	CFA franc	French, native languages
Ndjamena	CFA franc	French, native languages
Santiago	Peso	Spanish
Peking (Beijing)	Yuan	Chinese, Mongolian, Turkish, Tungus
Bogotá	Peso	Spanish
Moroni	CFA franc	Comoran, French
Brazzaville	CFA franc	French, native languages
San José	Colon	Spanish
Havana (La Habana)	Peso	Spanish
Nicosia (Levkosia)	Pound	Greek, Turkish, English
Prague (Praha)	Koruny	Czech, Slovak
Copenhagen (København)	Kroner	Danish

Nation	Area in sq. miles	Population 1/1/80 (est.)	Pop. per sq. mile	Form of government
Djibouti	8,494	143,000	17	Republic
Dominica	290	83,000	286	Republic*
Dominican Republic	18,816	5,330,000	283	Republic
Ecuador	109,483	8,190,000	75	Republic
Egypt†	386,661	40,980,000	106	Republic
El Salvador	8,124	4,505,000	555	Republic
Equatorial Guinea	10,830	335,000	31	Republic
Ethiopia	471,778	30,415,000	64	Provisional Military Government
Fiji	7,055	635,000	90	Monarchy (Federal)*
Finland	130,119	4,780,000	37	Republic
France	211,207	53,580,000	254	Republic
Gabon	103,347	545,000	5	Republic
Gambia	4,361	595,000	136	Republic*
German Democratic Republic	41,768	16,740,000	401	People's Republic
Germany, Federal Republic of (incl. West Berlin)	95,960	61,170,000	637	Federal Republic
Ghana	92,100	11,475,000	125	Republic*
Greece	50,944	9,490,000	186	Republic
Grenada	133	115,000	865	Parliamentary State*
Guatemala	42,042	6,890,000	164	Republic
Guinea	94,964	4,935,000	52	Republic
Guinea-Bissau	13,948	570,000	41	Republic
Guyana	83,000	840,000	10	Republic*
Haiti	10,714	4,950,000	462	Republic
Honduras	43,277	3,100,000	72	Republic
Hungary	35,920	10,775,000	300	People's Republic
Iceland	39,768	225,000	6	Republic
India (incl. part of Kashmir)	1,269,345	657,240,000	518	Republic*
Indonesia (incl. West Irian)	735,271	150,070,000	204	Republic
Iran	636,300	36,525,000	57	Republic
Iraq	167,925	12,955,000	77	Republic
Ireland	27,137	3,325,000	123	Republic
Israel†	8,019	3,810,000	475	Republic
Italy	116,303	57,080,000	491	Republic

Capital city	Currency	Predominant languages
Djibouti	Franc	Arabic, French
Roseau	East Caribbean dollar	English, French
Santo Domingo	Peso	Spanish
Quito	Sucre	Spanish, Quechua
Cairo (Al-Qāhirah)	Pound	Arabic
San Salvador	Colon	Spanish
Malabo	Ekuele	Spanish, native languages
Addis Abeba	Birr	Amharic, Arabic, Hamitic dialects
Suva	Dollar	English, Fijian, Hindustani
Helsinki	Markka	Finnish, Swedish
Paris	Franc	French
Libreville	CFA franc	French, native languages
Banjul (Bathurst)	Dalasi	English, native languages
East Berlin	Ostmark	German
Bonn	Deutsche Mark	German
Accra	Cedi	English, native languages
Athens (Athínai)	Drachma	Greek
Saint George's	East Caribbean dollar	English
Guatemala	Quetzal	Spanish, Indian languages
Conakry	Syli	Native languages. French
Bissau	Escudo	Portuguese, native languages
Georgetown	Dollar	English
Port-au-Prince	Gourde	Creole, French
Tegucigalpa	Lempira	Spanish
Budapest	Forint	Hungarian
Reykjavik	Króna	Icelandic
New Delhi	Rupee	Hindu and other Indo-Aryan languages Dravidian languages, English
Jakarta	Rupiah	Indonesian, Chinese, English
Tehrān	Rial	Farsi, Turkish dialects, Kurdish
Baghdād	Dinar	Arabic, Kurdish
Dublin	Pound	English, Irish
Jerusalem (Yerushalayim)	Pound	Hebrew, Arabic, English
Rome (Roma)	Lira	Italian

Nation	Area in sq. miles	Population 1/1/80 (est.)	Pop. per sq. mile	Form of government
Ivory Coast	124,504	8,135,000	65	Republic
Jamaica	4,243	2,190,000	516	Parliamentary State*
Japan	143,750	116,480,000	810	Monarchy
Jordan†	37,738	3,130,000	83	Monarchy
Kampuchea	69,898	6,785,000	97	People's Republic
Kenya	224,960	15,625,000	69	Republic*
Kiribati	342	62,000	181	Republic*
Korea, North	46,540	17,635,000	379	People's Republic
Korea, South	38,024	37,890,000	996	Republic
Kuwait	6,879	1,300,000	189	Sheikdom
Laos	91,428	3,680,000	40	People's Republic
Lebanon	4,015	3,115,000	776	Republic
Lesotho	11,720	1,330,000	113	Monarchy*
Liberia	43,000	1,825,000	42	Republic
Libya	679,362	2,930,000	4	Republic
Liechtenstein	61	26,000	426	Principality
Luxembourg	998	350,000	351	Grand Duchy
Madagascar	226,658	8,610,000	38	Republic
Malawi	45,747	5,820,000	127	Republic*
Malaysia	128,430	13,480,000	105	Constitutional Monarchy*
Maldives	115	150,000	1,304	Republic
Mali	478,766	6,545,000	14	Republic
Malta	122	340,000	2,787	Republic*
Mauritania	397,950	1,600,000	4	Republic
Mauritius (incl. Dependencies)	789	940,000	1,191	Parliamentary State*
Mexico	761,604	70,435,000	92	Federal Republic
Monaco	0.4	26,000	65,000	Principality
Mongolia	604,249	1,650,000	3	People's Republic
Morocco	172,415	19,815,000	115	Monarchy
Mozambique	302,329	10,325,000	34	People's Republic
Nauru	8	10,000	1,250	Republic*
Nepal	54,362	13,840,000	255	Monarchy
Netherlands	15,770	14,075,000	893	Monarchy
New Zealand	103,736	3,155,000	30	Monarchy*
Nicaragua	50,193	2,535,000	51	Republic

Capital city	Currency	Predominant languages
Abidjan	CFA franc	French, native languages
Kingston	Dollar	English
Tōkyō	Yen	Japanese
'Ammān	Dinar	Arabic
Phnum Pénh	Riel	Cambodian (Khmer), French
Nairobi	Pound	English, Swahili, native languages
Tarawa (island)	Australian dollar	Malay-Polynesian languages, English
P'yŏngyang	Won	Korean
Seoul (Sŏul)	Won	Korean
Kuwait (Al Kuwayt)	Dinar	Arabic
Viangchan (Vientiane)	Liberation kip	Lao, French
Beirut (Bayrūt)	Pound	Arabic, French, English
Maseru	South African rand	Sesotho, English
Monrovia	Dollar	Native languages, English
Tripoli (Tarābulus)	Dinar	Arabic
Vaduz	Swiss franc	German
Luxembourg	Franc	Luxembourgish, French, German
Antananarivo	Franc	French, Malagasy
Lilongwe	Kwacha	Chichewa, English
Kuala Lumpur	Ringgit	Malay, Chinese, English
Male	Rupee	Divehi, Arabic
Bamako	Franc	French, Bambara
Valletta	Pound	English, Maltese
Nouakchott	Ouguiya	Arabic, French
Port Louis	Rupee	English, French, Creole
Mexico City (Ciudad de México)	Peso	Spanish
Monaco	Franc	French, Italian
Ulaan Baatar	Tugrik	Mongolian
Rabat	Dirham	Arabic, Berber, French
Maputo	Escudo	Portuguese, native languages
Yaren	Australian pound	Nauruan, English
Kāthmāndu	Rupee	Nepali, Tibeto-Burman languages
Amsterdam and 's-Gravenhage (The Hague)	Guilder	Dutch
Wellington	Dollar	English, Maori
Managua	Córdoba	Spanish

Nation	Area in sq. miles	Population 1/1/80 (est.)	Pop. per sq. mile	Form of government
Niger	489,191	5,190,000	11	Republic
Nigeria	356,669	75,600,000	212	Republic*
Norway	125,182	4,085,000	33	Monarchy
Oman	82,030	880,000	11	Sultanate
Pakistan (incl. part of Kashmir)	310,404	82,570,000	266	Federal Republic
Panama	29,762	1,960,000	66	Republic
Papua New Guinea	178,260	3,110,000	17	Parliamentary State*
Paraguay	157,048	2,990,000	19	Republic
Peru	496,224	17,505,000	35	Republic
Philippines	115,831	48,315,000	417	Republic
Poland	120,725	34,490,000	294	People's Republic
Portugal	35,553	9,900,000	278	Republic
Qatar	4,247	215,000	51	Emirate
Romania	91,699	22,145,000	241	People's Republic
Rwanda	10,169	4,700,000	462	Republic
Saint Lucia	238	121,000	508	Parliamentary State*
St. Vincent	150	121,000	807	Parliamentary State*
San Marino	24	21,000	875	Republic
Sao Tome & Principe	372	86,000	231	Republic
Saudi Arabia	830,000	8,225,000	10	Monarchy
Senegal	75,750	5,575,000	74	Republic
Seychelles	171	66,000	386	Republic*
Sierra Leone	27,699	3,940,000	142	Republic*
Singapore	224	2,375,000	10,603	Republic*
Solomon Islands	10,983	225,000	20	Parliamentary State*
Somalia	246,201	3,930,000	16	Republic
South Africa (incl. Walvis Bay)	471,445	28,860,000	61	Federal Republic
Soviet Union (Union of Soviet Socialist Republics)	8,600,350	265,390,000	31	Federal Soviet Republic
Spain	194,885	37,410,000	192	Monarchy
Sri Lanka	25,332	14,870,000	587	Republic*
Sudan	967,500	18,175,000	19	Republic
Suriname	63,037	430,000	7	Republic
Swaziland	6,704	525,000	78	Monarchy*

Capital city	Currency	Predominant languages
Niamey	CFA franc	Hausa, Arabic, French
Lagos	Naira	Hausa, Ibo, Yoruba, English
Oslo	Krone	Norwegian (Riksmål and Landsmål)
Muscat (Masqat)	Rial	Arabic
Islāmābād	Rupee	Urdu, English
Panamá	Balboa	Spanish
Port Moresby	Kina	Papuan and Negrito languages, English
Asunción	Guaraní	Spanish, Guaraní
Lima	Sol	Spanish, Quechua
Manila	Peso	Pilipino, English
Warsaw (Warszawa)	Zloty	Polish
Lisbon (Lisboa)	Escudo	Portuguese
Ad-Dawhah	Riyal	Arabic
Bucharest (Bucureşti)	Leu	Romanian, Hungarian
Kigali	Franc	Kinyarwanda, French
Castries	East Caribbean dollars	English
Kingstown	East Caribbean dollars	English
San Marino	Italian lira, Vatican City lira	Italian
São Tomé	Escudo	Portuguese, native languages
Riyadh (Ar-Riyād)	Riyal	Arabic
Dakar	CFA franc	French, native languages
Victoria	Rupee	English, Creole
Freetown	Leone	English, native languages
Singapore	Dollar	Chinese, Malay, English, Tamil
Honiara	Dollar	Malay-Polynesian languages, English
Mogadisho	Shilling	Somali
Pretoria and Cape Town	Rand	English, Afrikaans, native languages
Moscow (Moskva)	Rouble	Russian and other Slavic languages, various Finno-Ugric, Turkic, and Mongol languages, Caucasian languages, Persian
Madrid	Peseta	Spanish, Catalan, Galician, Basque
Colombo	Rupee	Sinhala, Tamil, English
Khartoum (Al-Khurtūm)	Pound	Arabic, native languages, English
Paramaribo	Guilder	Dutch, Creole
Mbabane	Emalangeni	English, siSwati

Nation	Area in sq. miles	Population 1/1/80 (est.)	Pop. per sq. mile	Form of government
Sweden	173,732	8,325,000	48	Monarchy
Switzerland	15,941	6,250,000	392	Federal Republic
Syria †	71,498	8,460,000	118	Republic
Taiwan (Formosa) (Nationalist China)	13,885	18,410,000	1,326	Republic
Tanzania	364,900	17,250,000	47	Republic*
Thailand	198,456	46,695,000	235	Monarchy
Togo	21,600	2,500,000	116	Republic
Tonga	270	94,000	348	Monarchy*
Trinidad and Tobago	1,980	1,160,000	586	Republic*
Tunisia	63,170	6,360,000	101	Republic
Turkey	301,382	44,815,000	149	Republic
Tuvalu	9.2	10,000	1,087	Parliamentary State*
Uganda	91,520	13,420,000	147	Republic*
United Arab Emirates	32,278	775,000	24	Self-governing Union
United Kingdom of Great Britain and Northern Ireland	94,214	55,810,000	592	Monarchy*
United States	3,675,545	220,090,000	60	Federal Republic
Upper Volta	105,869	6,790,000	64	Republic
Uruguay	68,536	2,890,000	42	Republic
Vanuatu	5,700	106,000	19	Republic*
Vatican City (Holy See)	0.2	1,000	5,000	Ecclesiastical State
Venezuela	352,144	13,730,000	39	Federal Republic
Vietnam	127,242	51,620,000	406	People's Republic
Western Samoa	1,097	156,000	142	Constitutional Monarchy*
Yemen	75,289	5,840,000	78	Republic
Yemen, People's Democratic Republic of	128,559	1,935,000	15	People's Republic
Yugoslavia	98,766	22,145,000	224	Socialist Federal Republic
Zaire	905,567	29,650,000	33	Republic
Zambia	290,586	5,730,000	20	Republic*
Zimbabwe	150,804	7,255,000	48	Republic*

† Data for Israel, Jordan, Syria, and Egypt do not reflect de facto changes which have taken place since 1967.
* Commonwealth of Nations

Capital city	Currency	Predominant languages
Stockholm	Krona	Swedish
Bern (Berne)	Franc	German, French, Italian
Damascus (Dimashq)	Pound	Arabic, French
T'aipei	New Taiwan dollar	Chinese
Dar-es-Salaam	Shilling	Swahili, English, Arabic
Bangkok (Krung Thep)	Baht	Thai, Chinese
Lomé	CFA franc	Native languages, French
Nukualofa	Pa'anga	Tongan, English
Port of Spain	Dollar	English, Spanish
Tunis	Dinar	Arabic, French
Ankara	Lira	Turkish, Kurdish, Arabic
Funafuti (island)	Australian dollar	Malay-Polynesian languages, English
Kampala	Shilling	English, Swahili
Abū Zabī	Dirham	Arabic
London	Sterling pound	English, Welsh, Gaelic
Washington	Dollar	English
Ouagadougou	CFA franc	French, native languages
Montevideo	Peso	Spanish
Vila	Franc	Bislama, English, French
Vatican City	Italian lira	Italian, Latin
Caracas	Bolívar	Spanish
Hanoi	Dong	Vietnamese
Apia	Tala	Samoan, English
San'ā'	Rial	Arabic
Aden	Dinar	Arabic, English
Belgrade (Beograd)	Dinar	Serbo-Croatian, Slovenian, Macedonian
Kinshasa	Zaire	French. native languages
Lusaka	Kwacha	English, native languages
Salisbury	Dollar	English, native languages

FLAGS OF NATIONS

AFGHANISTAN

ALBANIA

ALGERIA

ANDORRA

ANGOLA

A flag is a distinctive design used as a symbol. A national flag is a symbolic design sacred to the nation for which it stands. The earliest national symbols were images or badges wrought in metal, stone, or wood and carried at the top of a spear. The first written reference to flags (or banners, as they were referred to then) in England was in a description by Bede, seventh century theologian and historian, of an interview between King Ethelbert and St. Augustine.

The word *flag* supposedly is derived from the Anglo-Saxon word *fleogan,* which means to fly or float in the wind. Interchangeable terms for flag are ensign, pennant, pennon, standard, and banner.

National flags usually are made of bunting, a durable woolen fabric. More recently many are made of a combination of nylon and bunting, which has increased the flag's life one and one half to three times. Bunting flags are sewn; small flags or those of other material may be printed; while those of an intricate design may be painted. Colors are also significant. Yellow represents gold; white represents silver.

The position in which a flag is displayed or carried is also significant. Dipping denotes honor or respect. Flags displayed at half-mast represent mourning; flags flown at the same level indicate respect among those whom each flag represents. To display the national flag of a visitor from another country, is an act of courtesy.

Flags shown are *national* flags in common use and vary slightly from official *state* flags, most particularly by omitting coats of arms in some cases.

ARGENTINA	AUSTRALIA	AUSTRIA	BAHAMAS	BAHRAIN
BANGLADESH	BARBADOS	BELGIUM	BENIN	BHUTAN
BOLIVIA	BOTSWANA	BRAZIL	BULGARIA	BURMA
BURUNDI	CAMBODIA (KAMPUCHEA)	CAMEROON	CANADA	CAPE VERDE
CENTRAL AFRICAN REPUBLIC	CHAD	CHILE	CHINA (MAINLAND)	CHINA (TAIWAN)
COLOMBIA	COMOROS	CONGO	COSTA RICA	CUBA
CYPRUS	CZECHOSLOVAKIA	DENMARK	DJIBOUTI	DOMINICA
DOMINICAN REPUBLIC	ECUADOR	EGYPT	EL SALVADOR	EQUATORIAL GUINEA

ETHIOPIA FIJI FINLAND FRANCE GABON

GAMBIA GERMAN DEM. REP. GERMANY, FED. REP. OF GHANA GREECE

GRENADA GUATEMALA GUINEA GUINEA-BISSAU GUYANA

HAITI HONDURAS HUNGARY ICELAND INDIA

INDONESIA IRAN IRAQ IRELAND ISRAEL

ITALY IVORY COAST JAMAICA JAPAN JORDAN

KENYA KIRIBATI KOREA, NORTH KOREA, SOUTH KUWAIT

LAOS LEBANON LESOTHO LIBERIA LIBYA

LIECHTENSTEIN

 LUXEMBOURG

 MADAGASCAR

 MALAWI

 MALAYSIA

 MALDIVES

 MALI

 MALTA

 MAURITANIA

 MEXICO

 MONACO

 MONGOLIA

 MOROCCO

 MOZAMBIQUE

 NAURU

 NEPAL

 NETHERLANDS

 NEW ZEALAND

 NICARAGUA

 NIGER

 NIGERIA

 NORWAY

 OMAN

 PAKISTAN

 PANAMA

 PAPUA NEW GUINEA

 PARAGUAY

 PERU

 PHILIPPINES

 POLAND

 PORTUGAL

 QATAR

 ROMANIA

 RWANDA

 SAINT LUCIA

 ST. VINCENT/
GRENADINES

 SAMOA

 SAN MARINO

 SAO TOME &
PRINCIPE

MAURITIUS

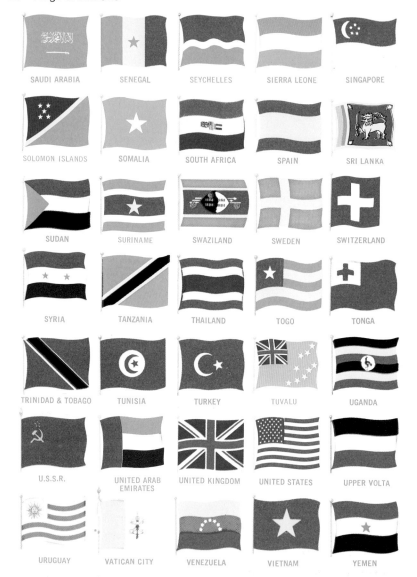

SAUDI ARABIA	SENEGAL	SEYCHELLES	SIERRA LEONE	SINGAPORE
SOLOMON ISLANDS	SOMALIA	SOUTH AFRICA	SPAIN	SRI LANKA
SUDAN	SURINAME	SWAZILAND	SWEDEN	SWITZERLAND
SYRIA	TANZANIA	THAILAND	TOGO	TONGA
TRINIDAD & TOBAGO	TUNISIA	TURKEY	TUVALU	UGANDA
U.S.S.R.	UNITED ARAB EMIRATES	UNITED KINGDOM	UNITED STATES	UPPER VOLTA
URUGUAY	VATICAN CITY	VENEZUELA	VIETNAM	YEMEN
YEMEN, P.D.R. OF	YUGOSLAVIA	ZAIRE	ZAMBIA	ZIMBABWE

Inhabited Localities

The symbol represents the number of inhabitants within the locality

At scales 1:6 000 000 to 1:12 000 000

- · 0—10,000
- ○ 10,000—25,000
- ◉ 25,000—100,000
- ▣ 100,000—250,000
- ▤ 250,000—1,000,000
- ■ >1,000,000

At 1:24 000 000 scale

- · 0—50,000
- ◉ 50,000—100,000
- ▣ 100,000—250,000
- ▤ 250,000—1,000,000
- ■ >1,000,000

Urban Area (area of continuous industrial, commercial, and residential development)

The size of type indicates the relative economic and political importance of the locality

| Écommoy | Lisieux | **Rouen** |
| Trouville | **Orléans** | **PARIS** |

Capitals of Political Units

BUDAPEST Independent Nation

Cayenne Dependency
(Colony, protectorate, etc.)

Lasa State, Province, etc.

Alternate Names

MOSKVA
'MOSCOW
English or second official language names are shown in reduced size lettering

Volgograd
(Stalingrad)
Historical or other alternates in the local language are shown in parentheses

Political Boundaries

International (First-order political unit)

—··—··— Demarcated and Undemarcated

Indefinite or Undefined

- - - - - - - Demarcation Line
(used in Korea)

Internal

State, Province, etc.
(Second-order political unit)

MURCIA Historical Region
(No boundaries indicated)

Transportation

———————— Primary Road

———————— Secondary Road

Canal du Midi Navigable Canal

—→ - - - - ←— Tunnel

- - - - - - - Ferry

Hydrographic Features

Intermittent Stream

Rapids, Falls

Irrigation or Drainage Canal

Reef

The Everglades Swamp

Glacier

VATNAJÖKULL

L. Victoria Lake, Reservoir

Tuz Gölü Salt Lake

Intermittent Lake, Reservoir

Dry Lake Bed

Topographic Features

Matterhorn △ 4478	Elevation Above Sea Level
76 ▽	Elevation Below Sea Level
Mount Cook ▲ 3764	Highest Elevation in Country
Khyber Pass ≍ 1067	Mountain Pass
133 ▼	Lowest Elevation in Country

Elevations are given in metres
The Highest and Lowest Elevation in a continent are underlined

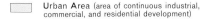 Sand Area

 Lava

 Salt Flat

ARCTIC OCEAN

90° 180° 165° 150° 135° 120° 105° 90° 75° 60° 45° 30° 15° 0°

GREENLAND
(Den.)

75°

Beaufort Sea

VICTORIA
ISLAND

BAFFIN ISLAND

Godthåb

ICELA

Arctic Circle

U.S.S.R.
UNITED
STATES

60°

Anchorage

Yellowknife

Hudson
Bay

UNIT
KINGD

Bering Sea

Gulf of
Alaska

ROCKY MTS

CANADA

NEWFOUNDLAND

IRELAND LON

ALEUTIAN ISLANDS

Vancouver

Winnipeg

FRAN

45°

NORTH

Montréal

ATLANTIC OCEAN

AMERICA

NEW YORK

P A C I F I C

SAN
FRANCISCO

CHICAGO
UNITED STATES

Washington

PORTUGAL SP.

LOS ANGELES

AÇORES AZORES
(Port.)

30°

O C E A N

Houston

Mississippi

BERMUDA
(U.K.)

MOROCCO

Tropic of Cancer

Gulf of Mexico

Miami

A

HAWAIIAN ISLANDS

MEXICO

CUBA

WESTERN
SAHARA

S

15°

(U.S.)

CIUDAD
DE MÉXICO

HAITI

DOMINICAN
REPUBLIC

MAURI-
TANIA

A

P

GUATEMALA

PUERTO RICO
(U.S.)

SENEGAL

MA

HONDURAS

Caribbean
Sea

GUINEA

UPP
VO

O

NICARAGUA

TRINIDAD AND
TOBAGO

SIERRA
LEONE

IVO
COA

L

PANAMA

VENEZUELA

0°

Equator

ARCHIPIÉLAGO DE COLÓN
GALAPAGOS ISLANDS
(Ec.)

COLOMBIA

GUYANA

FRENCH
SURI- GUIANA
NAME

Equator

ECUADOR

Amazon

Belém

Y

ANDES

PERU

BRAZIL

Recife

N

15°

E

AM.
SAMOA

SOUTH AMERICA

ATLANTIC OCE

FIJI

COOK
ISLANDS
(N.Z.)

FRENCH
POLYNESIA

BOLIVIA

Brasília

I

TONGA

PARAGUAY

RIO DE JANEIRO

Tropic of Capricorn

Asunción

SÃO PAULO

CHILE

International Date Line

30°

P A C I F I C

Santiago

URUGUAY
BUENOS AIRES

45°

O C E A N

ARGENTINA

FALKLAND ISLANDS
(U.K.)

60°

CABO DE HORNOS
CAPE HORN

Antarctic Circle

75°

Bellingshausen Sea

Weddell Sea

90° 180° 165° 150° 135° 120° 105° 90° 75° 60° 45° 30° 15° 0°

A   N   T   A   R

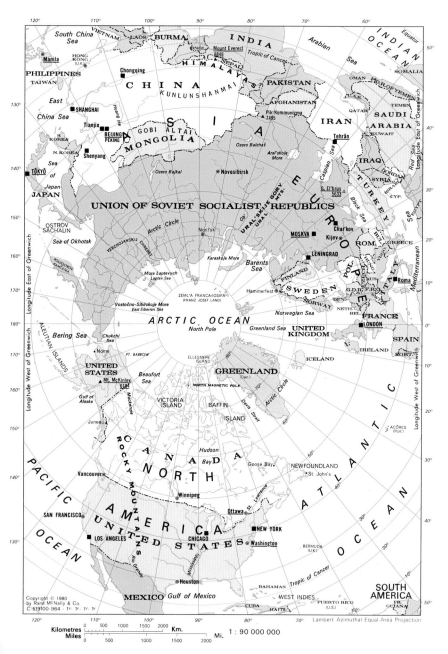

Kilometres 0 500 1000 1500 2000 Km.
Miles 0 500 1000 1500 2000 Mi.
1 : 90 000 000

Lambert Azimuthal Equal-Area Projection

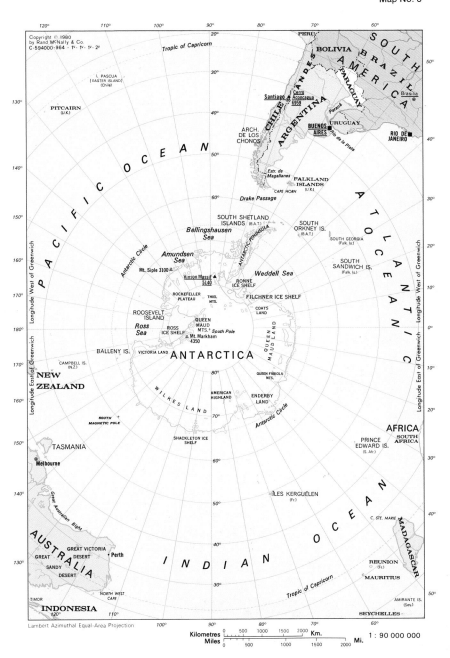

Copyright © 1980
by Rand McNally & Co.
C-594000-964 · 1ᵛ· 1ᵛ· 1ᵛ· 2ᵛ

Tropic of Capricorn

PERU
BOLIVIA
BRAZIL
SOUTH AMERICA
PARAGUAY
URUGUAY
ARGENTINA
CHILE
ANDES

I. PASCUA
(EASTER ISLAND)
(Chile)

PITCAIRN
(U.K.)

Santiago
Cerro
Aconcagua
6959

Brasilia

Paraná

BUENOS
AIRES

RIO DE
JANEIRO

ARCH.
DE LOS
CHONOS

Rio de la Plata

PACIFIC OCEAN

Estr. de
Magallanes

FALKLAND
ISLANDS
(U.K.)

CAPE HORN

Drake Passage

ATLANTIC OCEAN

SOUTH SHETLAND
ISLANDS (B.A.T.)

SOUTH
ORKNEY IS.
(B.A.T.)

SOUTH GEORGIA
(Falk. Is.)

Bellingshausen
Sea

ANTARCTIC PENINSULA

SOUTH
SANDWICH IS.
(Falk. Is.)

Antarctic Circle

Amundsen
Sea

Weddell Sea

Mt. Siple 3100△

Vinson Massif ▲
5140

RONNE
ICE SHELF

FILCHNER ICE SHELF

ROCKEFELLER
PLATEAU

THIEL
MTS.

COATS
LAND

ROOSEVELT
ISLAND

Ross
Sea

ROSS
ICE SHELF

QUEEN
MAUD
MTS.† South Pole
△ Mt. Markham
4350

QUEEN
MAUD
LAND

BALLENY IS.

VICTORIA LAND

ANTARCTICA

Longitude East of Greenwich

Longitude West of Greenwich

CAMPBELL IS.
(N.Z.)

QUEEN FÁBIOLA
MTS.

NEW
ZEALAND

W I L K E S   L A N D

AMERICAN
HIGHLAND

ENDERBY
LAND

SOUTH
MAGNETIC POLE

Antarctic Circle

SHACKLETON ICE
SHELF

AFRICA
SOUTH
AFRICA

TASMANIA

PRINCE
EDWARD IS.
(S. Afr.)

Melbourne

ÍLES KERGUÉLEN
(Fr.)

C. STE. MARIE

MADAGASCAR

Great Australian Bight

AUSTRALIA

GREAT VICTORIA
DESERT

GREAT
SANDY
DESERT

Perth

I N D I A N   O C E A N

REUNION
(Fr.)

MAURITIUS

TIMOR

NORTH WEST
CAPE

Tropic of Capricorn

AMIRANTE IS.
(Sey.)

INDONESIA

SEYCHELLES

Lambert Azimuthal Equal-Area Projection

Kilometres   0   500   1000   1500   2000   Km.

Miles   0   500   1000   1500   2000   Mi.

1 : 90 000 000

34

ATLANTIC

OCEAN

NORWEGIAN

SEA

ICELAND

Reykjavík

Akureyri

Seydisfjördur

VATNAJÖKULL

Hvannadalshnúkur

2119

FONTUR

Arctic Circle

Tromsø

LOFOTEN VESTER

Kebnek

2111

Jokkmok

NORWAY

Mo

Tärnaby

Steinkjer

Gaddede

Kristiansund

Örnsköldsvik

Trond-

heim

SWEDEN

Sundsvall

Glittertinden

2472

Florø

Gulf

FAEROE

ISLANDS

(Den.)

Bergen

Voss

Gävle

Uppsa

SHETLAND

ISLANDS

Oslo

Skien

Stavanger

Örebro

Kristiansand

Linköping

ORKNEY

ISLANDS

Wick

HEBRIDES

Inverness

Skagerrak

Göteborg

Borås

Växjö

GOTL

Stockho

NORTH

DENMARK

Balti

SCOTLAND

Aberdeen

København

Karlskrona

Sea

Glasgow

Edinburgh

Kaliningr

IRELAND

UNITED

Belfast

KINGDOM

Flensburg

Kiel

Ålborg

Malmö

Galway

(TR.)

N. IRELAND

ENGLAND

SEA

ISLE

OF

MAN

(U.K.)

Århus

Rostock

Gdańsk

Olszty

Dublin

Liverpool

Leeds

GERMAN

DEM.

Szczecin

Bydgoszcz

Cork

Birmingham

Manchester

Hamburg

Bremen

REP.

WALES

NETHERLANDS

Amsterdam

Hannover

BERLIN

Poznań

Cardiff

Bristol

LONDON

Münster

POLAN

Plymouth

Rotterdam

Essen

Leipzig

Wrocław

Portsmouth

Bruxelles

Bonn

FED. REP.

Dresden

Częstochowa

Kraków

English Channel

BELGIUM

Köln

OF

GER.

Frankfurt

Praha

Ostrava

Le Havre

Rouen

LUX.

Brno

Brest

PARIS

Metz

Mannheim

Nürnberg

CZECH.

Bratislava

Rennes

Le Mans

Orléans

Strasbourg

Stuttgart

Wien

Budape

Lorient

FRANCE

Dijon

Basel

München

Vienna

Nantes

Tours

Bern

Zürich

AUSTRIA

Graz

HUNGAR

La Rochelle

Limoges

Genève

SWITZ.

LIÈGE

Szeged

Clermont-

Ferrand

Mont

Blanc

4807

Milano

Verona

Venezia

Zagreb

Beograd

La Coruña

Oviedo

Bordeaux

Bay of

Biscay

Lyon

Grenoble

Torino

Bologna

Rijeka

YUGOSLAVI

Vigo

Bilbao

Orense

León

Toulouse

Nice

Genova

SAN

MARINO

Split

Sarajevo

PYRENEES

Avignon

MONACO

Livorno

Adriatic

PORTUGAL

Porto

Valladolid

Pamplona

ANDORRA

Montpellier

Marseille

Firenze

ITALY

Sea

Coimbra

Salamanca

Zaragoza

Barcelona

CORSE

CORSICA

(Fr.)

Roma

Foggia

Tirane

Lisboa

Madrid

Castellón

de la Plana

ISLAS BALEARES

BALEARIC ISLANDS

Ajaccio

Napoli

Bari

ALI

Badajoz

Tagus

SPAIN

Valencia

SARDEGNA

SARDINIA

(It.)

Salerno

Taranto

Lecce

CABO DE

SÃO VICENTE

Sevilla

Córdoba

Murcia

Alicante

Palma

Catanzaro

Ionian

Córdoba

Granada

Almería

Cartagena

Cagliari

Tyrrhenian

Palermo

Messina

Sea

Cádiz

Tarifa

Granada

(U.K.)

Málaga

Sea

Reggio di

Calabria

Gibraltar

Melilla

(Sp.)

MEDITERRANEAN

Annaba

(Bône)

Bizerte

Catania

Tanger

Alger

El

Asnam

Aigiers

Bizerte

Tunis

SEA

Casablanca

Rabat

Oran

Constantine

TUNISIA

MALTA

Valletta

Meknès

Fès

Oujda

MOUNTAINS

Sfax

MOROCCO

Sidi

bel Abbès

Djebel Chambi

1544

Safi

ATLAS

SAHARIEN

Biskra

ALGERIA

ATLA

Kilometres 0   200   400   600 Km.

Miles 0   200   400   600 Mi.

1 : 24 000 000

Copyright © 1980

by Rand McNally & Co.

C-550000-964   5⁰⁻ 5⁰⁻ 5⁰⁻ 8⁰

Miller Oblated Stereographic Projection

ATLANTIC OCEAN

NORTH SEA

SHETLAND ISLANDS
Melby House
Lerwick
Virkie

ORKNEY ISLANDS
MAINLAND
Stromness
Kirkwall
Burwick

ISLE OF LEWIS
SAINT KILDA
OUTER HEBRIDES
Little Minch
Durness
Thurso
Wick
Lochinver
Ben More Assynt △998
Helmsdale
Ullapool
Bonarbridge
Uig
Dingwall
Elgin
Fraserburgh
ISLAND OF SKYE
Kyle of Lochalsh
Loch Ness
Inverness
Huntly
INNER HEBRIDES
Mallaig
1343
Ben Nevis
Balmoral Castle
Aberdeen
Tobermory
Stonehaven
ISLAND OF MULL
Ben More 1174
GRAMPIAN MTS.
Arbroath
Perth
Dundee
Lochgilphead
Firth of Forth
Kirkcaldy
Greenock
Edinburgh
GLASGOW
Motherwell
Berwick-upon-Tweed
Port Ellen
ISLAND OF ARRAN
Kilmarnock
Galashiels
Campbeltown
Ayr
Hawick
NORTHUMBERLAND NATIONAL PARK
North Channel
Firth of Clyde
Moffat
SCOTLAND U.K.
Dumfries
Blyth
Coleraine
Newton Stewart
Carlisle
Newcastle upon Tyne
Londonderry
Lifford
Larne
Stranraer
Durham
Sunderland
Donegal
Omagh
Bangor
Whitehaven
Penrith
Bishop Auckland
Middlesbrough
Belmullet
Enniskillen
Portadown
ISLE OF MAN
Lake District National Park
YORKSHIRE DALES NATIONAL PARK
NORTH YORK MOORS NATIONAL PARK
Scarborough
Sligo
Cavan
Newry
Douglas
Barrow-in-Furness
PENNINES
Ballina
Castlebar
Roscommon
Dundalk
Castle-town
Lancaster
York
Kingston upon Hull
Clifden
Athlone
Drogheda
Blackpool
Black-burn
Leeds
CONNEMARA
Royal Canal
MEATH
IRELAND U.K.
Preston
MANCHESTER
Grimsby
ARAN ISLANDS
Galway
Tullamore
Dublin
IRISH SEA
Southport
Liverpool
Sheffield
Lincoln
Milltown Malbay
Ennis
Naas
Dun Laoghaire
Holy-head
Chester
Stoke-on-Trent
Nottingham
Skegness
Sheringham
Cromer
Shannon
Nenagh
LEINSTER
Wicklow
Caernarvon
PEAK DIST. NATIONAL PARK
Limerick
Tipperary
Arklow
Wrexham
Derby
Grantham
Norwich
Tralee
MUNSTER
Kilkenny
Stafford
Leicester
King's Lynn
Peterborough
Great Yarmouth
Dingle
1041
Carrauntoohil
Clonmel
Wexford
Barmouth
Aberystwyth
BIRMINGHAM
Coventry
Cambridge
Cahirciveen
Waterford
Rosslare
CAMBRIAN MTS.
Stratford-upon-Avon
Northampton
Ipswich
Bantry
Cork
Dungarvan
Cardigan
Worcester
Hereford
Gloucester
Banbury
Oxford
Luton
Chelmsford
St. George's Channel
Carmarthen
PEMBROKESHIRE COAST NATIONAL PARK
Milford Haven
Merthyr Tydfil
BRECON BEACONS NATIONAL PARK
Newport
LONDON
Southend-on-Sea
Swansea
Cardiff
Bristol
Reading
Windsor
Canterbury
Dover
EXMOOR NATIONAL PARK
Bath
Salisbury
Basingstoke
Guildford
Bridgwater
Yeovil
Brighton
Folkestone
Hastings
Exeter
Southampton
Portsmouth
Boulogne-sur-Mer
DARTMOOR NATIONAL PARK
Weymouth
Bournemouth
UNITED KINGDOM
Newquay
Plymouth
Torquay (Torbay)
English Channel
La Manche
FRANCE
Le Tréport
LAND'S END
Saint Austell
Falmouth
Cherbourg
Fécamp
Dieppe
Tôtes

Conic Projection, Two Standard Parallels

Kilometres 0 50 100 150 Km.
Miles 0 50 100 150 Mi.

1 : 7 500 000

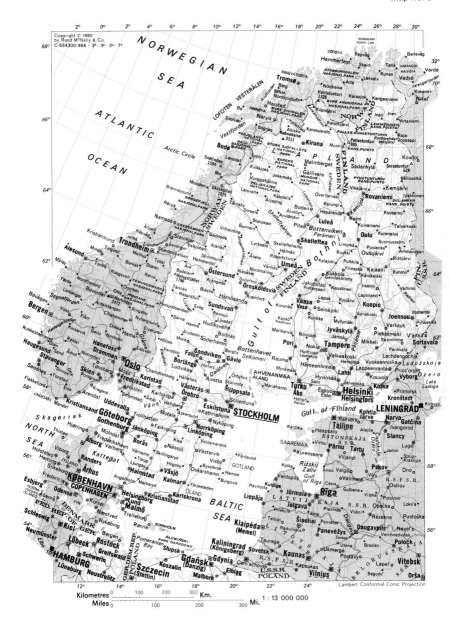

NORTH SEA

Deutsche Bucht

WADDENEILANDEN

OSTFRIESISCHE INSELN

NORTH FRISIAN ISLANDS

Waddenzee

FRIESLAND

Westerland
Husum
Sankt Peter
Heide
Meldorf
Brunsbüttel
Cuxhaven
Wilhelms-haven
Nordenham
Norden
Nordenham
Emden
Delfzijl

Flensburg
Sonderborg
Nakskov
Nykøbing
Vordingborg
Rødbyhavn
Gedser
Puttgarden
Ribnitz-Damgarten
Rostock

Schleswig
Rendsburg
Kieler Bucht
Kiel
Neustadt in Holstein
Bad Schwartau
Lübeck
Wismar
Güstrow
MECKLENBURG
Schwerin
Ludwigslust
Boizenburg
Lüchow
Wittenberge

Itzehoe
Neumünster
Elmshorn
Stade
HAMBURG
Buxtehude
Bremerhaven

Westerland
NORTH FRISIAN ISLANDS

Den Helder
Leeuwarden
Groningen
Drachten
Assen
Emmen
Meppen
Lingen
Haren
Cloppenburg
Quakenbrück
Walsrode
Uelzen
Salzwedel
Wittenberge
Stendal
Rathenow
Brandenburg

Alkmaar
IJsselmeer (Zuider Zee)
Kampen
Zwolle
Nordhorn
Nienburg
Langenhagen
Celle
Wolfsburg
NIEDERSACHSEN
Magdeburg

Zaandam
Haarlem
AMSTERDAM
Apeldoorn
Deventer
Enschede
Rheine
Espelkamp
Herford
Hannover
Braunschweig
Wolfenbüttel
Schönebeck

's-Gravenhage
The Hague
Utrecht
Arnhem
Münster
Osnabrück
Bielefeld
Hameln
Salzgitter

Vlaardingen
Rotterdam
Nijmegen
Bocholt
Winterswijk
Hamm
Detmold
Paderborn
Göttingen
Quedlinburg
Bernburg
Wittenberg
Dessau
Bitterfeld
Halle

Vlissingen
Flushing
Bergen op Zoom
Breda
Tilburg
Eindhoven
Recklinghausen
Lippstadt
Marburg an der Lahn
Siegen
Eisenach
Jena
Karl-Marx-Stadt (Chemnitz)
Leipzig
Zeitz
Gera
Zwickau

Oostende
Ostende
Roeselare
Gent
Gand
Antwerpen
Anvers
Mechelen
Lier
Mönchengladbach
Düsseldorf
Essen
Dortmund
Bochum
Wuppertal
Solingen
Köln
Cologne
Leverkusen
Kassel
Mühlhausen
Naumburg
Merseburg

Armen-tières
Roubaix
Kortrijk
Courtrai
BRUXELLES
BRUSSEL
Genk
Maastricht
Heerlen
Aachen
Bonn
Hennef
Marburg
Brilon
Kahler Asten 841△
SAUERLAND
Nordhausen
Eisleben

Lens
Lille
Charleroi
Liège
Verviers
Erfurt
THÜRINGER WALD
Saalfeld

Denain
Valenciennes
Nivelles
Dinant
Saint-Vith
Neuwied
Giessen
Bad Nauheim
Fulda
Meiningen
Plauen
Fichtelberg 1214△

Arras
Cambrai
Fourmies
Hirson
EIFEL
Koblenz
Frankfurt a.M.
Schweinfurt
Coburg
Hof
Karlovy Vary
Cheb

Péronne
Charleville-Mézières
Bastogne
Ettelbrück
Bitburg
Wiesbaden
Offenbach
Bamberg
Bayreuth
Kulmbach
Mariánské Lázně
Weiden in der Oberpfalz

Saint-Quentin
Laon
Signy-l'Abbaye
Bouillon
LUXEMBOURG
Trier
Bad Kreuznach
Mainz
Darmstadt
Idar-Oberstein
Würzburg
Kitzingen
Erlangen
Sulzbach-Rosenberg
Amberg

Noyon
Compiègne
Stenay
Longwy
Esch-sur-Alzette
Ludwigshafen
Mannheim
Bad Mergentheim
Fürth
Nürnberg

Soissons
Verdun-sur-Meuse
Thionville
Saarbrücken
Speyer
Heidelberg
Mosbach
Ansbach
Regensburg
BOHEMIAN

Reims
Château-Thierry
Marne
Bar-le-Duc
Neunkirchen
Forbach
Pirmasens
Heilbronn
Schwäbisch Hall

Meaux
Châlons-sur-Marne
Metz
Saint-Avold
Karlsruhe
Ludwigsburg
Schwäbisch Gmünd
Heidenheim
Straubing
Landau an der Isar

Provins
Esternay
Romilly-sur-Seine
Saint-Dizier
Nancy
Lunéville
Sarrebourg
Saverne
Pforzheim
Weissenburg in Bayern
Stuttgart
Ingolstadt

Montereau-faut-Yonne
Sens
Troyes
Bar-sur-Aube
Neufchâteau
Vittel
Saint-Dié
Épinal
Baden-Baden
Tübingen
Reutlingen
Ulm
Augsburg
Landshut
Burghausen

Auxerre
Les Riceys
Chaumont
Remiremont
Luxeuil-les-Bains
Strasbourg
Freudenstadt
Rottweil
Biberach an der Riss
Memmingen
Landsberg
Dachau
MÜNCHEN
MUNICH
Freising

Châtillon-sur-Seine
Tonnerre
Langeau
Vesoul
Belfort
Villingen-Schwenningen
Ravensburg
Leutkirch
Kaufbeuren
Weilheim
Rosenheim
Traunstein

Clamecy
Mirebeau-sur-Bèze
Montbéliard
Mulhouse
Schaffhausen
Konstanz
Friedrichshafen
Füssen
BAYERISCHE ALPEN

Corbigny
Dijon
Besançon
La Chaux-de-Fonds
Basel
Bâle
Zürich
2963 Madelegabel △
2963
Zugspitze
Reichenhall
Kitzbühel

Château-Chinon
Autun
Saint-Georges
Dole
Delémont
Biel
Solothurn
Luzern
Horgen
Vaduz
LIECHTENSTEIN
Innsbruck
Solbad Hall
Zell am See
HOHE TAUERN

Luzy
Chalon-sur-Saône
Poligny
Pontarlier
Lac de Neuchâtel
Vierwaldstätter See
Altdorf
Chur
1504
Brenner Pass 1374
Grossglockner

Moulins
Montceau
Lons-le-Saunier
Fribourg
Berne
Bern
Interlaken
Jungfrau 4158 △
2108 Passo del San Gottardo
RHAETIAN ALPS
Sankt Moritz
2756 Passo dello Stelvio
Merano
Meran
Bolzano
Bozen
AUSTRIA
ITALY

Paray-le-Monial
Lapalisse
Mâcon
Bourg-en-Bresse
Lausanne
Lake Geneva
Genève
BERNER ALPEN
2005 Simplon Pass
Chiavenna
PARCO NAZIONALE DELLO STELVIO

Vichy
Roanne

Kilometres 0 50 100 150 Km.
Miles 0 50 100 150 Mi.
1: 6 000 000

Kilometres 0 50 100 150 Km.
Miles 0 50 100 150 Mi.
1: 6 000 000

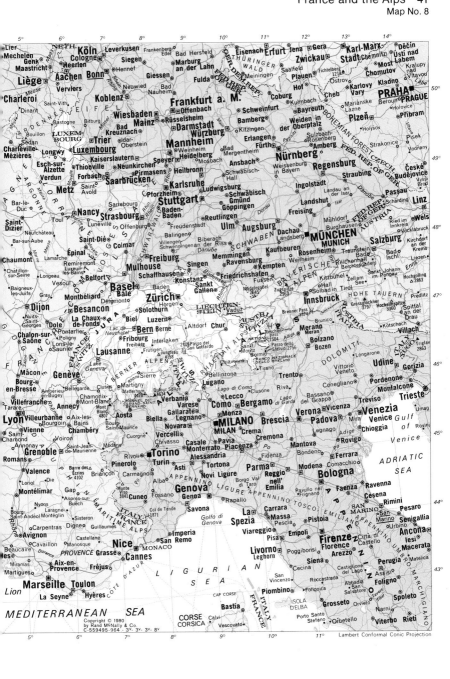

Lambert Conformal Conic Projection

MEDITERRANEAN SEA

ISLAS BALEARES
BALEARIC ISLANDS

Golfe du Lion

Kilometres 0 50 100 150 Km.
Miles 0 50 100 150 Mi.
1 : 6 000 000

Kilometres 0   50   100   150
Miles 0   50   100   150 Mi.
1: 6 000 000

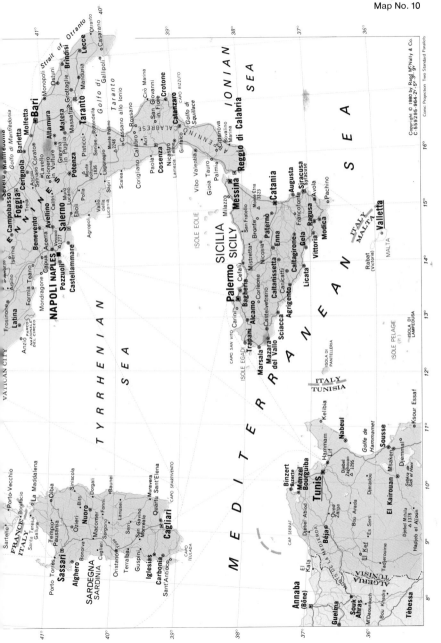

1 : 6 500 000

Kilometres 0   50   100   150 Km.
Miles 0   50   100   150 Mi.

1: 6 000 000

33°   34°   35°   36°   37°   38°   39°   40°   41°   42°   43°   44°   45°

•Ustje
ero   •Lodejnoje Polje   Annenskij Most•   Levino• •Ostrov   Ogibalovo•   Isakovo•   Velikodvorskaja• Sergijevskaja• Pavolvo•   60°
oga   Suchoti• Michajlovskij•
rica   Alechovšcina• •M'agozero   Kovžinski• •Lipin Bor   Krutec• Popovka• S'amža• Gora• Tot'ma• Zelencovo•   Starina
                           Zavod
          •S'as'stroj   Krasnaja Gora   Ozero   •Žitjevo   Fominskoje•   •Kn'azovo   •Nikol'skoje•
                    •Kost'kovo •Bol'šaja Chundala   Beloz'orsk   •Čeksino   Jurenino•
Volchov   Radogošča•   Pustin' Sofronovo•   Ustje• Sokol   Golubj•   Soligalič•   •Pankratovo
                              Čuny•   Bičevinka•   Leonicha•   Sujskoje•   •Kologriv
azevo   Tichvin   •Velikoje   Voskresenskoje• Moločnoje• Vologda   Vosja•   Bol'šaja   59°
                 Podborovje•   Babajevo•   Šeksna•   Korcevo•   •Čuchloma   Pas'ma
•Budogošč•   •Neboleči   Somino• Sazonovo•   Kaduj• Čerepovec   Fominskoje• Gr'azovec   Nikolo-Berezovec•   •Buj   Manturovo
'saja   Imeni• Vanskoje•   M'aksa   Baklanka•   Lopat'ovo•   Neja
era   Anciferovo•   Chvojnaja• Zel'abova•   L'ubim•   Galič
laja   Zarubino•   •Ustreka   DARVINSKIJ   Pošechonje•   Kommunar•
isera   Vesjegonsk•   ZAPOVEDNIK   Volodarsk   Danilov•   Severnoje• Voronjo   Makarjev•   58°
Okulovka•   •Vel'gija   Lesnoje• Bol'šoje• Rybinskoje   Ovinišče•   Ostrovskoje•   •Gorčucha
Krestcy   Borovič   Ramenje   Vodochranilišče   Volga•   Zavolžsk
Uglovka   Krasnyj Cholm•   Rybinsk   Volga Tutajev• Nekrasovskoje•   Kostroma
•Valdaj   Berezajka• Udoml'a•   •Sonkovo   •Gorčucha
Lyčkovo   Volga•   Jaroslavl   Nerechta•   Jurjevec•   Gorkovskoje
          •Bologoje   •Udoml'a   Bežeck•   •Uglič   Gavrilov-Jam•   Furmanov•   Kinešma• Vičuga•   Vodochranilišče   57°
olnovo- Trud•   •Vyšnij Voločok   Morkiny•   Kašin• Gora Tarchov• Rostov• Okt'abr'skij• Ivanovo   Sokol'skoje• Gorodec
Seliger• Firovo•   Gory•   Gora Tarchov• Petrovskoje•   •Puček   Zavolžje•
arevo   •Kalašnikovo   Vasiljevskij• Goricy Kal'azino• Cholm 294   Tejkovo•   •Šuja   •Archipovka   •Juža   GOR'KIJ
ALDAJSKAJA   •Ostaškov   Kuvšinovo• •Toržok Moch• Kimry• Belyj Gorodok• Pereslavl'-Zalesskij•   GORKY
OZVYŠENNOST'   Selizarovo•   Suchoverkovo•   Dubna•   Jurjev- Gavrilov Posad• V'azniki•   Dzeržinsk•   56°
eklino   Peno•   •Babino   Kalinin   Zaprudn'a•   Pol'skij•   Bogorodsk•
          Volga•   Turginovo•   Krasnozavodsk• •Aleksandrov   Orgtrud•   Stepancevo•   Pavlovo
•Nelidovo CENTRAL'NOLESNOJ Bachmutovo• Vysokovsk• Dmitrov• •Zagorsk •Kiržač Vladimir•   Vača•
        ZAPOVEDNIK   •Ržev   Stepurino• Solnečnogorsk•   Sobinka• Krasnoje   Černucha•   Murom   55°
Obuchova• Novos'olki•   Sačkovskaja•   Volokolamsk• Istra Mytišči• Krasnoarmejsk•   Echo•   •Kulebaki
Žarkovskij Tatarkino•   Sereda• Sjčovka•   Balašicha• Orechovo- Rošal'• Gus'-Chrustal'nyj•   Vyksa   Ardatov•
          Vladimirskij• Tupik•   Moskva•   MOSKVA   L'ubercy• Zujevo•   Čerusti•   Kolešicha•
        Cholm- •Novodugino   •Gagarin MOSCOW   Aprelevka•   Domodedovo• Jegorjevsk• Melenki•   MORDOVSKIJ
algazovo Zirkovkoi   Kasn'a•   Naro-   •Možajsk   Podol'sk•   Voskresensk•   Velikodvorskij• Semilovo• ZAPOVEDNIK
arcevo   •Safonovo   Fominsk   Obninsk•   Čechov• Kolomna   Spas-Klepiki•   Kasimov• Jelat'ma• Jermiš•   54°
olodn'a   Mytisino• Ugra• Kondrovo• Serpuchov• Kašira Beloomut•   Solotča• OKSKIJ ZAPOVEDNIK Poltevy• Pen'ki•
          Ozeriscе•   Klimov• Polotn'anyi•   •Aleksin •Jasnogorsk R'azan'   Murmino•   Spassk-R'azanskij• Javas•
SKO   •Jel'na   L'udkovo•   Zavod•   Serebr'anyje•   Mosolovo•   Zubova At'urjevo•
         Spas-Demensk• Dugna• Leninskij• Tula Prudy• Michajlov•   Sapožok• Pol'ana• Torbejevo•
hislaviči Jekimovici• Meščovsk• Peremyšl'• Sčokino• Venev•   •Uchlovo   Sarai• Vyša•
         •Kirov Vologe• Suchiniči• Čerepet'• Donskoj• Kimovsk• Skopin•   R'ažsk•   Algasovo• Zemetčino•   53°
•Roslavl' •L'udinovo   Kozel'sk• Bel'ov• Bogorodick• Tovarkovskij• Gorn'ak• Sapožok• Moršansk•   Bašmakovo•
Sum'ači Dubrovka• Dudorovici•   Odojev•   Mеščerino• Aleksandro-Nevskij• Staroжurjevo•   •Rudovka
•Miloslavsk D'at'kovo• Jelenskij• Bolchov• Turdej• Dankov•   Čaplygino• Pervomajskij•   Otjassy•
         •Fokino   Kletn'a• Korsakovo•   Lebed'an'•   Gorelovo•   Tambov
elynkoviči Belye Bereg• Mcensk• Novosil'• Jefremov•   Mičurinsk•   •Rasskazovo
Br'ansk• Mglin• •Sven' Or'ol•   Kujman'• Izmalkovo• Lipeck• Belomestnaja• Kotovsk•   Um'ot•   52°
Suraž• Počep•   Navl'a• Somovo• Kromy• Zmijovka•   Syrskij• Gr'azi•   Inžavino•
Klincy   Ramasucha• •Altuchovo Dmitrievsko- •Maloarchangel'sk Livny• Jelec Okt'abr'skij• Niжnaja• Ržaksa•
starodub Trubč'ovsk• Orlovskij•   Kolpny•   Verchnij• Matrenka• Sampur• Veselki•
         Belaja Ber'ozka• Železnogorsk• Svapa•   Dolgoje• Lomovec• Ok'tabr'skij• Talickij Čamlyk• Žerdevka•
Sem'onovka Znob'-Novgorodskoje• Sevsk• Fat'oz•   Urickoje•   VORONEŽSKIJ Uvarovo• Sapkino•
                                                      ZAPOVEDNIK

BARENTS SEA
Beloje More / White Sea
KOL'SKIJ POLUOSTROV / KOLA PENINSULA
Malyje Karmakuly
NOVAJA ZEML'A
KARSKOJE MORE / KARA SEA
OSTROV KOMSOMOLEC
OSTROV OKT'ABR'SKOJ REVOL'UCII
SEVERNAJA ZEML'A
OSTROV BOL'ŠEVIK
Mys Želanija
OSTROVA ARKTIČESKOGO INSTITUTA
ARCHIPELAG NORDENŠEL'DA
MYS ČEL'USKIN
Matočkin
Krasino
Peŝorskoje More
OSTROV KOLGUJEV
POLUOSTROV TAJMYR
Chatangskij Zaliv
Nord
Vajgač
Pasinskij Zaliv
Dikson
Novorybnoje
Narian-Mar
Chabarovo
Kara
Baidarackaja Guba
POLUOSTROV JAMAL
Japtiksal'a
Napalkovo
Gyda
Obskaja Guba
Tazovskij Guba
Karaul
Pasina
Voločanka
Chatanga
Chantangskij Zaliv
Dželinde
Vorkuta
Inta
Pečora
Suryikary
Novyj Port
Tareja
Agapa
Aian
Arctic Circle / Labytnangi
Uf'- Cilma
Krasnoselkup
Turuchansk
Gora Kamen' 1701
SREDNE SIBIRSKOJE
Uchta
Gora Čertaskij
Zeleznodoroznyj
Jakša
△ Gora Naradnaja 1895
Ob'
Nadym
Pur
Tarko-Sale
Igarka
Kureika
Nizn'aja Tunguska
Tunu
Goral'uca-Ongokton 1044
SIBIRSK
URAL'SKIJE GORY / URAL MOUNTAINS
Gora Konzakovskij
Serov
Berezniki
Nizn'ij Tagil
Sverdlovsk
Kamensk.
Ural'skij
Alapajevsk
ZAPADNO-SIBIRSKAJA NIZMENNOST'
Konda
ROSSIJSKAJA SOVETSKAJA FEDERATIVNAJA
PLOSKOGO
Murukta
Noril'sk
Chanty-Mansijsk
Surgut
Agan
Korliki
Verchneimbatskoje
Tura
Podkamennaja Tunguska
Bajkit
SOCIALISTIC
Tobol'sk
Ust'-Ilim
Vach
Laurat
Kazuyan
Karpasok
Sym
Podkamennaja Tunguska
RUSSIAN SOVIET FEDERATED SOCIA
Mutoraj
UNION
Tumen'
Tavda
Isim
Nazyvaevsk
Tara
Vasjugan'ja
Kolpasevo
Ket
Bajkit
Dušekan
Petropavlovsk
Kurgan
Volodarskoje
Krasnoarmejsk
Tatarsk
Om'
Čulym
Kazačinskoje
Jenisejsk
Angara
Boguéany
Yanavara
Lena
OF
SOVIET
Omsk
eKočetav
Irtyš
Kupino
Bolotnoje
Tom'
Anžero-Sudžensk
Ačinsk
Tasejevo
Čuna
Nizneilimsk
Kirensk
Ust'-Kut
Atbasar
Makinsk
Bestobe
Slavgorod
Kamen'-na-Obi
SOCIALIST
Celinograd
Ekibastuz
Novosibirsk
Kemerovo
Leninsk-Kuzneckij
Krasnojarsk
Kansk
Tajšet
Bratsk
Nizneudinsk
Bratskoje Vodochraniliŝče
Nizneangarsk
Temirtau
Pavlodar
Barnaul
Prokopievsk
Belovo
Jenisej
Černogorsk
Art'omovsk
Tulun
Žigalovo
Kumuri
Karaganda
Semipalatinsk
Bijsk
Novokuzneck
Abakan
Zima
Kaćug
KAZACHSKAJA S.S.R.
Agady
Rubcovsk
Tastaftol
Ust'-Kamengorsk
Gora Karagoš 2930
SAYAN MOUNTAINS
Čeremchovo
Angarsk
Irkutsk
Chuzir
Ozero Bajkal / Lake Bajkal
Karazal
Balchaš
Šemonaicha
Sebalino
Teli
Kyzyl
Chanch
Sosno Oz'orske
Ulan-Ude
Ozero Balchaš
Aktogaj
Ajaguz
Koš-Agač
Ulaangom
Chatgal
Petrovsk-Zabajkal'sk
Suchbaatar
Čiganak
Ustobe
Ozero Zaisan
Teli
Chovd
Chutag
Darchan
Satyorek
Taldy-Kurgan
CHINA XINJIANG WEIWUER ZIZHIQU / SINKIANG
Uliastaj
MONGOLIA
Orchon
Ondörchaan
Alma-Ata
Rybacie
Yining / Kuldja
Kelamayi
Altaj (Jesönbulag)
Cecerleg
Ulaanbaatar

Kilometres 0 200 400 600 Km.
Miles 0 200 400 600 Mi.
1 : 24 000 000

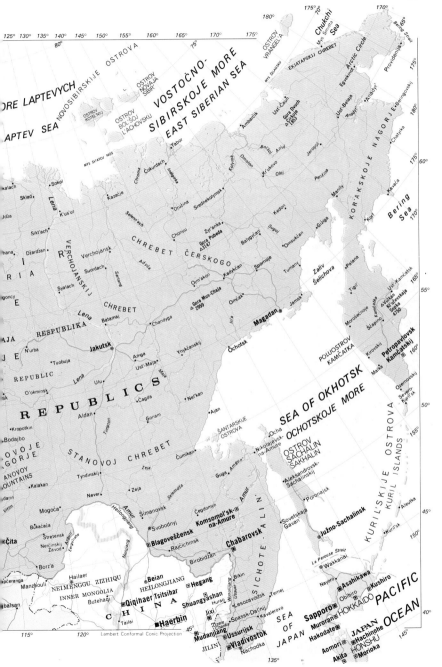

51

125° 130° 135° 140° 145° 150° 155° 160° 165° 170° 175°

180° 175° 70° 170°

80°

Chukchi Sea

OSTROVA

NOVOSIBIRSKIJE OSTROVA

OSTROV WRANGELA

Mys Smidta

Arctic Circle

Bering Strait 65°

ORE LAPTEVYCH

OSTROV NOVAJA SIBIR

VOSTOČNO-SIBIRSKOJE MORE

EKIATAPSKIJ CHREBET

Egvekinot

Providenija

175°

LAPTEV SEA

OSTROV KOTELNYJ

OSTROV BOL'ŠOJ L'ACHOVSKIJ

EAST SIBERIAN SEA

Uelen

Ust'-Čaun

Anadyr'

75°

KORÁKSKOJE NAGORJ E·Beringovskij

180°

kalach

MYS SVATOJ NOS

Ambarčik

Gora Davyd Gilde 1883

Anjuj

Anadyr'

Chatyrka

60°

Sokol

Chroma

Čokurdach

Indigirka

Kolyma

Bolšoj Anuj

Perzina

Sklad

Lena

K'us'ur

Kazačje

Družina

Srednekolymsk

Kolyma

Krjukovo

Oloj

Manily

Bering Sea

Kavača

Jdza

Sikt'ach

Selennjach

Chonuu

Zyŕanka Gora Pobeda 3147

Balygyčan

Sugoj

Omsukčan

Gižiga

Kgi

170°

hana

Džardžan

Verchojansk

CHREBET ČERSKOGO

Adyča

Omolon

Kedon

Tumany

Palana

55°

I

VERCHOJANSKIJ

Svjatach

Suordach

Sarang

Ojmakon

Kadykčan

Spornoje

Omčak

Zaliv Šelichova

Tigil'

Volkan Ključevskaja Sopka 4750

Ust'-Kamčatsk

165°

goncy

E

CHREBET

Lena

Batamaj

Chandyga

Gora Mus-Chala 2959

Inja

Omčak

Jamsk

Magadan

Morošečnoje

Šcapino

POLUOSTROV KAMČATKA

Kirovskij

Malka

Petropavlovsk-Kamčatski

160°

AJA

RESPUBLIKA

N'urba

Tuobuja

Anga

Ynykčanskij

Ochotsk

Severo-Kuril'sk

Ozernovskij

JE

Jakutsk

Ust'-Maja

Maja

50°

REPUBLIC

O'okminsk

Ulu

Nel'kan

KURIL'SKIJE OSTROVA

155°

sk

Lena

Čagda

Ajan

ŠANTARSKIJE OSTROVA

SEA OF OKHOTSK

REPUBLICS

Aldan

Gonam

OCHOTSKOJE MORE

KURIL ISLANDS

Kropotkin

Ocha

Nikolajevsk-na-Amure

OSTROV SACHALIN SAKHALIN

Aleutka

Kuril'sk

Bodajbo

OVOJE GORJE

STANOVOJ CHREBET

Zeja

Čumikan

Aleksandrovsk-Sachalinskij

45°

ANOVOY MOUNTAINS

Tyndinskij

Zeja

Selemdža

Guga

Poronajsk

Kuril'sk

150°

darin

Kalakan

Never

Amur

Simanovsk

Čegdomyn

SICHOTE-ALIN'

Sovetskaja Gavan'

Vitim

Mogoča

Svobodnyj

Komsomol'sk-na-Amure

Južno-Sachalinsk

Čita

Bukačača

Stretensk

Nerčinskij Zavod

Blagoveščensk

Chabarovsk

Birobidžan

La Perouse Strait

Wakkanai

Borz'a

Rajčichinsk

Bikin

Nevoro

Asahikawa

Kushiro

PACIFIC

peranga

Manzhouli

Hailaer

NEIMENGGU ZIZHIQU

Beian

HEILONGJIANG

Hegang

Lesozavodsk

Ternej

Obihiro

HOKKAIDO

balsan

INNER MONGOLIA

Butehaqi

Shuangyashan

Spassk-Dal'nij

Kavalerovo

Sapporo

Muroran

OCEAN

CHINA

Qiqihaer Tsitsihar

Jixi

SEA OF JAPAN

Hakodate

JAPAN

40°

Tailai

Haerbin

Mudanjiang

Ussurijsk

Nachodka

Aomori

Hachinohe

HONSHU

115° 120°

Lambert Conformal Conic Projection

JILIN

Vladivostok

135°

Akita

Morioka

145°

52

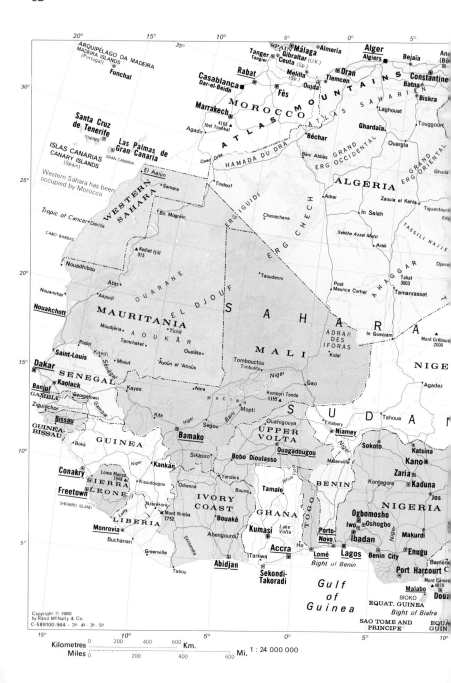

Copyright © 1980
by Rand McNally & Co.
C-589100-964 - 3ᵛ· 4ᵛ· 3ᵛ· 5ᵛ

Kilometres
Miles
Km.
Mi. 1 : 24 000 000

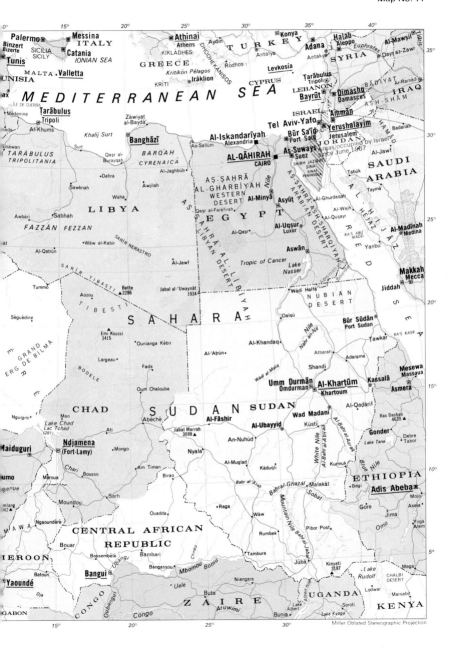

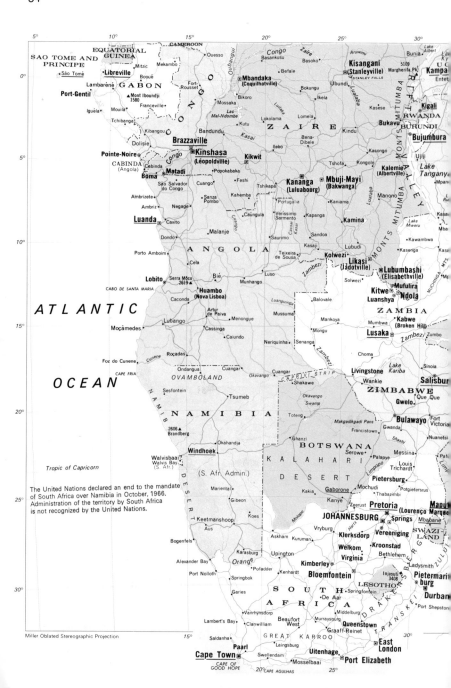

Kilometres 0   200   400   600 Km.
Miles 0   200   400   600 Mi.

1 : 24 000 000

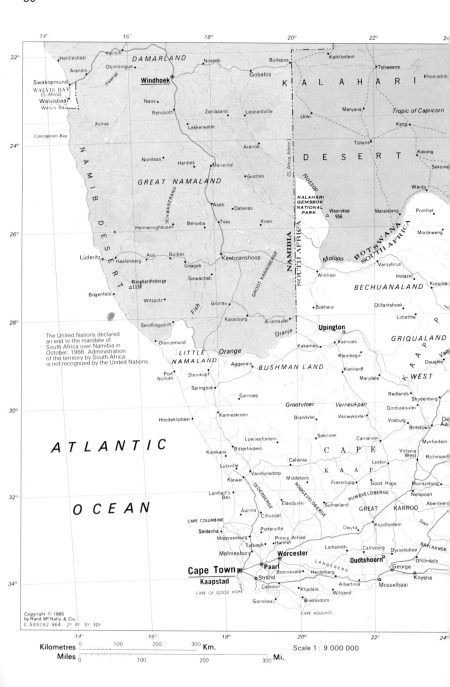

14° 16° 18° 20° 22° 24°

22°
Hentiesbaai • Karibib
Arandis • Otjimbingue
DAMARLAND
Nossob • Buitepos
Kalkfontein
Tshwaane
Khomodim
Swakopmund
WALVIS BAY
(S. Africa)
Walvisbaai
Walvis Bay
Windhoek
Gobabis
K A L A H A R I
Naos •
Rehoboth
Zaniasand • Leonardville
Urwi •
Manyana
Tropic of Capricorn
Kang •
Conception Bay
Lekkerwater
Tshane •
24°
Aranos •
D E S E R T
Kokong
Sekoma
Nomtsas •
Haribes •
Mariental •
Gochas •
Kalahari
GREAT NAMALAND
(S. Africa Admin.)
Werda •
Kalahari
Gemsbok
National
Park
Vloorskop
956
Maralaleng •
Pomfret
Asab • Daberas •
Berseba • Tses •
Koes •
Morokweng
Helmeringhausen •
26°
Lüderitz
Haalenberg
Aus • Guibes
Goageb
Keetmanshoop
NAMIBIA
SOUTH AFRICA
Witdraai •
Molopo
BOTSWANA
SOUTH AFRICA
Vanzylsrus •
Klinghardtsberge
1138
Gawachab •
Bokhara •
Hotazel •
Kuruma •
Bogenfels •
Witzputz •
Grünau •
BECHUANALAND
Olifantshoek •
28°
Sendlingsdrift •
Karasburg •
Ariamsvlei •
Oranjemund •
Upington
Kakamas •
Keimoes •
GRIQUALAND
Lohatlha •
The United Nations declared
an end to the mandate of
South Africa over Namibia in
October, 1966. Administration
of the territory by South Africa
is not recognized by the United Nations.
LITTLE
NAMALAND
Orange
Aggeneis •
Kleinbegin •
Kenhardt •
Marydale •
Douglas •
WEST
Port
Nolloth •
Steinkopf •
BUSHMAN LAND
Redlands •
Strydenburg •
Springbok •
Gamoep •
30°
A T L A N T I C
Hondeklipbaai •
Kamieskroon •
Groatvloer
Verneukpan
Brandvlei •
Vanwyksvlei •
Omdraaisvlei •
Vosburg •
Britstown •
Sakrivier •
Loeriesfontein •
Carnarvon •
Victoria
West
Myntfontein •
Richmond
Bitterfontein •
Komkans •
Calvinia •
C A P E
Loxton •
O C E A N
Lutzville •
K A A P
Fraserburg •
Good Hope •
Murraysburg •
32°
Klawer •
Vanrhynsdorp •
Middelpos •
Aberdeen •
Lambert's
Bay •
Aurora •
Elandsvlei •
Sutherland •
NUWEVELDBERGE
Kruidfontein •
Nelspoort •
GREAT   KARROO
CAPE COLUMBINE
Citrusdal •
Dwyka •
Saldanha •
Porterville •
Prince Alfred
Hamlet
Moorreesburg •
Ladismith •
Calitzdorp •
Dysselsdorp •
Tulbagh •
Uniondale •
Malmesbury •
Worcester
Oudtshoorn
George
Knysna
Cape Town
Paarl
Strand •
Bonnievale •
Heidelberg •
Mosselbaai •
Kaapstad
Caledon •
Albertinia •
34°
CAPE OF GOOD HOPE
Klipdale •
Witsand •
Gansbaai •
Bredasdorp •
CAPE AGULHAS

Kilometres |0   100   200   300| Km.   Scale 1 : 9 000 000
Miles |0   100   200   300| Mi.

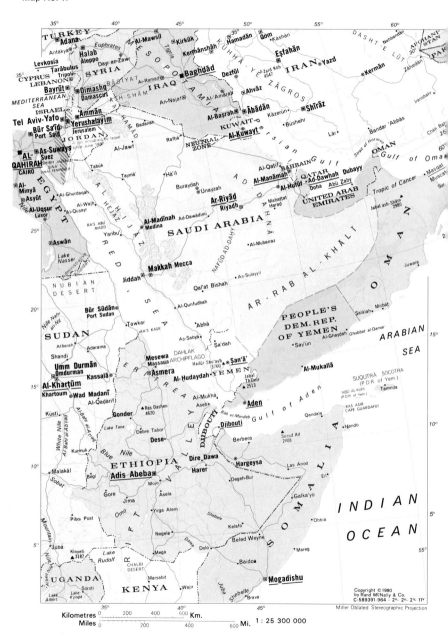

Kilometres 0 200 400 600 Km.
Miles 0 200 400 600 Mi. 1 : 25 300 000

Copyright © 1980
by Rand McNally & Co.
C-589391-964
Miller Oblated Stereographic Projection

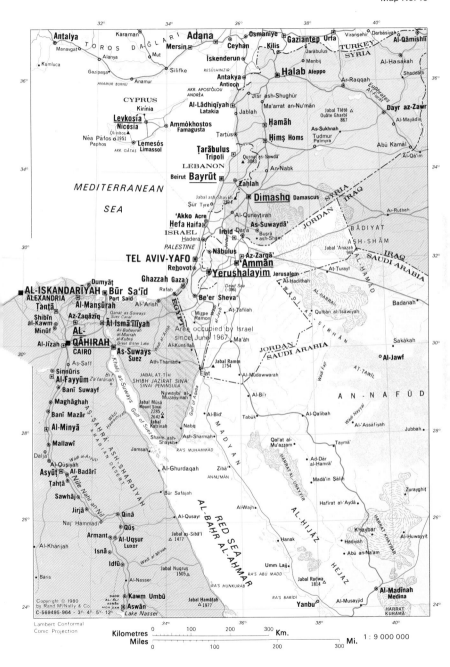

Lambert Conformal
Conic Projection

Kilometres 0   100   200   300 Km.

Miles 0   100   200   300 Mi.

1 : 9 000 000

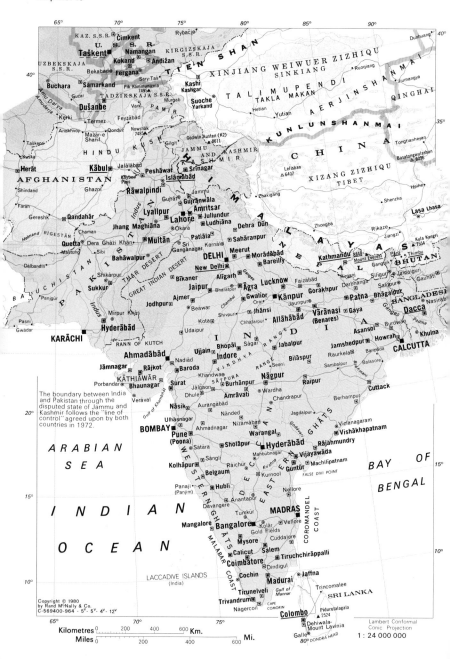

The boundary between India and Pakistan through the disputed state of Jammu and Kashmir follows the "line of control" agreed upon by both countries in 1972.

Kilometres   200   400   600 Km.
Miles   200   400   600 Mi.

Lambert Conformal
Conic Projection
1 : 24 000 000

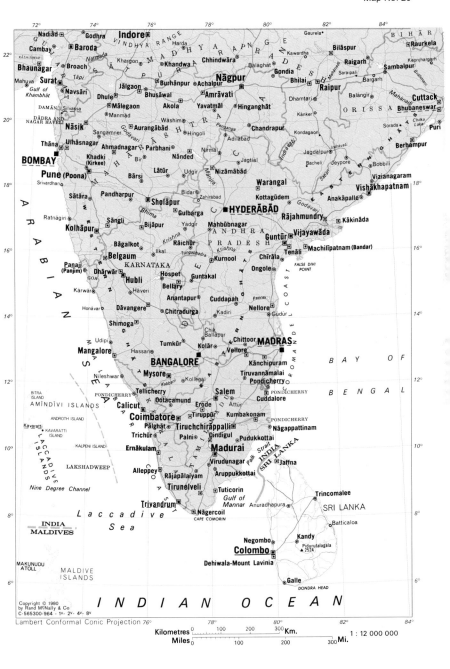

Lambert Conformal Conic Projection 76°

Kilometres 0 — 100 — 200 — 300 Km.
Miles 0 — 100 — 200 — 300 Mi.

1 : 12 000 000

62

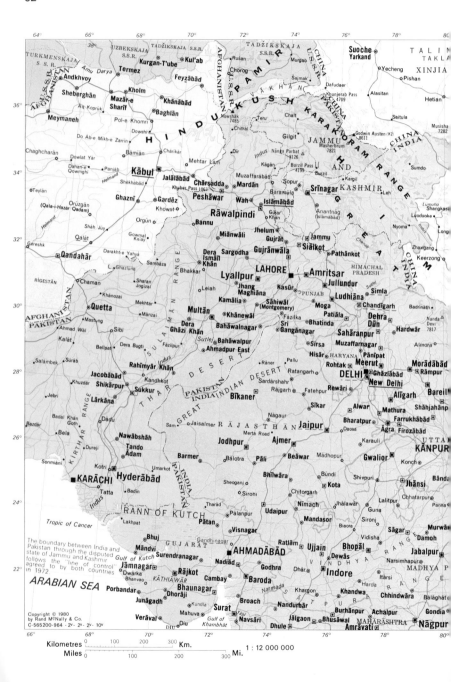

Kilometres 0 100 200 300 Km.

Miles 0 100 200 300 Mi.

1 : 12 000 000

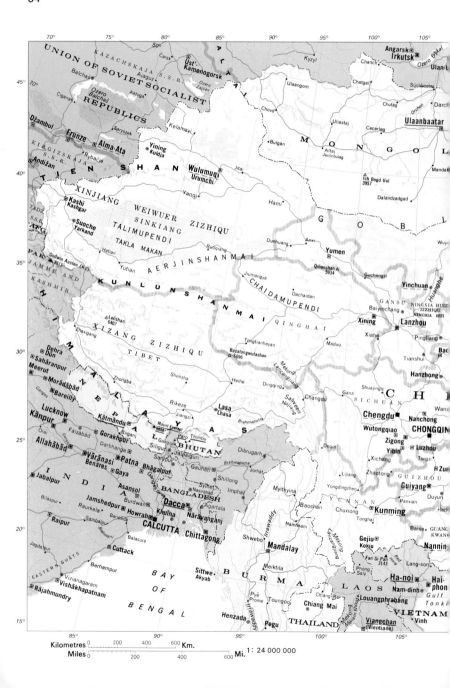

Kilometres 0 200 400 600 Km.

Miles 0 200 400 600 Mi.

1 : 24 000 000

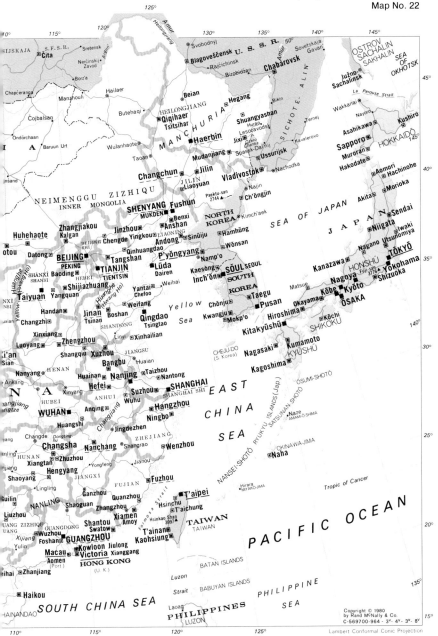

Lambert Conformal Conic Projection

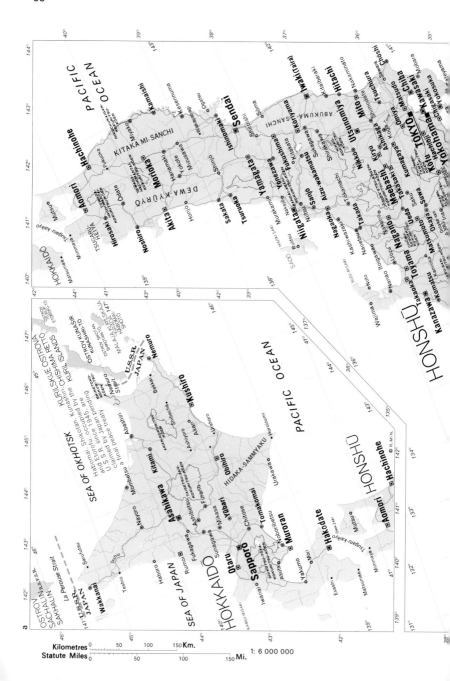

PACIFIC OCEAN

HOKKAIDO

Wakkanai

OSTROV SACHALIN N.s.s.R.
SAKHALIN
U.S.S.R.
JAPAN
La Perouse Strait

SEA OF OKHOTSK

KURILSKIE OSTROVA
KURIL'SKII CHISHIMA RETTO
Kunashir, occupied by the KURIL ISLANDS
Habomai, Shikotan, Kunashiri
and Etorofu, occupied since 1945,
are claimed by Japan U.S.S.R. has
claimed a final peace treaty

U.S.S.R.
JAPAN

Nemuro
Nemuro Strait

Kushiro

Kitami

Asahikawa

Otaru
Sapporo

Yubari
Obihiro

Muroran
Tomakomai

HIDAKA-SAMMYAKU

Hakodate

Tsugaru-kaikyo

Aomori

HONSHU

Hachinohe

PACIFIC OCEAN

SEA OF JAPAN

HOKKAIDO

PACIFIC OCEAN

HOKKAIDO

Aomori
Hirosaki
Noshiro
Akita

Hachinohe

KITAKA MI-SANCHI

Morioka

Kamaishi

DEWA-KYURYO

Yamagata

Sakata
Tsuruoka

Sendai

Ishimaki

Niigata
Nagaoka
Takada

Nagano
Matsumoto
Ueda

Yonezawa
Fukushima

Aizu-wakamatsu

Koriyama

ABUKUMA-SANCHI

Iwaki (Taira)

Hitachi
Mito

Utsunomiya
Nikko

Kiryu
Ashikaga

Maebashi
Takasaki
Kumagaya

Suwa

Kofu

Toyama
Takaoka
Kanazawa
Komatsu

Kashiwazaki

HONSHU

Choshi
Chiba
Matsudo
TOKYO
Kawasaki
Yokohama
Yokosuka

PACIFIC OCEAN

Kilometres 0   50   100   150 Km.
Statute Miles 0   50   100   150 Mi.
1: 6 000 000

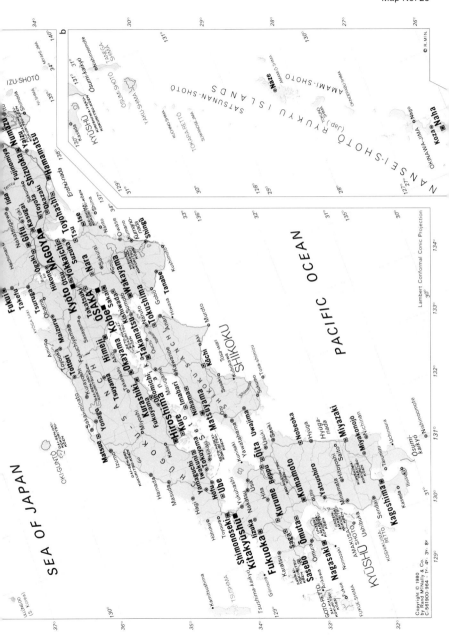

SEA OF JAPAN

PACIFIC OCEAN

KYUSHU

SHIKOKU

IZU-SHOTŌ

NANSEI-SHOTŌ RYUKYU ISLANDS (Jap.)

SATSUNAN-SHOTŌ

AMAMI-SHOTŌ

ŌSUMI-SHOTŌ

TOKARA-RETTŌ

OKI-GUNTŌ

GOTŌ-RETTŌ

AMAKUSA-SHOTŌ

Lambert Conformal Conic Projection

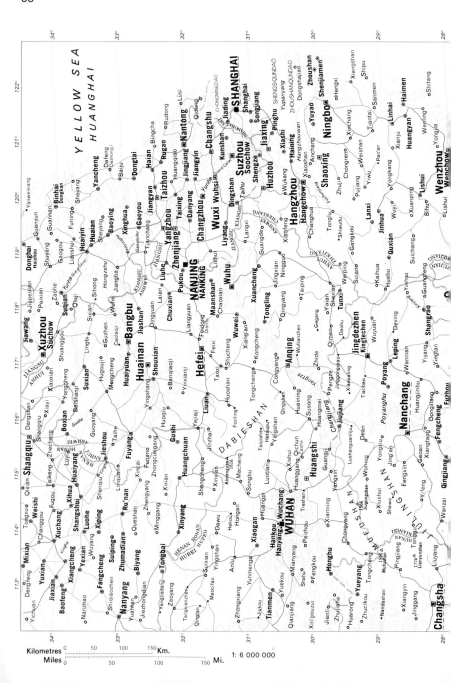

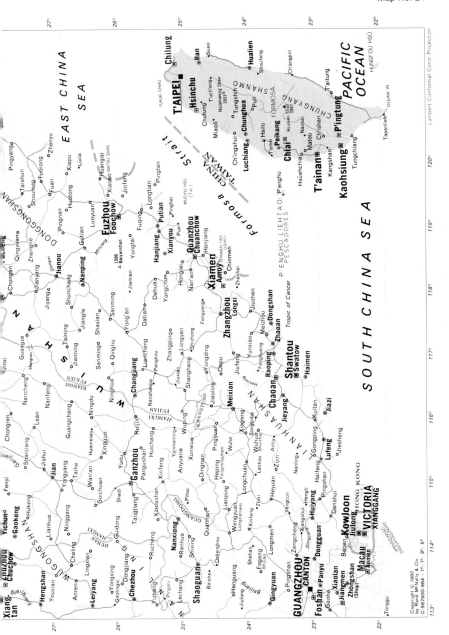

Lambert Conformal Conic Projection

Copyright © 1980
by Rand McNally & Co.
C-567600-984 - 1ʸ - 1ʸ - 3ʸ - 5ʸ

EAST CHINA SEA

PACIFIC OCEAN

SOUTH CHINA SEA

Formosa Strait (TAIWAN CHINA Strait)

TAIPEI
Chilung
Ilan
Suao
Hsinchu
Chutung
Tuchiang
Hualien
Shoufeng
Chunghua
Pufi
Changpin
Miaoli
Hsiaikang
Hsilo
Nanhsi
Tratung
Peikang
Matou
Chishan
Luchiang
Chiai
Kangshan
Kaohsiung
Tungchiang
Pingtung
Tapanlieh
Oluan Pi

P'ENGHU LIEHTAO
(PESCADORES)
Penghu

Tropic of Cancer

Fuzhou
Foochow
Nanping
Jianou
Putian
Fuqing
Hanjiang
Xianyou
Quanzhou
Chuanchow
Xiamen
Amoy
Zhangzhou
Longxi
Dongshan
Zhaoan
Shantou
Swatow
Haimen
Chaoan
Jieyang
Meixian

Fujian
Jiangxi
Nanchang
Ganzhou
Shaoguan
Changjiang

GUANGZHOU
CANTON
Foshan
Panyu
Dongguan
Macau
Aomen
Kowloon
Jiulong
HONG KONG
VICTORIA
XIANGGANG
Qingyuan

CHINA GUANGXI
ZHUANGZU
Chittagong   YUNNAN   Gejiu Kokiu   Nanning   ZIZHIQU Yulin   Foshan GUANGZHOU Shantou
BANGLA-   CANTON   Swatow
DESH   Mandalay   3143   ZHUANGZU   Macau New Kowloon VICTORIA
            Shwebo   Fan-si-pan   Nanning Beihai   Aomen   HONG KONG
Sittwe   Myingyan   Phöngsali   Ha-noi   (Port.) (U.K.)
(Akyab)   BURMA   Keng Tung   Red Hong Hai-phong   Haikou
                                         Nam-dinh   HAINANDAO
          Prome   Chiang Rai LAOS
          (Pyè)   Louangphrabang   Gulf of
Henzada   *Chiang   Tonkin
          RANGOON Mai   Viangchan   Vinh
          Pegu   (Vientiane)   Udon   Dong-hoi
Moulmein   THAILAND Thani Khon Kaen
                                              Hue
          Nakhon   Da-nang
          Sawan   Nakhon
Tavoy   Ratchasima   Pakxé   VIETNAM
                                           Qui-nhon   SOUTH CHINA
          KRUNG THEP
Mergui   BANGKOK   KAMPUCHEA
MERGUI   Stoeng Treng
ARCHIPELAGO   Gulf of   Phnum Pénh   Nha-trang   SEA
          Thailand   Mékong
Chumphon   Kâmpóng Saóm   Gia-dinh
                    Rach-gia Phan-thiet
ISTHMUS   Can-tho   THANH-PHO HO CHI MINH
OF   (SAI-GON)
KRA   Nakhon Si   Puerto Princesa
       Thammarat   PALAWAN
Phuket   Songkhla

ANDAMAN ISLANDS (Ind·a)
ANDAMAN SEA
Port Blair
NICOBAR ISLANDS (India)
Great Channel
Banda Aceh

Alor Setar   Kudat
          Kota Baharu   Kota Kinabalu Gunung
George Town   Kinabalu
(Pinang)   Bandar Seri Begawan 4094 Sandakan
                    KEPULAUAN   BRUNEI   Bukit
Medan   MALAYSIA   BUNGURAN   (U.K.)   Pagon
        MALAYA   UTARA   1850 Tarakan
Pematangsiantar   Kuala Lumpur
        Meleka   MALAYSIA
Sibolga   TANDJUNG   Sibu   2053 Kong Kemul
PULAU   DATU   Kuching Kapuas Kayan Talok
NIAS   SINGAPORE SINGAPORE   Rajang
                 KEPULAUAN LINGGA   BORNEO SU
Pakanbaru   Pontianak KALIMANTAN
SUMATERA   Sampit Mehawi Samarinda
Padang SUMATRA   Balikpapan
        Gunung   Jambi   BELITUNG
        Kerinci   Pangkalpinang   Banjarmasin
        3800   Palembang   Sampit
Bengkulu   Lahat
                              GREATER   SU
          Telukbetung   INDONESIA   ISLAND
INDIAN   OCEAN   LAUT JAWA   JAVA SEA
                 JAKARTA   MADURA
          Bogor Cirebon Semarang
          BANDUNG   Surabaya SURABAYA
          Tasikmalaya Surakarta Madiun Malang
          Yogyakarta   BALI LOMBOK Laut
                 JAWA   Denpasar   SUMBAWA
                 JAVA   BALI LOMBOK LESSER

CHRISTMAS ISLAND
(Austr.)

Kilometres 0 200 400 600 Km.
Miles 0   200   400   600 Mi.
1 : 24 000 000

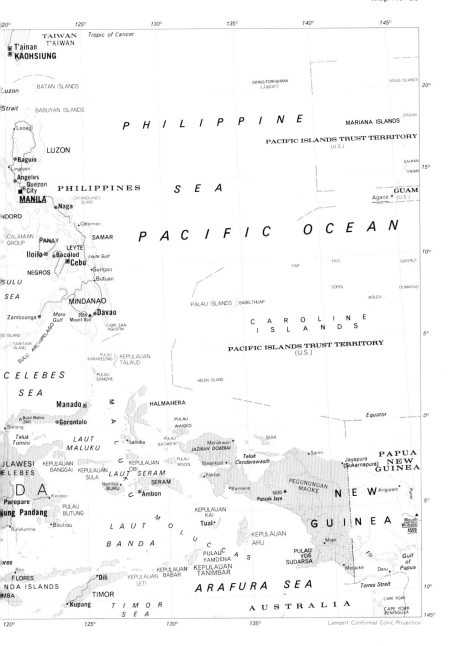

1: 12 000 000

110°　　　　　115°　　　　　120°　　　　　125°　　　　　130°

Surakarta ● Malang
Yogyakarta ● Blitar ● Jember ● BALI　SUMBAWA　SUNDA ISLANDS　TIMOR　　　A r a f
JAWA JAVA　　　LOMBOK　LESSER　SUMBA　Laut Sawu　Kupang　Timor　MELVILLE
I N D O N E S I A　　　　SUMBAWA　PULAU ROTI　　　　ISLAND
　　　　　　　　　　　　　　PULAU　　　　Sea　BATHURST
　　　　　　　　　　　　　　SAWU　　　　　　ISLAND
10°　　　　　　　　　　CARTIER ISLAND　　　　　　Darwin　ARNHEM
I N D I A N　　　　　　CAPE　Joseph　Rum Jungle ●　LAND
　　　　　　　　　　LONDONDERRY　Bonaparte　Katherine
　　　　　　　　　　　BONAPARTE　Gulf
　　　　　　　　　　　ARCHIPELAGO　　　Victoria　Birdum
　　　　　　　　　　　　　Wyndham
O C E A N　　　　CAPE LEVEQUE　KIMBERLEY PLATEAU　Newcastle
15°　　ROWLEY　　　　△ Mount Ord　　　Waters
　　　SHOALS　　　　936　Halls　NORTHERN
　　　　　　Broome　Fitzroy　Creek
　　DAMPIER　Port　EIGHTY MILE BEACH
　　ARCHIPELAGO　Hedland　GREAT SANDY DESERT　TERRITORY
　　　　● Roebourne　　　　Barrow Creek ●
20°　Onslow ●　Fortescue　● Nullagine　Lake Mackay
NORTH WEST CAPE　HAMERSLEY RANGE　　(Dry Salt Lake)　Mount Zeil
　　　　　1235　　Lake　　　　1511　● Alic
　　　　　Mount Bruce　Disappointment　Mount Leisler　Spring
　　　　WESTERN　(Dry Salt Lake)　901　MACDONNELL
　　Lake Macleod　GIBSON DESERT　　　　A U S T R
105°　　△ Mount Augustus　Mount　Lake Carnegie
　BERNIER ISLAND　1105　Essendon　(Dry)　Mount Aloysius
　Carnarvon ●　　906　　　1085　Mount Woodroffe
25°　DIRK HARTOG　Wooramel ●　Wiluna ●　　　　1439
　ISLAND　Meekatharra ●　GREAT VICTORIA DESERT
　　　　Mount　A U S T R A L I A
　　　　Magnet　Lake Carey　SOUTH
　Geraldton ●　Lake　(Dry Salt Lake)
　Dongara ●　Barlee　Leonora ●
　　　　D A R L I N G   R A N G E
30°　　Dalwallinu ●　Kalgoorlie ●　Forrest ●　Ooldea ●
　Perth ●　Southern　Norseman ●　Eucla ●
　　Northam ●　Cross　　　　CAPE ADIEU
　Bunbury ●　Ravensthorpe ●　● Esperance
CAPE NATURALISTE　Augusta ●　CAPE　Great Australian Bight
CAPE LEEUWIN　Albany ●　ARID
　　CAPE VANCOUVER
35°
　　　　I N D I A N　　O C E A
40°　Copyright © 1980
by Rand McNally & Co.
C-590200-964 - 4ᵛ·· 5ᵛ·· 5ᵛ·· 9ᵛ
　105°　　110°　　115°　　120°　　125°　　130°
Kilometres 0　200　400　600 Km.
Statute Miles 0　200　400　600 Mi.　　1 : 24 000 000

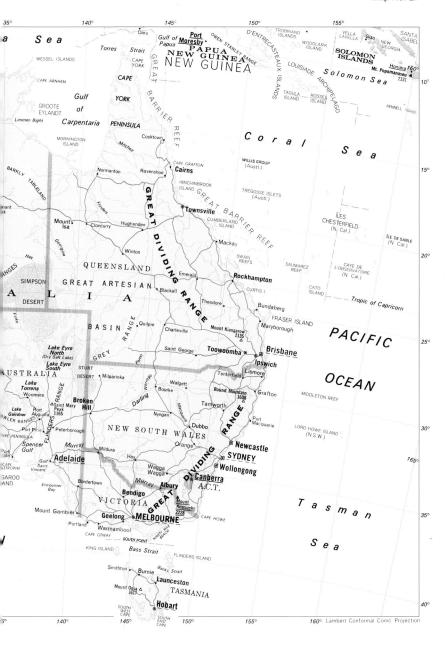

35°   140°   145°   150°   155°

a   S e a

WESSEL ISLANDS

Torres   Strait

Daru

Gulf of
Papua

**Port
Moresby**

OWEN STANLEY RANGE

**PAPUA
NEW GUINEA**

NEW GUINEA

D'ENTRECASTEAUX ISLANDS

TROBRIAND
ISLANDS

WOODLARK
ISLAND

VELLA
LAVELLA   Gizo

NEW
GEORGIA

SANTA
ISABEL

**SOLOMON
ISLANDS**

Honiara 160°

Mt. Popomanaseu
2331

CAPE ARNHEM

CAPE
YORK

CAPE

GROOTE
EYLANDT

Gulf

of

LOUISIADE ARCHIPELAGO

TAGULA
ISLAND

ROSSEL
ISLAND

S o l o m o n   S e a

RENNELL

10°

Limmen Bight

MORNINGTON
ISLAND

Carpentaria   PENINSULA

YORK

C o r a l

S e a

BARKLY
TABLELAND

Cooktown

CAPE GRAFTON

WILLIS GROUP
(Austl.)

ILES
CHESTERFIELD
(N. Cal.)

ÎLE DE SABLE
(N. Cal.)

Normanton   Ravenshoe   **Cairns**

HINCHINBROOK
ISLAND

TREGOSSE ISLETS
(Austl.)

15°

Mount
Isa

Cloncurry

Hughenden

Mitchell

Flinders

Townsville

CUMBERLAND
ISLAND

GREAT BARRIER REEF

B A R R I E R   R E E F

G R E A T

Winton

QUEENSLAND

•Mackay

SWAIN
REEFS

SAUMAREZ
REEF

CAYE DE
L'OBSERVATOIRE
(N. Cal.)

20°

SIMPSON

DESERT

GREAT   ARTESIAN

Georgina

Emerald

Blackall

•**Rockhampton**

CURTIS I.

CATO
ISLAND

Tropic of Capricorn

A L I A

B A S I N

Theodore

Bundaberg

FRASER ISLAND

PACIFIC

Hay

RANGES

Lake Eyre
North
(Dry Salt Lake)

Lake Eyre
South

Quilpie

GREY

Charleville

RANGE

Saint George

Mount Kiangarow
1135

Toowoomba

Maryborough

Brisbane

OCEAN

25°

AUSTRALIA

Finke

Lake
Torrens

Woomera

STURT

DESERT

Milparinka

Paroo

Warrego

Bourke

Walgett

Ipswich

Lismore

Tenterfield

Grafton

MIDDLETON REEF

LORD HOWE ISLAND
(N.S.W.)

AUSTRALIA

Lake
Gairdner

GAWLER RANGES

Port
Augusta

Saint Mary
Peak
1165

Peterborough

**Broken
Hill**

Darling

Nyngan

Round Mountain
1608

Tamworth

RANGE

DIVIDING

30°

165°

YORKE PENINSULA

EYRE PENINSULA

Port Pirie

Spencer
Gulf

Murray

NEW   SOUTH   WALES

Dubbo

Orange

Macquarie

Port
Macquarie

Port
Lincoln

Adelaide

Mildura

Hay

Wagga
Wagga

Newcastle

SYDNEY

KANGAROO
ISLAND

CAPE
CATASTROPHE

Gulf
Saint
Vincent

Encounter
Bay

Bordertown

Murray

Albury

Canberra
A.C.T.

Wollongong

GREAT

DIVIDING RANGE

T a s m a n

35°

Mount Gambier

Bendigo

VICTORIA

Mount
Kosciusko
2228

S e a

Portland

Geelong

Warrnambool

CAPE OTWAY

MELBOURNE

CAPE HOWE

NINETY MILE BEACH

SOUTH POINT

KING ISLAND

Bass Strait

FLINDERS ISLAND

Smithton   Burnie

Banks Strait

Launceston

TASMANIA

Mount Ossa
1617

SOUTH
WEST
CAPE

Hobart

SOUTH
EAST
CAPE

40°

5°   140°   145°   150°   155°   160° Lambert Conformal Conic Projection

Kilometres 0   100   200   300 Km.

Miles 0   100   200   300 Mi.

1 : 12 000 000

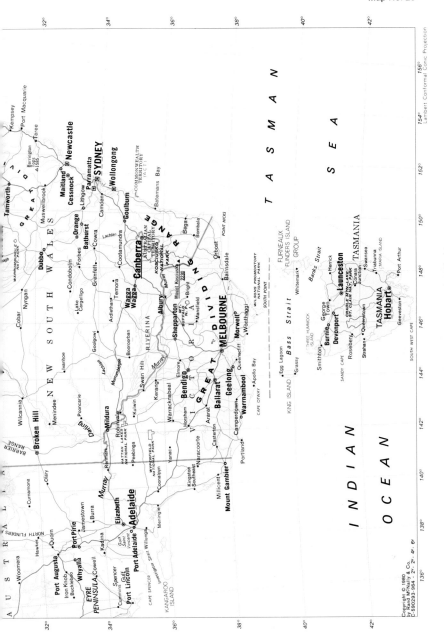

Lambert Conformal Conic Projection

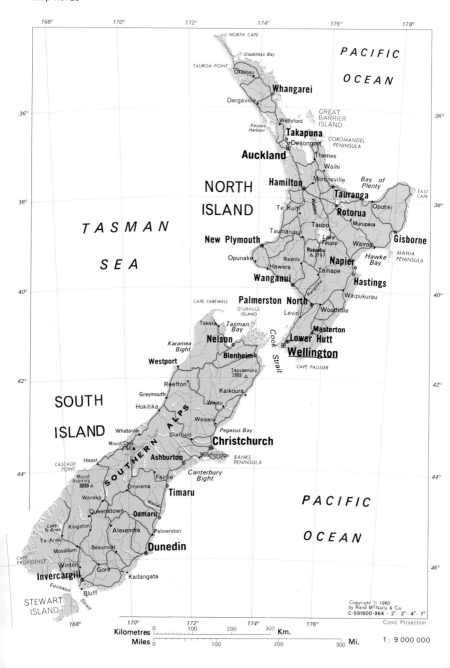

NORTH CAPE
Doubtless Bay
TAUROA POINT
Okahau
Whangarei
Dargaville
Wellsford
Kaipara Harbour
GREAT BARRIER ISLAND
Takapuna
Devonport
COROMANDEL PENINSULA
Auckland
Thames
Waihi
Hamilton
Morrinsville
Bay of Plenty
Tauranga
EAST CAPE

PACIFIC OCEAN

Te Kuiti
Rotorua
Opotiki
Murupara

NORTH ISLAND

Taupo
Waikato
Taumarunui
New Plymouth
Lake Taupo
Ruapehu △ 2797
Wairoa
Gisborne
MAHIA PENINSULA

TASMAN

Opunake
Raetihi
Hawera
Taihape
Rangitikei
Napier
Hawke Bay

SEA

Wanganui
Hastings
Waipukurau

36°   36°
38°   38°
40°   40°
42°   42°
44°   44°
46°

Palmerston North
CAPE FAREWELL
D'URVILLE ISLAND
Levin
Woodville
Takaka
Tasman Bay
Cook Strait
Masterton
Nelson
Lower Hutt
Wellington
Karamea Bight
Blenheim
CAPE PALLISER
Westport
Tapuaenuku 2885 △
Reefton
Kaikoura
Greymouth
Wau
Hokitika
Waipara
SOUTH
Whataroa
Sheffield
Pegasus Bay
ISLAND
Mount Cook 3764 △
Christchurch
Southbridge
BANKS PENINSULA
CASCADE POINT
Haast
Ashburton
Mount Aspiring 3039 △
Fairlie
Canterbury Bight
Wanaka
Omarama
Timaru
Waitaki
Queenstown
Oamaru
Lake Te Anau
Kingston
Alexandra
Palmerston
Te Anau
Mossburn
Beaumont
Dunedin
CAPE PROVIDENCE
Winton
Gore
Invercargill
Kaitangata
Foveaux
Bluff
STEWART ISLAND
Strait

SOUTHERN ALPS

PACIFIC OCEAN

Copyright © 1980
by Rand McNally & Co.
C-591600-964 - 2° - 2° - 4° - 7°
Conic Projection

168° 170° 172° 174° 176° 178°

Kilometres
0 100 200 300 Km.
Miles
0 100 200 300 Mi.
1 : 9 000 000

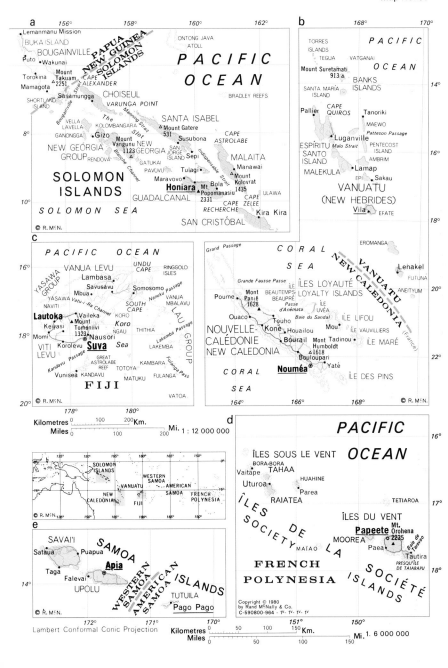

a

Lemanmanu Mission
BUKA ISLAND
BOUGAINVILLE
Puto • Wakunai
PAPUA NEW GUINEA
SOLOMON ISLANDS
Torokina
Mamagota
Mount Takuam
2251
CAPE ALEXANDER
SHORTLAND ISLAND
Sasamungga
CHOISEUL
VARUNGA POINT
ONTONG JAVA ATOLL
PACIFIC OCEAN
BRADLEY REEFS
VELLA LAVELLA
The KOLOMBANGARA Slot
Mount Gatere
GANONGGA • Gizo
NEW GEORGIA GROUP
Vangunu 1123 NEW
RENDOVA GEORGIA
SANTA ISABEL
Manning Strait
531
Susubona
SAN JORGE ISLAND
CAPE ASTROLABE
GATUKAI
PAVUVU
Sepi
Indispensable Strait
MALAITA
Manawai
SOLOMON ISLANDS
Maravovo
Tulagi
Blanche Channel
Mount Kolovrat 1435
Honiara Mt. Bola
GUADALCANAL Popomanasiu 2331
CAPE RECHERCHE
CAPE ZELEE
ULAWA
Kira Kira
SOLOMON SEA
SAN CRISTÓBAL
© R. MᶜN.

b

TORRES ISLANDS
TEGUA VATGANAI
Mount Suretamati 913 △
SANTA MARÍA ISLAND
Pallier
CAPE QUIROS
PACIFIC OCEAN
BANKS ISLANDS
Tanoriki
MAEWO
Patteson Passage
Luganville
ESPÍRITU SANTO ISLAND
Malo Strait
PENTECOST ISLAND
AMBRIM
MALEKULA
EPI Sakau
Lamap
VANUATU
(NEW HEBRIDES)
Vila EFATE

c

PACIFIC OCEAN
VANUA LEVU
UNDU CAPE
RINGGOLD ISLES
YASAWA GROUP
Lambasa
Savusavu
Somosomo
Nanuku Passage
VANUA MBALAVU
YASAWA Vatu-i-Ra Channel
NAVITI
SOUTH CAPE
KORO
Koro
THITHIA
LAU GROUP
Lautoka Vaileka
Mount Tomanivi 1323
Keiyasi
NGAU
Sea
LAKEMBA
Lakemba Passage
VITI LEVU
Momi
Korolevu
Nausori
Suva
GREAT ASTROLABE REEF
KAMBARA
Fulanga Pass
FULANGA
Kandavu Passage
Vunisea KANDAVU
TOTOYA
MATUKU
VATOA
FIJI
© R. MᶜN.

Grand Passage
CORAL SEA
EROMANGA
VANUATU
NEW CALEDONIA
Lenakel
FUTUNA
ANEITYUM
ÎLES LOYAUTÉ LOYALTY ISLANDS
Grande Fausse Passe
ÎLE
BEAUTEMPS-BEAUPRÉ
Poume
Mont Panié 1628
Passe d'Anémata
ÎLE UVÉA
Ouaco
Touho
Koné Houailou
Mou
ÎLE LIFOU
ÎLE VAUVILLIERS
NOUVELLE-CALÉDONIE NEW CALEDONIA
Bourail Mont Tadinou Humboldt
△1618
ÎLE MARÉ
Bouloupari
Nouméa
Yaté
CORAL SEA
ÎLE DES PINS
VANUATU
NEW CALEDONIA (France)
© R. MᶜN.

Kilometres 0 100 200 Km.
Miles 0 100 200 Mi. 1 : 12 000 000

SOLOMON ISLANDS
VANUATU WESTERN SAMOA
AMERICAN SAMOA
NEW CALEDONIA FIJI
FRENCH POLYNESIA
© R. MᶜN.

d

PACIFIC OCEAN
ÎLES SOUS LE VENT
BORA-BORA TAHAA
Vaitape
Uturoa
HUAHINE
Parea
RAIATEA
TETIAROA
ÎLES DU VENT
Papeete Mt. Orohena 2235
MOOREA
Paea
MAIAO
Tautira
PRESQU'ÎLE DE TAIARAPU
Baie de Taravao
FRENCH POLYNESIA
ÎLES DE LA SOCIÉTÉ
SOCIETY ISLANDS

Copyright © 1980
by Rand McNally & Co.
C-590800-964 - 1ᵛ- 1ᵛ- 1ᵛ- 1ᵛ

e

SAVAI'I
Sataua • Puapua
Taga
Falevai
Apia
SAMOA ISLANDS
WESTERN SAMOA
AMERICAN SAMOA
UPOLU
TUTUILA
Pago Pago
© R. MᶜN.

Lambert Conformal Conic Projection

Kilometres 0 50 100 150 Km.
Miles 0 50 100 150 Mi. 1 : 6 000 000

116°   114°   112°   110°   108°   106°   104°

32°

San Diego   Yuma   ARIZONA   Casa Grande   Silver City   WHITE SANDS NATIONAL MONUMENT   Alamogordo   Artesia   Hobbs
Tijuana   Mexicali   San Luis   Río Colorado   ORGAN PIPE CACTUS NATIONAL MONUMENT   Tucson   Lordsburg   Las Cruces   NEW MEXICO   Carlsbad
Ensenada   Lukeville   SAGUARO NATIONAL MONUMENT   CHIRICAHUA NATIONAL MONUMENT   Anthony   CARLSBAD CAVERNS NATIONAL PARK   Kermit   Ode
El Golfo de   López   Collada   UNITED   Bisbee   Ciudad Juárez   El Paso   Guadalupe Peak 2667   Andrews
Santa Clara   Puerto   STATES   Nogales   Douglas   Sierra Blanca   Pecos   Cran
PARQUE NACIONAL   Peñasco   El Cozón   MEXICO   Nogales   Guadalupe   Río Grande   Fort Stockton
SIERRA DE SAN   Nogales   Cananea   Ascensión   Van Horn
PEDRO MÁRTIR   San Felipe   Bravo del Norte
Vicente   Caborca   Altar   Santa   Arizpe   Nueva   Villa   Alpine
30°   Guerrero   El Desemboque   Ana   Nacozari   Casas   Ahumada
Rosario   Benjamín   Mata Ortiz   Grandes   San Antonio   BIG BEND NATIONAL PARK   Sanderson
Punta   Puerto   Hill   de Bravo   Presidio   PARQ NACIONAL DEL CARM
Prieta   Libertad   Carbó   Moctezuma   Las Varas   El Sueco   Maclovío   El Carricito
ISLA ÁNGEL   El Desemboque   Ures   Cerro Puerta   Herrera   Tacubaya
DE LA   Kino   Sahuaripa   de Lajas   Aldama
GUARDA   Hermosillo   Dolores   Chihuahua
28°   ISLA CEDROS   Bahía   El Arco   Tasfota   Suaqui   Yécora   Ciudad   Cuauhtémoc   Delicias   Julimes
Sebastián   Grande   Guerrero   Ciudad   Saucillo
Vizcaíno   Ocampo   Creel   Camargo   La Esmeralda
Guaymas   PARQUE NACIONAL   Valle de   Ciudad   El Carricito
San Ignacio   Santa Rosalía   Ciudad   Esperanza   BARRANCA   Zaragoza   Jiménez
PUNTA   Obregón   DEL COBRE   Hidalgo   Ceballos
26°   ABREOJOS   Mulegé   Navojoa   del Parral   Carrillo
Comondú   Huatabampo   Cerro Agua   San Per
Loreto   Yavaros   Agua Caliente   Caliente   Las Nieves   Barcelona   de las Colon
ISLA   Grande de Gastelum   3315   Torreón
Santo   CARMEN   Cerro Mohinora   San   Gómez   Parras d
Domingo   Los Mochis   San Blas   3992   Bernardo   La Zarca   Palacio   la Fuent
ISLA SANTA   Tameapa   Abasolo   Pedricena   Juan Euger
MAGDALENA   San Luis   Guasave   Copalquin   Los   Acacio
ISLA DE SANTA   Gonzaga   ISLA   Pericos   Herreras   Camacho
MARGARITA   El Médano   SAN JOSÉ   Culiacán   Tejamen   Miguel
24°   ISLA   Quilá   Coacoyle   Francisco   Auza
CERRALVO   Altata   l. Madero   Durango
Tropic of Cancer   La Paz   El Avión   Tayoltita   Ciudad   Río
Todos Santos   El Quelite   Nombre   Villa   Grande Can
de Dios   Vicente Guerrero
Agua   Cerro   3080
San José   Caliente   Mazatlán   Candelaria   Fresnillo
del Cabo   Rosario   Zacatecas
22°   CABO   Teacapán   Jerez de   Garcia Salinas
SAN LUCAS   Tecuala   Rosamorada   Cerro Lechuguilla   Jalpa
Santiago   ISLAS   Aguascalientes
PACIFIC   Ixcuintla   MARÍAS   Cerro   Jalostotitlán
ISLA MARÍA MADRE   El Vigía
ISLA MARÍA MAGDALENA   Tepic   2740
20°   ISLA MARÍA CLEOFAS   Ahuacatlán   Guadalajara   Atotonilc
OCEAN   Puerto   el Alto
Vallarta   Mascota   Ocotlán   Zamora de
CABO CORRIENTES   Cocula   de Chapala   Hidalgo
ISLAS   Autlán de   Sayula   Ciudad
REVILLAGIGEDO   Navarro   PARQUE NACIONAL   Guzmán
(Mex.)   ISLA   VOLCÁN DE COLIMA   PARQUE NACIO
SOCORRO   Colima   PICO DE TANCÍT
Manzanillo   Apatzingán
18°

Pomaro

16°

114°   112°   110°   108°   106°   104°

Kilometres 0   100   200   300 Km.
Miles 0   100   200   300 Mi.   1 : 13 300 000

GULF OF MEXICO

26° Fort Myers○● UNITED STATES ⊙ West Palm Beach GRAND BAHAMA
FLORIDA GREA
The Everglades □● Fort Lauderdale ABAC
MIAMI● Miami Beach ELEUTH
EVERGLADES NATIONAL PARK Nassau
24° Key West⊙ FLORIDA KEYS Straits NEW
ANDROS ISLAND PROVIDENCE

LA HABANA Straits of Florida GREAT BAHAMA BAN
HAVANA Nicholas Channel W E
22° Marianao □● Cárdenas
Pinar del Río○ Artemisa○ Güines Matanzas Sagua Old Bahama Channel
Golfo de Batabanó ○Santa Fe Santa Clara□● Placetas
CABO SAN ANTONIO CABO CORRIENTES Cienfuegos Sancti Spíritus Ciego de Avila Florida○ Nuevitas
ISLA DE LA JUVENTUD (ISLA DE PINOS) CUBA Camagüey⊙ Ba
Holguín
Manzanillo○ Bay

Pico Turquino CAYMAN ISLANDS G R E A T E R Santi
1994 de C
Georgetown (U.K.)

Río Lagartos. CABO CATOCHE
Progreso○ CABO SAN ANTONIO
Mérida⊙ Tizimín ●Puerto Juárez
Celestún○ Halachó○ Chichen Itzá ○Cozumel
○Ticul ISLA DE COZUMEL
Tenabo○ ○Peto ○Tulum
92° Campeche⊙ ○Hopelchén
YUCATAN ●Felipe Carrillo Puerto
Champotón● PENÍNSULA
Ciudad del Carmen● MEXICO Ciudad Chetumal
Frontera○ ○Escárcega de Matamoros Chetumal Bay
18° Usumacinta ○Tiradero Orange Walk● BELIZE (U.K.)
Palenque○ ○Piedras Negras ○Belize
○Ocozingo ●San Benito Belmopan
Comitán○ ○Sayaxché 1122 Victoria Peak Gulf of Honduras ISLAS DE LA BAHÍA
○San Luis
16° 4220 GUATEMALA Puerto Barrios○ Puerto La
Volcán Tajumulco El Estor○ Cortés○ ○Ceiba ○Limón Brus
Huehuetenango○ El Progreso○ San Pedro Sula● Laguna
Tapachula○ SIERRA DE LAS MINAS ○Yoro
Cerro Las CORDILLERA DE AGALTA Patuca CABO GRACIAS
○Tiquisate Guatemala⊙ Minas 2865 A DIOS CARI
14° Escuintla○ HONDURAS Juticalpa○ Coco
Santa Ana● San San Waspán
Nueva Salvador Ramón○
San Salvador San San Miguel● Tegucigalpa⊙ Puerto
EL SALVADOR Vicente La Cerro Mogotón○ Cabezas
Union 2107 △Cerro Piu
Chinandega○ Estelí○ 1800 ○Prinzapolca
León○ El Sauce○ ○Matagalpa ○La Cruz
12° Managua⊙ NICARAGUA ○Río Grande ISLA DE SAN ANDRÉS (COL.)
Diriamba○ Granada ○Rama
Lago de Nicaragua Punta Gorda CORN ISLANDS (NIC.)
Rivas○ San○ ○San Andrés
ISLA DE Carlos
OMETEPE ●San Juan del Norte
Liberia○ Volcán Miravalles
2028
10° PACIFIC PENÍNSULA COSTA RICA Limón
OCEAN DE NICOYA Puntarenas○ ○Cartago
CABO BLANCO San José⊙ Colón⊙ ISTMO DE PANAMÁ
▲Cerro Chirripó Bocas del Toro○ Portobelo○ Lor
Puerto 3819 Golfo de los ○Chepo ○Mulatupo Ce
Cortés○ 3475 Mosquitos La Chorrera○ Monte
8° PEN. DE OSA Volcán Barú PANAMA ●Panamá ○Acandí
Puerto David○ Río Hato○ ISLA ●La Palma
Armuelles○ Aguadulce○ Gulf DEL REY ○Yaviza ○Turbo
PUNTA BURICA Golfo of Jaqué○
Chiriquí PENÍNSULA Panama
ISLA DE DE
COIBA AZUERO

Copyright © 1980
by Rand McNally & Co.
C-530100-964 - 2ᵛ- 6ᵛ- 5ᵛ- 12ᵛ

Kilometres 0 100 200 300 Km.
Miles 0 100 200 300 Mi. 1 : 12 000 000

Lambert Conformal Conic Projection

84

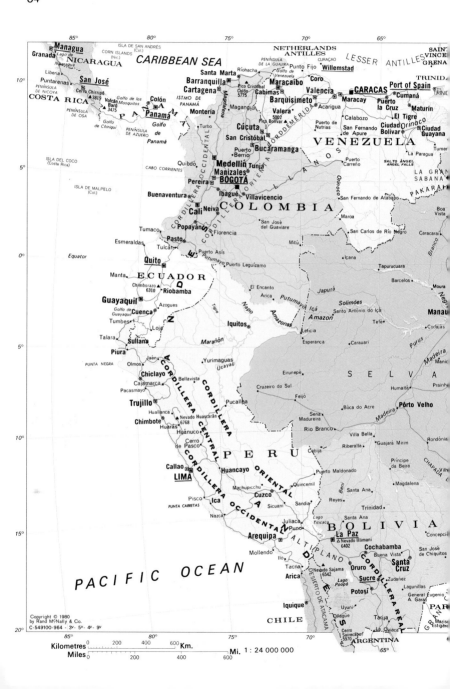

Copyright © 1980
by Rand McNally & Co.
C-549100-964 · 3ᵛ· 5ᵛ· 4ᵛ· 9ᵛ

Kilometres 0 200 400 600 Km.
Miles 0 200 400 600   Mi.   1 : 24 000 000

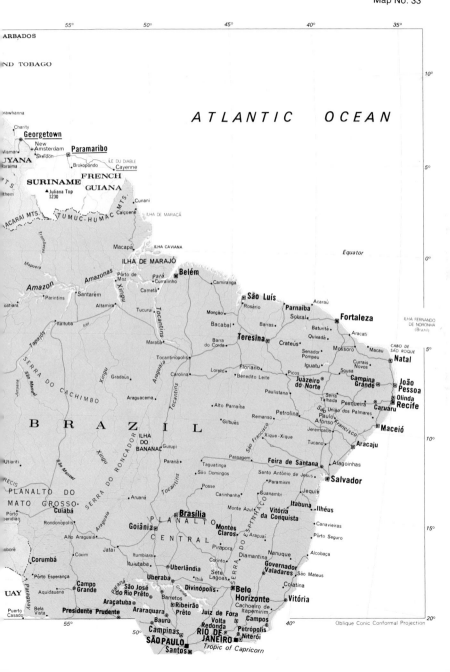

ARBADOS

ND TOBAGO

ATLANTIC   OCEAN

orawhanna

Charity
Georgetown
New
Amsterdam
Wismar• •Skeldon
GUYANA
Roraima
•them
MACARAI MTS.

•Brokopondo
Paramaribo
ÎLE DU DIABLE
•Cayenne
FRENCH
SURINAME GUIANA
▲Juliana Top
1230
TUMUC-HUMAC MTS.
•Cunani
Calçoene
ILHA DE MARACÁ

Triomfvaras
Mapuera
•oathiara

Macapá
ILHA CAVIANA
Equator

ILHA DE MARAJÓ

Amazon
Pôrto de
Moz.
•Curralinho
Belém
•Camiranga
Amazonas
Pará
Cametá
•Parintins •Santarém
Altamira
São Luís
•Rosário
Acaraú
•Itaituba
Irirí
Tucuruí
Monção•
Parnaíba
Fortaleza
Sobral• •Barras
Bacabal•
Baturité
Aracati
Marabá•
Barra
do
Corda
Teresina
Crateús• Quixadá•
Mossoró •Macau
CABO DE
SÃO ROQUE
Natal

ILHA FERNANDO
DE NORONHA
(Brazil)

Tapajós
SERRA DO CACHIMBO
São Manuel
Gradaús•
Tocantinópolis
Carolina
Floriano•
Loreto• •Bénedito Leite
Picos
Senador
Pompeu
Iguatú•
Currais
Novos
Sousa
Juazeiro
do Norte
Campina
Grande
João
Pessoa
Olinda
Recife
Araguacema
Serra
Talhada
Pesqueira Caruaru
•Alto Parnaíba
Paulistana•
•Remanso
Petrolina•
São União dos Palmares
Paulo
Afonso•
Maceió

B R A Z I L
ILHA
DO
BANANAL
•Gilbués
•Gurupi
São Francisco
Xique-Xique
Jeremoabo•
Tucano•
Aracaju

Utiariti•
SERRA DO RONCADOR
Paraná•
Passagem•
Taguatinga•
São Domingos•
Feira de Santana
Afogoinhas•

•Posse
Santo Antônio de Jesus•
Jequié•
Salvador

PLANALTO DO
MATO GROSSO•
•Aruanã
Carinhanha•
•Paramirim
Itabuna •Ilhéus
Pôrto
eridião
•Rondonópolis
Cuiabá
Monte Azul•
•Guanambi
Vitória
da Conquista
•Canavieiras

oboré
Alto Araguaí•
•Coxim
Brasília
PLANALTO
Goiânia
Montes
Claros
•Araçuai
•Pôrto Seguro

Corumbá
Jataí•
C E N T R A L
Pirapora•
Nanuque•
Alcobaça

•Pôrto Esperança
Itumbiara•
Ituiutaba•
Diamantina•
SERRA DO ESPINHAÇO
Governador
Valadares •São Mateus

UAY
Aquidauana•
Uberlândia
Corinto•
Sete
Lagoas•
Colatina•

Puerto
Casado•
Campo
Grande
São José
do Rio Prêto
Uberaba
Itbiá•
Divinópolis•
Belo
Horizonte
•Vitória

Bela
Vista•
Presidente Prudente•
Araraquara•
Ribeirão
Prêto
Araçatuba•
Barretos•
Juiz de Fora•
Cachoeiro de
Itapemirim•

Campinas•
Bauru•
Volta
Redonda
Campos
RIO DE
Petrópolis•
JANEIRO
Niterói
SÃO PAULO
Santos•
Tropic of Capricorn
Oblique Conic Conformal Projection

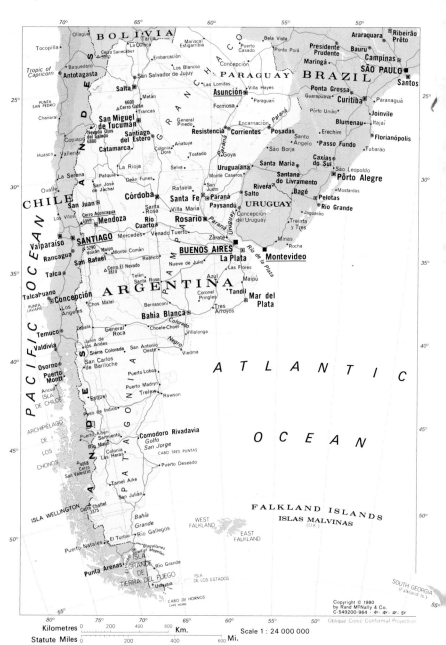

Kilometres 0   200   400   600 Km.

Statute Miles 0   200   400   600 Mi.

Scale 1 : 24 000 000

Oblique Conic Conformal Projection

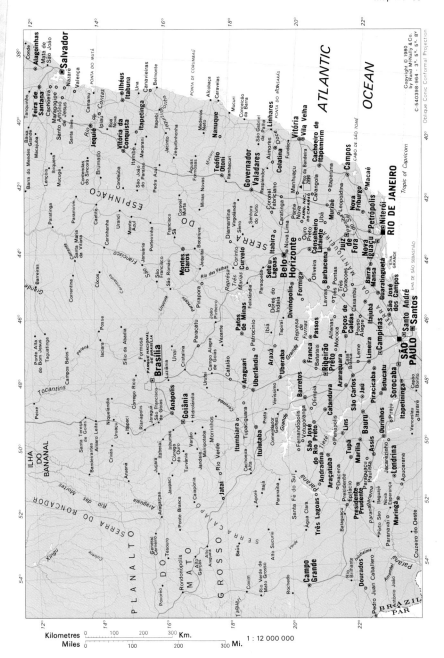

ATLANTIC

OCEAN

Kilometres 0 100 200 300 Km.

Miles 0 100 200 300 Mi.

1 : 12 000 000

Kilometres 0 200 400 600 Km.

Miles 0 200 400 600 Mi.

1 : 24 000 000

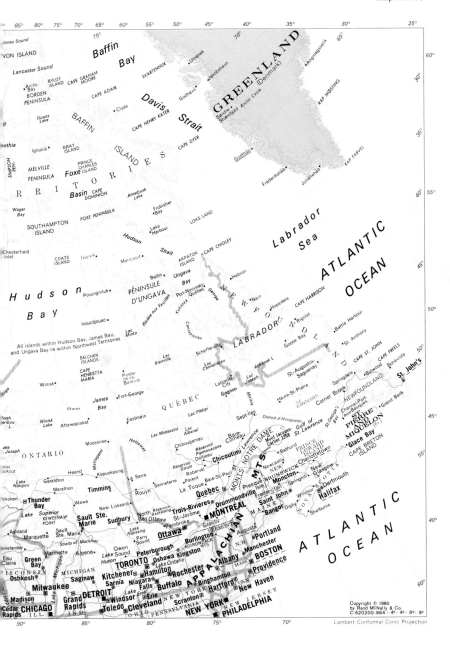

SCOTT ISLANDS
50°
135°   130°   125°   120°   115°   110°   105°   100°   55

Williams Roberts Peak **Edmonton**
Waddington 2700   341   Wetaskiwin   Flin Flon   Lake
Mount 3994   Lloydminster   Winnipeg MANITO
Campbell Good Hope COAST BRITISH Mount Columbia Red Deer   Prince Albert
River Mountain   3747
Mount 3954   COLUMBIA   SASKATCHEWAN
VANCOUVER **Vancouver** Kamloops   Biggar **Saskatoon**   Swan River Red
ISLAND   Revelstoke Mount ALBERTA   Yorkton Dauphin River
Victoria Kelowna Assiniboine Fort Kindersley Moose Lake
2428 Bellingham Grand 3618 Macleod Medicine Hat Jaw **Regina** Manitoba Gir
45° Mount Olympus Nelson   Lethbridge   Virden Morden **Winnipeg**
CAPE DISAPPOINTMENT **Seattle** **Spokane** Kalispell CANADA Williston NORTH Grand Forks
Tacoma Olympia WASHINGTON **UNITED STATES** Minot DAKOTA
P A C I F I C **Yakima** Lewiston Missoula Great Falls Sidney Bismarck Wahpe
Portland Columbia Walla Walla MONTANA Baker Lemmon Aberdeen Linton
Salem BLUE Butte Helena Yellowstone SOUTH
Eugene Mount Hood Salmon 3043 Livingston Miles Rapid Pierre Brookin
40° 3424 MOUNTAINS RIVER Dillon Billings City BLACK City DAKOTA
Coos Bay OREGON Baker MOUNTAINS Yellowstone Sheridan HILLS Chamberlain Siou
O C E A N Ontario IDAHO Lake Grand Teton WYOMING Lead Valentine Missouri Fall
Crescent Klamath Nampa **Boise** 4197 Casper Chadron NEBRASKA
City Falls Idaho Falls Scottsbluff Sioux
Redding Mount Shasta Twin Falls Preston Laramie North Platte City
4317 Pocatello Rock Cheyenne Columbus Linc
Ukiah Elko GREAT Springs Ogallala Grand
30° **Reno** Humboldt Great **Ogden** Sterling South Platte Island Beat
Chico Carson City NEVADA Salt **Provo** Boulder Denver McCook
San Francisco **Oakland** BASIN **Salt Lake City** Goodland KANSAS Manhat
Sacramento Ely UTAH Grand **Colorado Springs** Garden Hutchinson
San Jose Boundary Peak Tonopah Junction Pikes Peak COLORADO **Pueblo** City **Wichita**
Salinas 4006 Richfield 4301 Dodge City Liberal
Fresno Cedar City Lake Uncompahgre Trinidad Alva Ponca
San Luis Obispo Powell Peak 4361 Farmington Dalhart City
35° **Las Vegas** Colorado Los Alamos Wheeler Peak OKLAHOMA Lawt
Santa Barbara **Bakersfield** Lake Humphreys 4011 Santa Fe **Amarillo** **Oklahoma**
Lancaster Mead Peak Gallup Tucumcari Clinton **City**
LOS ANGELES San Needles 3851 Albuquerque TEXAS **Wichita Falls** Den
Long Beach Bernardino Flagstaff Holbrook NEW **Lubbock** Mineral Wells **Dall**
San Diego ARIZONA Silver City MEXICO Roswell Abilene **Fort**
30° **Tijuana Mexicali** Phoenix Mesa Alamogordo Midland San **Worth**
Ensenada Cerro de La **Tucson** El Paso Odessa Angelo TEXAS Killeen
Encantada San Felipe Ciudad Fort Stockton Pecos EDWARDS **Austin** Bry
UNITED STATES 3069 Juarez PLATEAU **San**
MEXICO Santa Ana Nueva Del Rio **Antoni**
25° Hermosillo Moctezuma Casas Grandes Rio **Laredo** Corpu
BAJA PUNTA San Chihuahua Conchos Eagle Pass Victoria Christ
ISLA DE EUGENIA Ignacio SIERRA Delicias Rio Grande del Norte Nuevo Brown
GUADALUPE (Mex) **Ciudad** Hidalgo Nueva Rosita **Laredo** vill
ISLA SANTA MAGDALENA **Obregon** del Parral Ciudad Jiménez Sabinas **Reynosa** Matamor
Los MADRE Gomez Hidalgo **Monterrey** San
Mochis Palacio **Torreon** Saltillo Linares Fernande
Culiacán Concepcion Ciudad Victo
20° del Oro ORIENTAL
Rio Grande Durango Matehuala
Mazatlan OCCIDENTAL Cerritos **Tampic**
Tropic of Cancer San José del Cabo San Tamazunchale
La Paz ISLAS **Tepic** Aguascalientes Luis Potosí
MARIAS **Guadalajara** **Léon** **Querétaro**
Acaponeta CABO CORRIENTES

Kilometres 0 200 400 600 Km.
Miles 0   200 400 600 Mi.   1 : 24 000 000

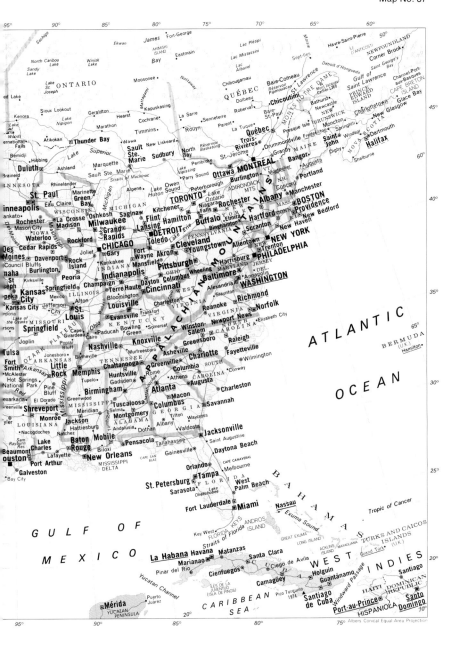

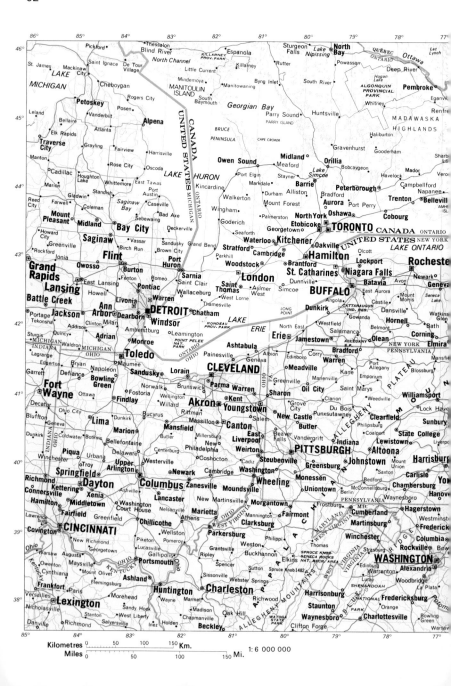

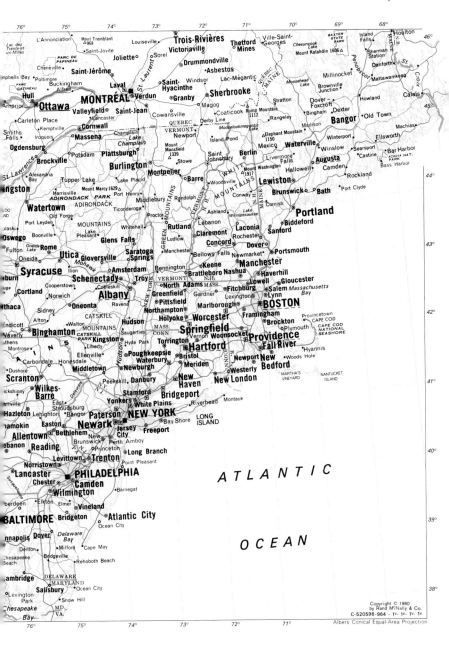

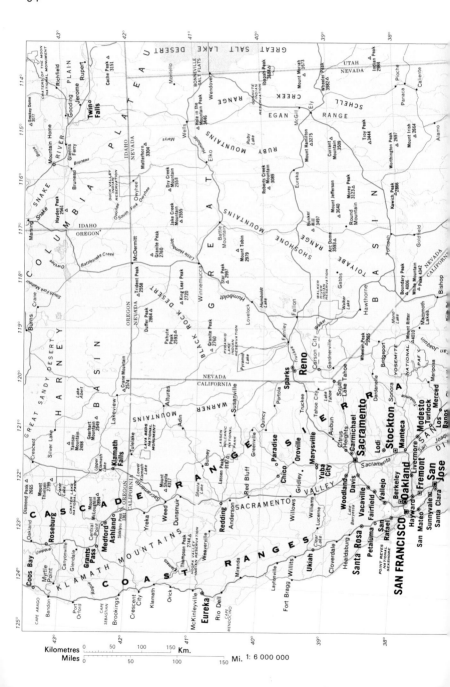

Kilometres 0 50 100 150 Km.
Miles 0   50   100   150 Mi. 1: 6 000 000

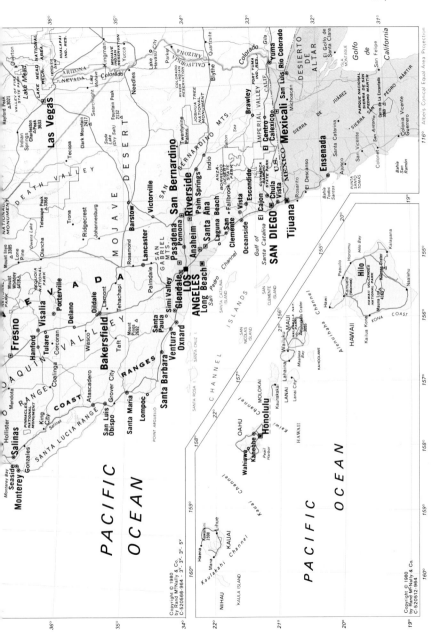

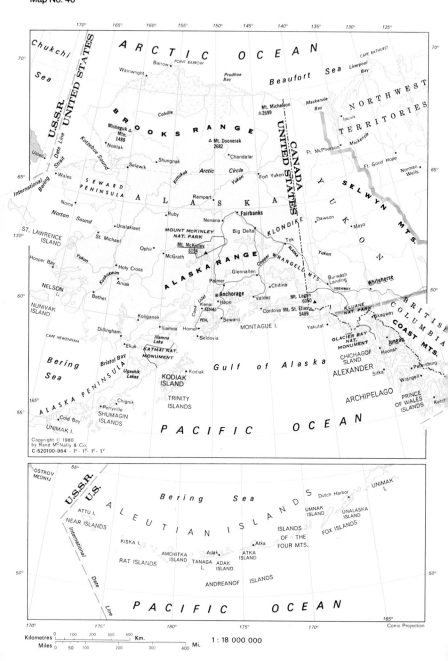

Kilometres 0 100 200 300 400 Km.

Miles 0 50 100 200 300 400 Mi.

1 : 18 000 000

Conic Projection

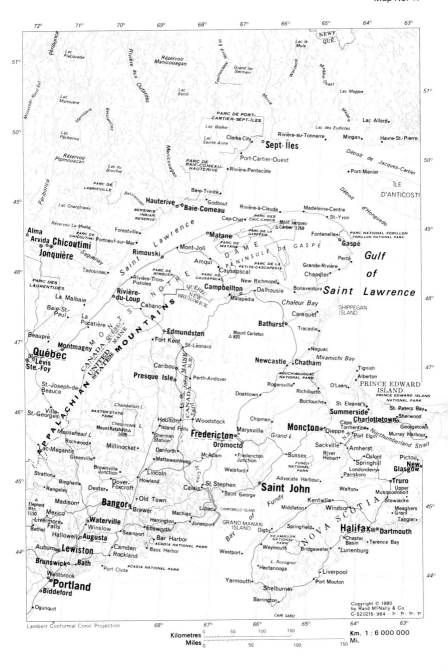

Lambert Conformal Conic Projection

Kilometres
0   50   100   150

Miles
0   50   100

Km. 1 : 6 000 000
Mi.

Kilometres 0 50 100 150 Km.

Miles 0 50 100 150 Mi.

1 : 6 000 000

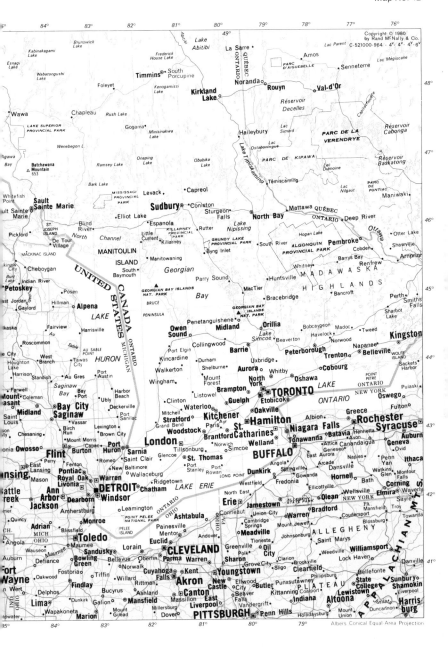

Albers Conical Equal Area Projection

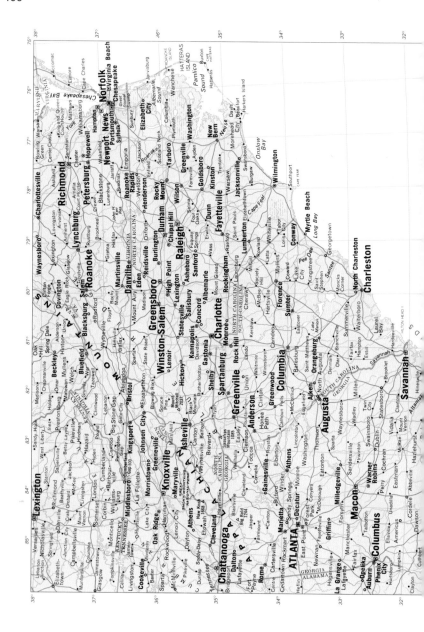

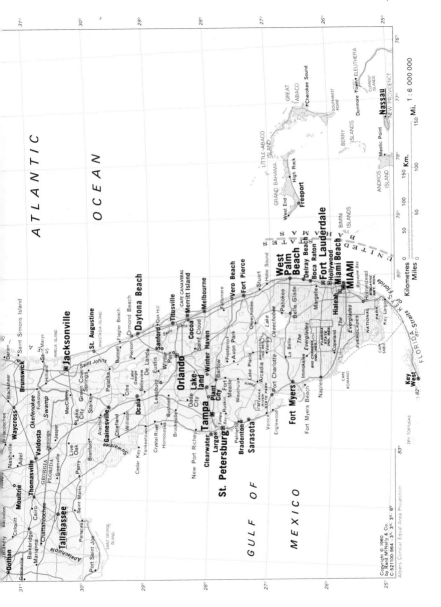

ATLANTIC

OCEAN

GULF

OF

MEXICO

1 : 6 000 000

Kilometres 0   50   100   150 Km.
Miles 0   50   100   150 Mi.   1 : 6 000 000

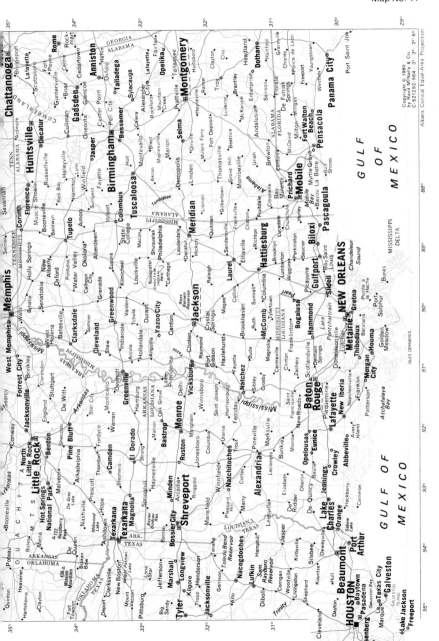

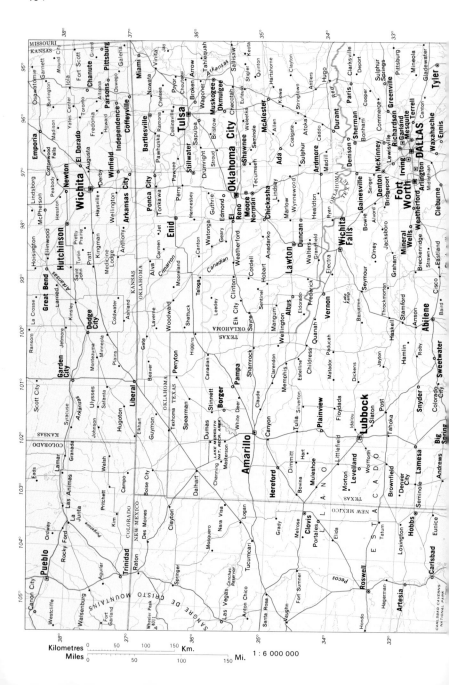

Kilometres 0 50 100 150 Km.

Miles 0 50 100 150 Mi.

1 : 6 000 000

Texas

GULF OF MEXICO

Copyright © 1980
by Rand McNally & Co.
C-521400-964 - 3ᵛ - 3ᵛ - 3ᵛ - 4ᵛ

97°Albers Conical Equal-Area Projection

Baytown
Pasadena
HOUSTON
Bellaire
Rosenberg
Wharton
Galveston
GALVESTON ISLAND
Freeport
Lake Jackson
Bay City
Columbus
La Grange
Brenham
Prairie View
Bellville
Navasota
Conroe
College Station
Bryan
Madisonville
Centerville
Franklin
Cameron
Rockdale
Giddings
Somerville
Taylor
Bartlett
Rogers
Marlin
McGregor
Temple
Belton
Killeen
Copperas Cove
Gatesville
Valley Mills
Clifton
Waco
Hubbard
Mexia
Palestine
Rusk
Alto
Crockett
Lovelady
Trinity
Livingston
Shepherd
Cleveland
Dayton
Huntsville
Buffalo
Oakwood
Teague
Hamilton
Mullin
Comanche
Brownwood
Winters
Ballinger
San Angelo
Eden
Brady
Mason
Eldorado
Sonora
Ozona
Sheffield
Iraan
McCamey
Crane
Monahans
Odessa
Midland
Kermit
Pecos
Barstow
Fort Stockton
Sanderson
Marathon
Alpine
Marfa
Fort Davis
Mt. Livermore △2555
Van Horn
GUADALUPE MOUNTAINS NATIONAL PARK
Presidio
Ojinaga
Candelaria
Pilares
Ruidosa
Barranca Azul
El Mulato
Santiago Peak 1988 △
BIG BEND NATIONAL PARK
UNITED STATES
MEXICO
TEXAS

Austin
San Marcos
New Braunfels
San Antonio
Kerrville
Fredericksburg
Ingram
Bandera
Camp Wood
Rocksprings
Junction
Menard
San Saba
Burnet
Marble Falls
Johnson City
Georgetown
Cherokee
Llano
Lampasas
Seguin
Lockhart
Luling
Gonzales
Nixon
Yorktown
Cuero
Victoria
Goliad
Beeville
Refugio
Sinton
Rockport
Aransas Pass
Corpus Christi
Kingsville
Alice
Robstown
Mathis
George West
Kenedy
Pleasanton
Charlotte
Devine
Hondo
Uvalde
Sabinal
Spofford
Bracketville
Del Rio
Ciudad Acuña
Eagle Pass
Piedras Negras
Crystal City
La Pryor
Carrizo Springs
Cotulla
Freer
San Diego
Benavides
Premont
Falfurrias
Encino
San Isidro
Hebbronville
San Ygnacio
Laredo
Nuevo Laredo

BALCONES ESCARPMENT
EDWARDS PLATEAU
TEXAS PLAINS
NUECES
Rio Grande Bravo del Norte
Colorado
Brazos
Trinity

GULF OF MEXICO
PADRE ISLAND
Laguna Madre
MATAGORDA ISLAND

McAllen
Reynosa
Pharr
Edinburg
San Juan
Weslaco
Harlingen
San Benito
Brownsville
Matamoros
Valle Hermoso
Rio Bravo
Raymondville
Diecisiete de Marzo
General Bravo
China
Cerralvo
Los Aldamas
Doctor Gonzales
Guadalupe
Monterrey
PARQUE NACIONAL CUMBRES DE MONTERREY
Sabinas Hidalgo
Villaldama
Bustamante
Lampazos de Naranjo
Cerro Carrizal 1943
Candela
Monclova
San Buenaventura
Abasolo
Ciudad Frontera
Cuatro Ciénegas
Ocampo
Sacramento
Nadadores
San Pedro de las Colonias
Torreón
Gómez Palacio
Bermejillo
Tlahualilo de Zaragoza
Mapimí
Ceballos
La Esperanza
Providencia
Barcelona
La Jarita
Santa Elena
Virulento
Nuevo Sauchillo
Coracitos
Cerro Antonico △2135
La Zara
San Luis del Cordero

SIERRA MADRE ORIENTAL
BOLSÓN DE MAPIMÍ
SERRANÍAS DEL BURRO
Mesa de Palomas 1995 △
Laguna del Rey

Sabinas
Nueva Rosita
Ciudad Melchor Múzquiz
Santa María
La Cruz
Jiménez
Nava
Villa Unión
El Remolino
Las Cuevas
Palo Blanco
Dolores
San Martín de las Vacas
Tezoc Hipolito
Caderejta Jiménez
Cadereyta
Villagrán
Paredón
Villa de Villaldama
Ciudad de Villaldama
Vallecillo
Sombreretillo
Los Nogales
Mier
Ciudad Mier
Paras
Ciudad Guerrero
Parás

25° 26° 27° 28° 29° 30° 31°
94° 95° 96° 97° 98° 99° 100° 101° 102° 103° 104°

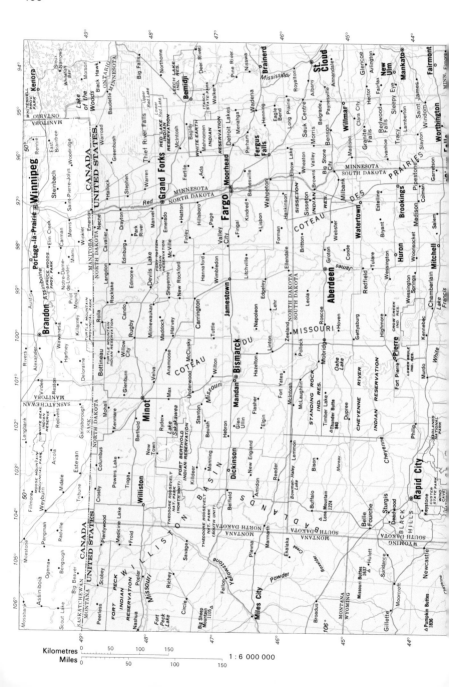

Kilometres 0 50 100 150
Miles 0 50 100 150
1 : 6 000 000

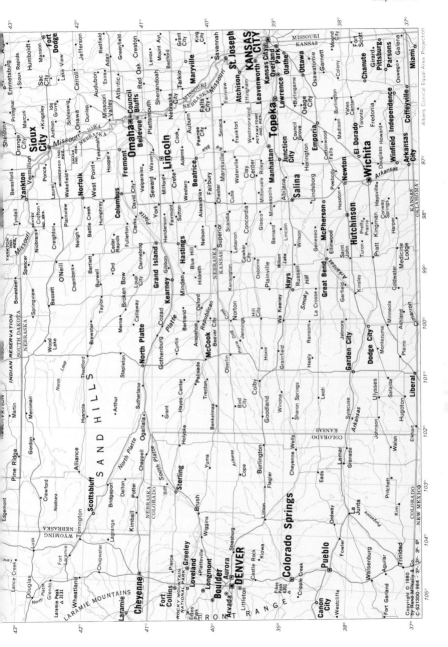

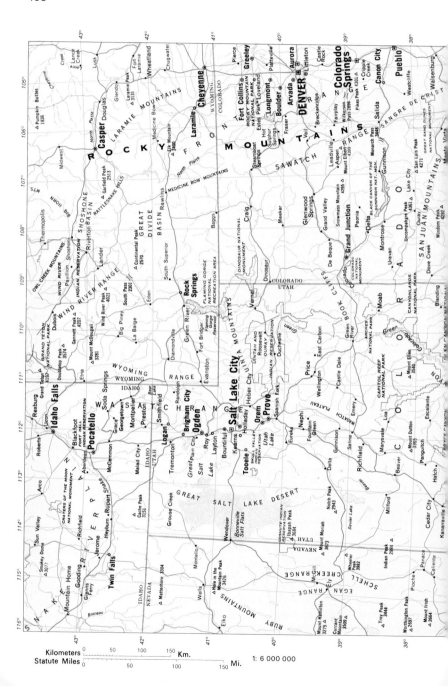

Kilometers
Statute Miles

0 50 100 150 Km.

0   50   100   150 Mi.

1: 6 000 000

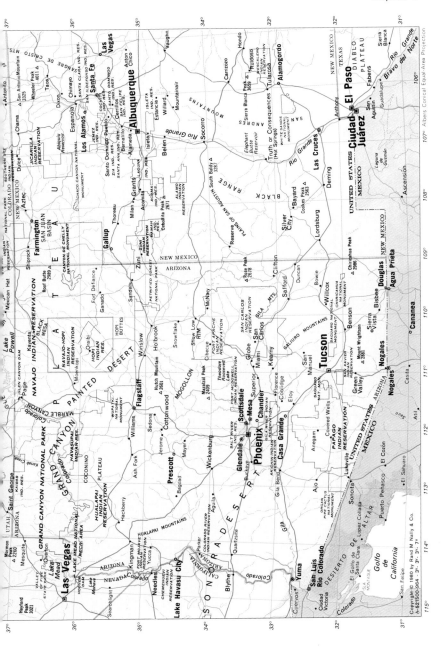

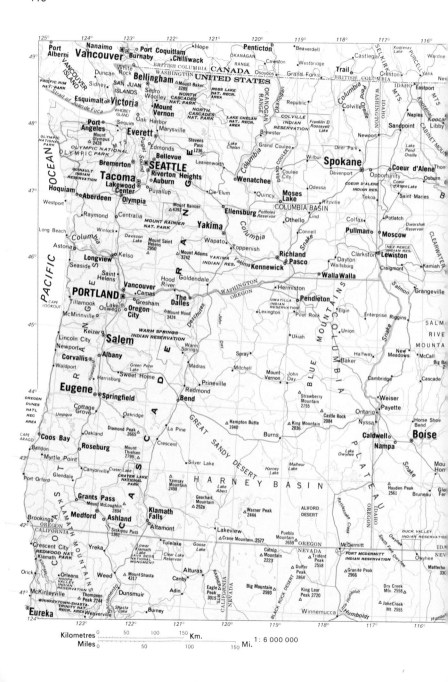

Kilometres 0   50   100   150 Km.
Miles 0   50   100   150 Mi.   1 : 6 000 000

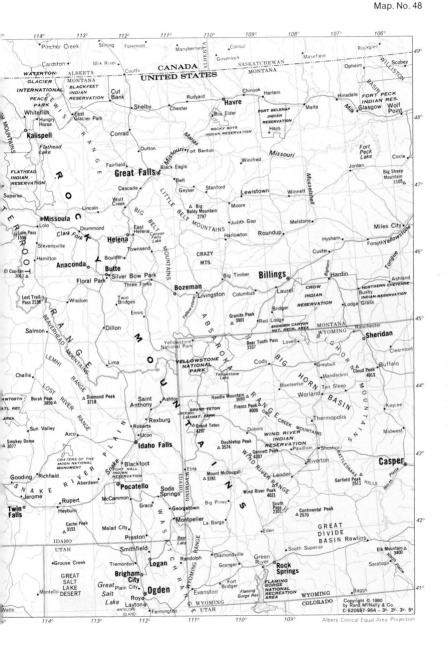

114° 113° 112° 111° 110° 109° 108° 107° 106°

Pincher Creek • Stirling • Foremost • Manyberries • Consul • Masefeld • Rocklen • 49°

Cardston • Milk River • Coutts • Govenlock • SASKATCHEWAN • Ophein • Scobey

WATERTON- ALBERTA • CANADA • MONTANA • BASIN • PECK • WILLISTON

GLACIER • MONTANA • UNITED STATES • Hinsdale • FORT • PECK • INDIAN • RES. • Wolf

INTERNATIONAL • BLACKFEET • Chinook • Harlem • Glasgow • Point

PEACE • INDIAN • Cut • Rudyard • Havre • Malta • 48°

PARK • RESERVATION • Bank • Shelby • Chester • Box Elder • FORT BELKNAP • INDIAN • RESERVATION

Whitefish • East • Conrad • ROCKY BOYS • Hays

Hungry • Glacier Park • INDIAN RESERVATION

Horse • Dutton • Fort Benton • Winifred • Missouri • Fort • Circle

Kalispell • Flathead • Fairfield • Missouri • Peck • Lake

Lake • Great Falls • Black Eagle • Jordan • Big Sheep

FLATHEAD • Cascade • Belt • Stanford • Lewistown • Winnett • Mountain • 1105 • 47°

INDIAN • Geyser • Musselshell

RESERVATION • Wolf • △ Big • Moore • Melstone

Superior • Creek • Lincoln • Baldy Mountain • Judith Gap • Miles City

Missoula • 2797 • Harlowton • Roundup • Hysham • Forsyth Yellowstone

Lolo • Clark Fork • East • Canyon • LITTLE BELT • MOUNTAINS • Custer • 46°

Lolo Pass • Drummond • Helena • Ferry • Townsend • CRAZY • Big Timber • Billings • Hardin • Ashland

1596 • Helena • Lake • MTS. • Bozeman • CROW • NORTHERN CHEYENNE

Stevensville • Boulder • BIG • Livingston • Columbus • Laurel • INDIAN • Busby • INDIAN-RESERVATION

Hamilton • Anaconda • Butte • Silver Bow Park • Bridger • RESERVATION • Lodge • Grass

El Capitan • Floral Park • Three Forks • Granite Peak • Red Lodge • BIGHORN CANYON • MONTANA • Ranchester

3043 △ • Wisdom • Twin • Ennis • △ 3901 • Bear Tooth Pass • NAT. RECR. AREA • WYOMING • Sheridan • 45°

Lost Trail • Bridges • Yellowstone • 3337 • Lovell • BIG • Clearmont

Pass 2138 • Salmon • Dillon • National Park • Cody • Greybull • Cloud Peak • Buffalo

Lima • YELLOWSTONE • Manderson • 4013

Challis • NATIONAL • Yellowstone • Meeteetse • Ten Sleep • HORN • Kaycee

SAWTOOTH • Borah Peak • △ Diamond Peak • PARK • Lake • Worland • BASIN • 44°

N'TL REC. • 3859 △ • 3718 • Saint • Ashton • Needle Mountain • Thermopolis • Midwest

AREA • Anthony • 3690 • Dubois • WIND RIVER

Sun Valley • Rexburg • GRAND TETON • Francs Peak • INDIAN

Smokey Dome • Arco • Roberts • NAT. PARK • 4009 • RESERVATION • Casper

△ 3077 • Ucon • △ Grand Teton • Doubletop Peak • Pavillion • Shoshoni • 43°

CRATERS OF THE • Idaho Falls • 4197 • △ 3574 • Gannett Peak • Riverton • RATTLESNAKE

Gooding • Richfield • MOON NATIONAL • Etna • 4207 • Lander • HILLS • Garfield Peak • 2513

MONUMENT • FORT HALL • Mount McDougall • Wind River Peak • South • 2570

Jerome • Aberdeen • INDIAN • △ 3281 • 4021 • Pass • Continental Peak • GREAT

Twin • Rupert • RESERVATION • Pocatello • Soda • Georgetown • Big Piney • 2301 • △ 2570 • DIVIDE

Falls • Heyburn • McCammon • Springs • Grace • La Barge • Eden • BASIN • Rawlins • 42°

Cache Peak • Montpelier • Elk Mountain

△ 3151 • Malad City • Georgetown • Diamondville • South Superior • △ 3400

IDAHO • Preston • Smithfield • Randolph • Granger • Green River • Rock • Saratoga

UTAH • Bear • River • Springs

Grouse Creek • Tremonton • Lake • Fort • FLAMING • Baggs • 41°

GREAT • Logan • Bridger • GORGE • WYOMING

Montello • SALT • Brigham • Plain City • Evanston • NATIONAL • COLORADO

LAKE • City • Flaming • RECREATION

Wells • DESERT • Great • Ogden • Gorge Res. • AREA

Salt • Royo • Laylon • ANTELOPE • UTAH

Lake • Farmington • ISLAND

114° 113° 112° 111° 110° 109°

Introduction to the Index

The Index includes in a single alphabetical list some 7,000 names appearing on the maps. Each name is followed by a map reference and by the location of the feature on the map. The map location is designated by latitude and longitude coordinates. If a page contains several maps, a lowercase letter identifies the inset map.

Most map features are indexed to the largest-scale map on which they appear. Countries, mountain ranges, and other extensive features are generally indexed to the map that shows them in their entirety.

NAME FORMS Names in the Index, as on the maps, are generally in the local language and insofar as possible are spelled according to official practice. Diacritical marks are included, except that those used to indicate tone, as in Vietnamese, are usually not shown. Most features that extend beyond the boundaries of one country have no single official name, and these are usually named in English. Many conventional English names and former names are cross referenced to the primary map name. All cross references are indicated by the symbol→. A name that appears in a shortened version on the map due to space limitations is given in full in the Index, with the portion that is omitted on the map enclosed in brackets.

ALPHABETIZATION Names are alphabetized in the order of the letters of the English alphabet. Spanish *ll* and *ch*, for example, are not treated as distinct letters. Furthermore, diacritical marks are disregarded in alphabetization—German or Scandinavian *ä* or *ö* are treated as *a* or *o*.

The names of physical features may appear inverted, since they are always alphabetized under the proper, not the generic, part of the name, thus: "Gibraltar, Strait of ᙀ". Otherwise every entry, whether consisting of one word or more, is alphabetized as a single continuous entity. "Lakeland," for example, appears after "La Crosse" and before "La Salle." Names beginning with articles (Le Havre, Den Helder, Al-Qāhirah, As-Suways) are not inverted. Names beginning "Mc" are alphabetized as though spelled "Mac," and names beginning "St." and "Sainte" as though spelled "Saint."

In the case of identical names, towns are listed first, then political divisions, then physical features. Entries that are completely identical (including symbols, discussed below) are distinguished by abbreviations of their official country names and are sequenced alphabetically by country name. The many duplicate names in Canada, the United Kingdom, and the United States are further distinguished by abbreviations of the names of their primary subdivisions. (See list of abbreviations on pages 112—115.)

ABBREVIATIONS AND CAPITALIZATION Abbreviation and styling have been standardized for all languages. A period is used after every abbreviation even when this may not be the local practice. The abbreviation "St." is used only for "Saint." "Sankt" and other forms of the term are spelled out.

All names are written with an initial capital letter except for a few Dutch names, such as 's-Gravenhage. Capitalization of noninitial words in a name generally follows local practice.

SYMBOL The symbols that appear in the Index graphically represent the broad categories of the features named, for example, ʌ for mountain (Everest, Mount ʌ). Superior numbers following some symbols in the Index indicate finer distinctions, for example, ʌ¹ for volcano (Fuji-san ʌ¹). A complete list of the symbols and those with superior numbers is given on page 115.

LIST OF ABBREVIATIONS

	LOCAL NAME	ENGLISH
Afg.	Afghānestān	Afghanistan
Afr.	—	Africa
Ala., U.S.	Alabama	Alabama
Alaska, U.S.	Alaska	Alaska
Alg.	Algérie	Algeria
Alta., Can.	Alberta	Alberta
Am. Sam.	American Samoa	American Samoa
And.	Andorra	Andorra
Ang.	Angola	Angola
Anguilla	Anguilla	Anguilla
Ant.	—	Antarctica
Antig.	Antigua	Antigua
Arc. O.	—	Arctic Ocean
Arg.	Argentina	Argentina
Ariz., U.S.	Arizona	Arizona
Ark., U.S.	Arkansas	Arkansas
Ar. Sa.	Al-'Arabīyah as-Sa'ūdīyah	Saudi Arabia
As.	—	Asia
Atl. O.	—	Atlantic Ocean
Austl.	Australia	Australia
Ba.	Bahamas	Bahamas
Baḥr.	Al-Baḥrayn	Bahrain
Barb.	Barbados	Barbados
B.A.T.	British Antarctic Territory	British Antarctic Territory
B.C., Can.	British Columbia	British Columbia
Bdi.	Burundi	Burundi
Bel.	Belgique Belgïe	Belgium
Belize	Belize	Belize
Benin	Benin	Benin
Ber.	Bermuda	Bermuda

Abbr.	Name	Name
Ber. S.	—	Bering Sea
Bhārat	Bhārat	India
B.I.O.T.	British Indian Ocean Territory	British Indian Ocean Territory
Blg.	Bålgarija	Bulgaria
Bngl.	Bangladesh	Bangladesh
Bol.	Bolivia	Bolivia
Bots.	Botswana	Botswana
Bra.	Brasil	Brazil
B.R.D.	Bundesrepublik Deutschland	Federal Republic of Germany
Bru.	Brunei	Brunei
Br. Vir. Is.	British Virgin Islands	British Virgin Islands
Calif., U.S.	California	California
Cam.	Cameroun	Cameroon
Can.	Canada	Canada
Can./End.	Canton and Enderbury	Canton and Enderbury
Carib. S.	—	Caribbean Sea
Cay. Is.	Cayman Islands	Cayman Islands
Centraf.	République centrafricaine	Central African Republic
Česko.	Československo	Czechoslovakia
Chile	Chile	Chile
Christ. I.	Christmas Island	Christmas Island
C. Iv.	Côte d'Ivoire	Ivory Coast
C.M.I.K.	Chosŏn Minjujuŭi In'min Konghwaguk	North Korea
Cocos Is.	Cocos (Keeling) Islands	Cocos (Keeling) Islands
Col.	Colombia	Colombia
Colo., U.S.	Colorado	Colorado
Comores	Comores	Comoros
Congo	Congo	Congo
Conn., U.S.	Connecticut	Connecticut
Cook Is.	Cook Islands	Cook Islands
C.R.	Costa Rica	Costa Rica
Cuba	Cuba	Cuba
C.V.	Cabo Verde	Cape Verde
Dan.	Danmark	Denmark
D.C., U.S.	District of Columbia	District of Columbia
D.D.R.	Deutsche Demokratische Republik	German Democratic Republic
Del., U.S.	Delaware	Delaware
Den.	Danmark	Denmark
Djibouti	Djibouti	Djibouti
Dom.	Dominica	Dominica
D.Y.	Druk-Yul	Bhutan
Ec.	Ecuador	Ecuador
Eire	Eire	Ireland
Ellás	Ellás	Greece
El Sal.	El Salvador	El Salvador
Eng., U.K.	England	England
Esp.	España	Spain
Eur.	—	Europe
Falk. Is.	Falkland Islands	Falkland Islands (Islas Malvinas)
Fiji	Fiji	Fiji
Fla., U.S.	Florida	Florida
Før.	Føroyar	Faeroe Islands
Fr.	France	France
Ga., U.S.	Georgia	Georgia
Gabon	Gabon	Gabon
Gam.	Gambia	Gambia
Gaza	—	Gaza Strip
Ghana	Ghana	Ghana
Gib.	Gibraltar	Gibraltar
Gren.	Grenada	Grenada
Grn.	Grønland	Greenland
Guad.	Guadeloupe	Guadeloupe
Guam	Guam	Guam
Guat.	Guatemala	Guatemala
Guer.	Guernsey	Guernsey
Gui.-B.	Guinea-Bissau	Guinea-Bissau
Gui. Ecu.	Guinea Ecuatorial	Equatorial Guinea
Guinée	Guinée	Guinea
Guy.	Guyana	Guyana
Guy. fr.	Guyane française	French Guiana
Haï.	Haïti	Haiti
Haw., U.S.	Hawaii	Hawaii
H.K.	Hong Kong	Hong Kong
Hond.	Honduras	Honduras
H. Vol.	Haute-Volta	Upper Volta
Idaho, U.S.	Idaho	Idaho
I.I.A.	Ittiḥād al-Imārāt al-'Arabīyah	United Arab Emirates
Ill., U.S.	Illinois	Illinois
Ind., U.S.	Indiana	Indiana
Ind. O.	—	Indian Ocean
Indon.	Indonesia	Indonesia
I. of Man	Isle of Man	Isle of Man
Iowa, U.S.	Iowa	Iowa
Īrān	Īrān	Iran
'Irāq	Al-'Irāq	Iraq
Ísland	Ísland	Iceland
It.	Italia	Italy
Jam.	Jamaica	Jamaica
Jersey	Jersey	Jersey
Jugo.	Jugoslavija	Yugoslavia
Kam.	Kampuchea	Kampuchea
Kans., U.S.	Kansas	Kansas
Kenya	Kenya	Kenya
Kípros	Kípros Kıbrıs	Cyprus
Kiribati	Kiribati	Kiribati
Kuwayt	Al-Kuwayt	Kuwait
Ky., U.S.	Kentucky	Kentucky
La., U.S.	Louisiana	Louisiana
Lao	Lao	Laos
Leso.	Lesotho	Lesotho
Liber.	Liberia	Liberia
Libiyā	Lībiyā	Libya
Liech.	Liechtenstein	Liechtenstein
Lubnān	Al-Lubnān	Lebanon
Lux.	Luxembourg	Luxembourg
Macau	Macau	Macau
Madag.	Madagasikara	Madagascar
Magreb	Al-Magreb	Morocco
Magy.	Magyarország	Hungary
Maine, U.S.	Maine	Maine
Malawi	Malawi	Malawi
Malay.	Malaysia	Malaysia
Mald.	Maldives	Maldives
Mali	Mali	Mali
Malta	Malta	Malta
Man., Can.	Manitoba	Manitoba
Mart.	Martinique	Martinique
Mass., U.S.	Massachusetts	Massachusetts
Maur.	Mauritanie	Mauritania
Maus.	Mauritius	Mauritius
Md., U.S.	Maryland	Maryland
Medit. S.	—	Mediterranean Sea

Abbr.	Local	English
Méx.	México	Mexico
Mich., U.S.	Michigan	Michigan
Mid. Is.	Midway Islands	Midway Islands
Minn., U.S.	Minnesota	Minnesota
Mişr	Mişr	Egypt
Miss., U.S.	Mississippi	Mississippi
Mo., U.S.	Missouri	Missouri
Moç.	Moçambique	Mozambique
Monaco	Monaco	Monaco
Mong.	Mongol Ard Uls	Mongolia
Mont., U.S.	Montana	Montana
Monts.	Montserrat	Montserrat
Mya.	Myanma	Burma
N.A.	—	North America
Namibia	Namibia	Namibia
Nauru	Nauru	Nauru
N.B., Can.	New Brunswick	New Brunswick
N.C., U.S.	North Carolina	North Carolina
N. Cal.	Nouvelle-Calédonie	New Caledonia
N. Dak., U.S.	North Dakota	North Dakota
Nebr., U.S.	Nebraska	Nebraska
Ned.	Nederland	Netherlands
Ned. Ant.	Nederlandse Antillen	Netherlands Antilles
Nepāl	Nepāl	Nepal
Nev., U.S.	Nevada	Nevada
Newf., Can.	Newfoundland	Newfoundland
N.H., U.S.	New Hampshire	New Hampshire
Nic.	Nicaragua	Nicaragua
Nig.	Nigeria	Nigeria
Niger	Niger	Niger
Nihon	Nihon	Japan
N. Ire., U.K.	Northern Ireland	Northern Ireland
Niue	Niue	Niue
N.J., U.S.	New Jersey	New Jersey
N. Mex., U.S.	New Mexico	New Mexico
Nor.	Norge	Norway
Norf. I.	Norfolk Island	Norfolk Island
N.S., Can.	Nova Scotia	Nova Scotia
N.W. Ter., Can.	Northwest Territories	Northwest Territories
N.Y., U.S.	New York	New York
N.Z.	New Zealand	New Zealand
Oc.	—	Oceania
Ohio, U.S.	Ohio	Ohio
Okla., U.S.	Oklahoma	Oklahoma
Ont., Can.	Ontario	Ontario
Oreg., U.S.	Oregon	Oregon
Öst.	Österreich	Austria
Pa., U.S.	Pennsylvania	Pennsylvania
Pac. O.	—	Pacific Ocean
Pāk.	Pākistān	Pakistan
Pan.	Panamá	Panama
Pap. N. Gui.	Papua New Guinea	Papua New Guinea
Para.	Paraguay	Paraguay
P.E.I., Can.	Prince Edward Island	Prince Edward Ísland
Perú	Perú	Peru
Pil.	Pilipinas	Philippines
Pit.	Pitcairn	Pitcairn
P.I.T.T.	Pacific Islands Trust Territory	Pacific Islands Trust Territory
Pol.	Polska	Poland
Poly. fr.	Polynésie française	French Polynesia
Port.	Portugal	Portugal
P.R.	Puerto Rico	Puerto Rico
P.S.N.Á.	Plazas de Soberanía en el Norte de África	Spanish North Africa
Qatar	Qaṭar	Qatar
Que., Can.	Québec	Quebec
Rep. Dom.	República Dominicana	Dominican Republic
Réu.	Réunion	Reunion
R.I., U.S.	Rhode Island	Rhode Island
Rom.	Romãnia	Romania
Rw.	Rwanda	Rwanda
S.A.	—	South America
S. Afr.	South Africa Suid-Afrika	South Africa
Sah. Occ.	Sahara Occidentale	Western Sahara
Sask., Can.	Saskatchewan	Saskatchewan
S.C., U.S.	South Carolina	South Carolina
S. Ch. S.	—	South China Sea
Schw.	Schweiz; Suisse; Svizzera	Switzerland
Scot., U.K.	Scotland	Scotland
S. Dak., U.S.	South Dakota	South Dakota
Sén.	Sénégal	Senegal
Sey.	Seychelles	Seychelles
Shq.	Shqipëri	Albania
Sing.	Singapore	Singapore
S.L.	Sierra Leone	Sierra Leone
S. Lan.	Sri Lanka	Sri Lanka
S. Mar.	San Marino	San Marino
Sol. Is.	Solomon Islands	Solomon Islands
Som.	Somaliya	Somalia
Sp.	España	Spain
S.S.R.	Sovetskaja Socialističeskaja Respublika	Soviet Socialist Republic
S.S.S.R.	Sojuz Sovetskich Socialističeskich Respublik	Union of Soviet Socialist Republics
St. Hel.	St. Helena	St. Helena
St. K.-N.	St. Kitts-Nevis	St. Kitts-Nevis
St. Luc.	St. Lucia	St. Lucia
S. Tom./P.	São Tomé e Príncipe	Sao Tome and Principe
St. P./M.	St.-Pierre-et-Miquelon	St. Pierre and Miquelon
St. Vin.	St. Vincent	St. Vincent
Sūd.	As-Sūdān	Sudan
Suomi	Suomi	Finland
Sur.	Suriname	Surinam
Sūriy.	As-Sūriyah	Syria
Sval.	Svalbard og Jan Mayen	Svalbard and Jan Mayen
Sve.	Sverige	Sweden
Swaz.	Swaziland	Swaziland
T.a.a.f.	Terres australes et antarctiques françaises	French Southern and Antarctic Territories
Taehan	Taehan-Min'guk	South Korea
T'aiwan	T'aiwan	Taiwan
Tan.	Tanzania	Tanzania
Tchad	Tchad	Chad
T./C. Is.	Turks and Caicos Islands	Turks and Caicos Islands
Tenn., U.S.	Tennessee	Tennessee
Tex., U.S.	Texas	Texas
Thai.	Prathet Thai	Thailand
Togo	Togo	Togo

Tok. Is.	Tokelau Islands	Tokelau Islands
Tonga	Tonga	Tonga
Trin.	Trinidad and Tobago	Trinidad and Tobago
Tun.	Tunisie	Tunisia
Tür.	Türkiye	Turkey
Tuvalu	Tuvalu	Tuvalu
Ug.	Uganda	Uganda
U.K.	United Kingdom	United Kingdom
'Umān	'Umān	Oman
Ur.	Uruguay	Uruguay
Urd.	Al-Urdunn	Jordan
U.S.	United States	United States
U.S.S.R.	Sojuz Sovetskich Socialisticeskich Respublik	Union of Soviet Socialist Republics
Utah, U.S.	Utah	Utah
Va., U.S.	Virginia	Virginia
Van.	Vanuatu	Vanuatu
Vat.	Città del Vaticano	Vatican City
Ven.	Venezuela	Venezuela
Viet.	Viet-nam	Vietnam
Vir. Is., U.S.	Virgin Islands	Virgin Islands (U.S.)
Vt., U.S.	Vermont	Vermont
Wake I.	Wake Island	Wake Island
Wales, U.K.	Wales	Wales
Wal./F.	Wallis et Futuna	Wallis and Futuna
Wash., U.S.	Washington	Washington
Wis., U.S.	Wisconsin	Wisconsin
W. Sam.	Western Samoa	Western Samoa
W. Va., U.S.	West Virginia	West Virginia
Wyo., U.S.	Wyoming	Wyoming
Yai.	Yaitopya	Ethiopia
Yaman	Al-Yaman	Yemen
Yam. S.	Al-Yaman ash-Sha'bīyah	People's Democratic Republic of Yemen
Yis.	Yisra'el	Israel
Yukon, Can.	Yukon	Yukon
Zaïre	Zaïre	Zaire
Zam.	Zambia	Zambia
Zhg.	Zhongguo	China
Zimbabwe	Zimbabwe	Zimbabwe

KEY TO SYMBOLS

- $\wedge$ **Mountain**
- $\wedge^1$ Volcano
- $\wedge^2$ Hill
- $\not\wedge$ **Mountains**
- $\not\wedge^1$ Plateau
- $\not\wedge^2$ Hills
- $)($ **Pass**
- $\vee$ **Valley, Canyon**
- $\smile$ **Plain**
- $\smile^1$ Basin
- $\smile^2$ **Delta**
- $\succ$ **Cape**
- $\succ^1$ Peninsula
- $\succ^2$ Spit, Sand Bar
- **I** **Island**
- I^1 Atoll
- I^2 Rock
- **II** **Islands**
- II^1 Rocks
- $\bullet$ **Other Topographic Features**
- $\bullet^1$ Continent
- $\bullet^2$ Coast, Beach

- $\bullet^3$ **Isthmus**
- $\bullet^4$ Cliff
- $\bullet^5$ Cave, Caves
- $\bullet^6$ Crater
- $\bullet^7$ Depression
- $\bullet^8$ Dunes
- $\bullet^9$ Lava Flow
- $\simeq$ **River**
- $\simeq^1$ River Channel
- Ξ **Canal**
- Ξ^1 Aqueduct
- $\llcorner$ **Waterfall, Rapids**
- $\mathcal{U}$ **Strait**
- $\mathcal{C}$ **Bay, Gulf**
- $\mathcal{C}^1$ Estuary
- $\mathcal{C}^2$ Fjord
- $\mathcal{C}^3$ Bight
- $\circleddash$ **Lake, Lakes**
- $\circleddash^1$ Reservoir
- $\equiv$ **Swamp**
- $\boxtimes$ **Ice Features, Glacier**

- $\overline{\tau}$ **Other Hydrographic Features**
- $\overline{\tau}^1$ Ocean
- $\overline{\tau}^2$ Sea
- $\overline{\tau}^3$ Anchorage
- $\overline{\tau}^4$ Oasis, Well, Spring
- $\div$ **Submarine Features**
- $\div^1$ Depression
- $\div^2$ Reef, Shoal
- $\div^3$ Mountain, Mountains
- $\div^4$ Slope, Shelf
- $\square$ **Political Unit**
- $\square^1$ Independent Nation
- $\square^2$ Dependency
- $\square^3$ State, Canton, Republic
- $\square^4$ Province, Region, Oblast
- $\square^5$ Department, District, Prefecture
- $\square^6$ County
- $\square^7$ City, Municipality
- $\square^8$ Miscellaneous
- $\square^9$ Historical

- $\mathcal{U}$ **Cultural Institution**
- $\mathcal{U}^1$ Religious Institution
- $\mathcal{U}^2$ Educational Institution
- $\mathcal{U}^3$ Scientific, Industrial Facility
- $\perp$ **Historical Site**
- $\blacktriangle$ **Recreational Site**
- $\boxtimes$ **Airport**
- $\blacksquare$ **Military Installation**
- $\rightarrow$ **Miscellaneous**
- $\rightarrow^1$ Region
- $\rightarrow^2$ Desert
- $\rightarrow^3$ Forest, Moor
- $\rightarrow^4$ Reserve, Reservation
- $\rightarrow^5$ Transportation
- $\rightarrow^6$ Dam
- $\rightarrow^7$ Mine, Quarry
- $\rightarrow^8$ Neighborhood
- $\rightarrow^9$ Shopping Center

Name	Map No.	Lat °′	Long °′
Al-Fāshir	14	13.38 N	25.21 E
Al-Fayyūm	14	29.19 N	30.50 E
Alfenas	35	21.25 S	45.57 W
Alfred	38	45.34 N	74.53 W
Algeciras	9	36.08 N	5.30 W
Alger (Algiers)	14	36.47 N	3.03 E
Algeria □¹	14	28.00 N	3.00 E
Algiers			
→ Alger	14	36.47 N	3.03 E
Algoma	42	44.36 N	87.27 W
Al-Ḥijāz ◆¹	18	24.30 N	38.30 E
Al-Ḥudaydah	17	14.48 N	42.57 E
Alicante	9	38.21 N	0.29 W
Alice	45	27.45 N	98.04 W
Alicedale	16	33.19 S	26.05 E
Alice Springs	27	23.42 S	133.53 E
Alīgarh	21	27.54 N	78.05 E
Al-Iskandarīyah (Alexandria)	14	31.12 N	29.54 E
Al-Ismāʿīlīyah	18	30.35 N	32.16 E
Aliwal North	16	30.45 S	26.45 E
Al-Jīzah	14	30.01 N	31.13 E
Al-Kʾarṭūm (Khartoum)	14	15.36 N	32.32 E
Al-Khandaq	14	18.36 N	30.34 E
Alkmaar	7	52.37 N	4.44 E
Al-Kuwayt	17	29.20 N	47.59 E
Al-Lādhiqīyah (Latakia)	18	35.31 N	35.47 E
Allāhābād	21	25.27 N	81.51 E
Allegheny Mountains ⩘	38	38.30 N	80.00 W
Allentown	38	40.36 N	75.29 W
Alliance	46	42.06 N	102.52 W
Alma	41	48.33 N	71.39 W
Alma-Ata	13	43.15 N	76.57 E
Al-Madīnah (Medina)	17	24.28 N	39.36 E
Al-Maḥallah al-Kubrā	14	30.58 N	31.10 E
Al-Manāmah	17	26.13 N	50.35 E
Al-Mawṣil	17	36.20 N	43.08 E
Almería	9	36.50 N	2.27 W
Al-Minyā	14	28.06 N	30.45 E
Al-Mukallā	17	14.32 N	49.08 E
Alor Setar	26	6.07 N	100.22 E
Alpena	42	45.04 N	83.26 W
Alpine	45	30.22 N	103.40 W
Alps ⩘	8	46.25 N	10.00 E
Al-Qaḍārif	14	14.02 N	35.24 E
Al-Qāhirah (Cairo)	14	30.03 N	31.15 E
Al-Qāmishlī	18	37.02 N	41.14 E
Al-Qaṭrūn	14	24.56 N	14.38 E
Alsace □⁹	8	48.30 N	7.30 E
Alta	6	69.55 N	23.12 E
Altamaha ⩱	43	31.19 N	81.17 W
Altamont	48	42.12 N	121.44 W
Altamura	10	40.50 N	16.33 E
Altiplano ⩘¹	33	18.00 S	68.00 W
Alton	44	38.54 N	90.10 W
Altoona	38	40.30 N	78.24 W
Altus	45	34.38 N	99.20 W
Al-Ubayyiḍ	14	13.11 N	30.13 E
Al-Uqṣur (Luxor)	14	25.41 N	32.39 E
Alvarado	31	18.46 N	95.46 W
Amana	42	41.48 N	91.52 W
Amarillo	45	35.13 N	101.49 W
Amatikulu	16	29.06 S	31.27 E
Amazon (Solimões) (Amazonas) ⩱	33	0.05 S	50.00 W
Amberg	7	49.27 N	11.52 E
Ambon	25	3.43 S	128.12 E
Ambositra	15	20.31 S	47.15 E
Ambre, Cap d' ⊁	15	11.57 S	49.17 E
Amecameca [de Juárez]	31	19.07 N	98.46 W
America Samoa □²	1	14.20 S	170.00 W
Ames	42	42.02 N	93.37 W
Amga	13	60.53 N	132.00 E
Amherst	43	37.35 N	79.03 W
Amherstburg	42	42.06 N	83.06 W
Amiens	8	49.54 N	2.18 E
Amīndīvi Islands ‖	20	11.23 N	72.23 E
ʿAmmān	18	31.57 N	35.56 E
Ammókhostos (Famagusta)	18	35.07 N	33.57 E
Amory	44	33.59 N	88.29 W
Amos	42	48.35 N	78.07 W
Åmot	6	59.35 N	8.00 E
Amqui	41	49.28 N	67.26 W
Amrāvati	21	20.56 N	77.45 E
Amritsar	21	31.35 N	74.53 E
Amsterdam, Ned.	7	52.22 N	4.54 E
Amsterdam, N.Y., U.S.	38	42.57 N	74.11 W
Amu Darya (Amudarja) ⩱	19	42.30 N	59.15 E
Amundsen Gulf C	36	71.00 N	124.00 W
Amundsen Sea ⸗²	3	72.30 S	112.00 W
Amur (Heilongjiang) ⩱	13	52.56 N	141.10 E
Anaconda	48	46.08 N	112.57 W
Anaheim	39	33.51 N	117.57 W
Anakāpalle	20	17.41 N	83.01 E
Anápolis	35	16.20 S	48.58 W
Anchorage	40	61.13 N	149.53 W
Ancona	10	43.38 N	13.30 E
Andalucia □⁹	9	37.36 N	4.30 W
Andaman Islands ‖	26	12.00 N	92.45 E
Andaman Sea ⸗²	26	10.00 N	95.00 E
Anderson, Ind., U.S.	44	40.10 N	85.41 W
Anderson, S.C., U.S.	43	34.31 N	82.39 W
Andes ⩘	1	20.00 S	68.00 W
Andkhvoy	21	36.56 N	65.08 E
Andong	22	40.08 N	124.20 E
Andorra	9	42.30 N	1.31 E
Andorra □¹	4	42.30 N	1.30 E
Andradina	35	20.54 S	51.23 W
Andreanof Islands ‖	40	52.00 N	176.00 W
Andrews	45	32.19 N	102.33 W
Andros ‖	11	37.45 N	24.42 E
Andros Island ‖	32	24.26 N	77.57 W
Angarsk	13	52.34 N	103.54 E
Angel, Salto (Angel Falls) ↳	33	5.57 N	62.30 W
Angel de la Guarda, Isla ‖	31	29.20 N	113.25 W
Angeles	25	15.09 N	120.35 E
Angel Falls			
→ Ángel, Salto ↳	33	5.57 N	62.30 W
Ångermanälven ⩱	6	62.48 N	17.56 E
Angermünde	7	53.01 N	14.00 E
Angers	8	47.28 N	0.33 W
Angmagssalik	36	65.36 N	37.41 W
Angola □¹	15	12.30 S	18.30 E
Angoram	25	4.04 S	144.04 E
Angoulême	8	45.39 N	0.09 E
Anguilla □²	32	18.15 N	63.05 W
Aniak	40	61.35 N	159.33 W
Anina	11	45.05 N	21.51 E
Ankara	4	39.56 N	32.52 E
Annaba (Bône)	14	36.54 N	7.46 E
An-Nafūd ◆²	18	28.30 N	41.00 E
An-Najaf	17	31.59 N	44.20 E
Annapolis	38	38.59 N	76.30 W
Annapurna ⋀	21	28.34 N	83.50 E
Ann Arbor	42	42.18 N	83.45 W
Annecy	8	45.54 N	6.07 E
An-Nuhūd	14	12.42 N	28.26 E
Anqing	24	30.31 N	117.02 E
Ansbach	7	49.17 N	10.34 E
Anshan	22	41.08 N	122.59 E
Antalaha	15	14.53 S	50.16 E
Antananarivo	15	18.55 S	47.31 E
Antarctica ⋅¹	3	90.00 S	0.00
Antarctic Peninsula ⊁¹	3	69.30 S	65.00 W
Antelope Island ‖	48	40.57 N	112.12 W
Antequera	9	37.01 N	4.33 W
Anticosti, Île d' ‖	41	49.30 N	63.00 W
Antigua □¹	32	17.03 N	61.48 W
Antofagasta	34	23.39 S	70.24 W
Antonito	47	37.05 N	106.00 W
Antsirabe	15	19.51 S	47.02 E
Antwerp			
→ Antwerpen	7	51.13 N	4.25 E
Antwerpen (Anvers)	7	51.13 N	4.25 E
Anvers			
→ Antwerpen	7	51.13 N	4.25 E
Anžero-Sudžensk	13	56.07 N	86.00 E
Aomori	23a	40.49 N	140.45 E
Aôral, Phnum ⋀	26	12.02 N	104.10 E
Aosta	10	45.44 N	7.20 E
Apatzingán [de la Constitución]	31	19.05 N	102.21 W
Apeldoorn	7	52.13 N	5.58 E
Apennines			
→ Appennino ⩘	10	43.00 N	13.00 E
Apia	30e	13.50 S	171.44 W
Apo, Mount ⋀	25	6.59 N	125.16 E
Apostle Islands ‖	42	46.50 N	90.30 W
Apostólou Andréa, Akrotírion ⊁	18	35.42 N	34.35 E
Appalachian Mountains ⩘	37	41.00 N	77.00 W
Appennino (Appennines) ⩘	10	43.00 N	13.00 E
Appleton	42	44.16 N	88.25 W
Aqaba, Gulf of C	18	29.00 N	34.40 E
ʿArab, Baḥr al- ⩱	14	9.02 N	29.28 E
Arabian Sea ⸗²	1	15.00 N	65.00 E
Aracaju	33	10.55 S	37.04 W

Name	Map No.	Lat° '	Long° '
Araçatuba	33	21.12 S	50.25 W
Arad	11	46.11 N	21.20 E
Arafura Sea ᴥ²	25	11.00 S	135.00 E
Aragón □⁹	9	41.00 N	1.00 W
Araguaia ≃	33	5.21 S	48.41 W
Araguari	35	18.38 S	48.11 W
Aral'skoje More ᴥ²	4	45.00 N	59.00 E
Aran Islands II	5	53.07 N	9.43 W
Aranyaprathet	26	13.41 N	102.30 E
Arapahoe	46	40.18 N	99.54 W
Araraquara	33	21.47 S	48.10 W
Araxá	35	19.35 S	46.55 W
Arbroath	5	56.34 N	2.35 W
Arcadia, Fla., U.S.	43	27.14 N	81.52 W
Arcadia, La., U.S.	44	32.33 N	92.55 W
Arc Dome ᴧ	39	38.51 N	117.22 W
Archangel			
→ Archangel'sk	4	64.34 N	40.32 E
Archangel'sk	4	64.34 N	40.32 E
Arches National Park ✦	47	38.42 N	109.45 W
Arco	48	43.38 N	113.18 W
Arctic Ocean ᴥ¹	2	85.00 N	170.00 E
Ardennes ᴧ¹	8	50.10 N	5.45 E
Ardmore	45	34.10 N	97.08 W
Arecibo	32	18.28 N	66.43 W
Arendal	6	58.27 N	8.48 E
Arequipa	33	16.24 S	71.33 W
Arezzo	10	43.25 N	11.53 E
Argentina □¹	34	34.00 S	64.00 W
Argonne ᴧ¹	8	49.30 N	5.00 E
Árgos	11	37.39 N	22.44 E
Arguello, Point ⅄	39	34.35 N	120.39 W
Árgun' (Eergu'nahe) ≃	22	53.20 N	121.28 E
Århus	6	56.09 N	10.13 E
Arica	33	18.29 S	70.20 W
Arizona □³	37	34.00 N	112.00 W
Arkadelphia	44	34.07 N	93.04 W
Arkansas □³	37	34.50 N	93.40 W
Arkansas ≃	37	33.48 N	91.04 W
Arles	8	43.40 N	4.38 E
Armentières	8	50.41 N	2.53 E
Arnhem	7	51.59 N	5.55 E
Ar-Ramādī	17	33.25 N	43.17 E
Arran, Island of I	5	55.35 N	5.15 W
Arras	8	50.17 N	2.47 E
Ar-Riyāḍ (Riyadh)	17	24.38 N	46.43 E
Ar-Rub' al-Khālī ᴧ²	17	20.00 N	51.00 E
Artemisa	32	22.49 N	82.46 W
Artesia	45	32.51 N	104.24 W
Art'omovsk	13	54.21 N	93.26 E
Aru, Kepulauan II	25	6.00 S	134.30 E
Aruba I	32	12.30 N	69.58 W
Arusha	15	3.22 S	36.41 E
Arvada	47	39.50 N	105.05 W
Arvida	41	48.25 N	71.11 W
Asahikawa	23a	43.46 N	142.22 E
Asansol	21	23.41 N	86.59 E
Asbestos	38	45.46 N	71.57 W
Ascensión	31	31.06 N	107.59 W
Ascoli Piceno	10	42.51 N	13.34 E
Asenovgrad	11	42.01 N	24.52 E
Ashburton	29	43.55 S	171.45 E
Asheboro	43	35.42 N	79.49 W
Asheville	43	35.34 N	82.33 W
Ashikaga	23	36.20 N	139.27 E
Ashland, Ky., U.S.	38	38.28 N	82.38 W
Ashland, Oreg., U.S.	48	42.12 N	122.42 W
Ashland, Wis., U.S.	42	46.35 N	90.53 W
Ashtabula	38	41.52 N	80.48 W
Asia ᴧ¹	1	50.00 N	100.00 E
Asia Minor ᴧ¹	4	39.00 N	32.00 E
Asmera	17	15.20 N	38.53 E
Aspen	47	39.11 N	106.49 W
Assen	7	52.59 N	6.34 E
Assiniboine, Mount ᴧ	36	50.52 N	115.39 W
As-Suwaydā'	18	32.42 N	36.34 E
As-Suways (Suez)	14	29.58 N	32.33 E
Asti	10	44.54 N	8.12 E
Astoria	48	46.11 N	123.80 W
Astrachan'	4	46.21 N	48.03 E
Asunción	34	25.16 S	57.40 W
Aswān	14	24.05 N	32.53 E
Aswān High Dam ᴧ⁶	17	24.05 N	32.53 E
Asyūṭ	14	27.11 N	31.11 E
Atacama, Desierto de ᴧ²	33	20.00 S	69.15 W
Atar	14	20.31 N	13.03 W
Atbasar	13	51.48 N	68.20 E

Name	Map No.	Lat° '	Long° '
Atchafalaya Bay ᴄ	44	29.25 N	91.20 W
Atchison	46	39.34 N	95.07 W
Athabasca	36	54.43 N	113.17 W
Athabasca, Lake ᴤ	36	59.07 N	110.00 W
Athens			
→ Athínai, Ellás	11	37.58 N	23.43 E
Athens, Ga., U.S.	43	33.57 N	83.23 W
Athens, Ohio, U.S.	38	39.20 N	82.06 W
Athens, Pa., U.S.	38	41.57 N	76.31 W
Athens, Tenn., U.S.	43	35.27 N	84.36 W
Athens, Tex., U.S.	45	32.12 N	95.51 W
Athínai (Athens)	11	37.58 N	23.43 E
Atikokan	42	48.45 N	91.37 W
Atka Island I	40	52.15 N	174.30 W
Atlanta	43	33.45 N	84.23 W
Atlantic City	38	39.22 N	74.26 W
Atlantic Ocean ᴥ¹	1	0.00	25.00 W
Atlas Mountains ᴧ	14	33.00 N	2.00 W
Atotonilco el Alto	31	20.33 N	102.31 W
Aṭ-Ṭafīlah	18	30.50 N	35.36 E
Attapu	26	14.48 N	106.50 E
Attu Island I	40	52.55 N	173.00 E
Auburn, Maine, U.S.	41	44.06 N	70.14 W
Auburn, Nebr., U.S.	46	40.23 N	95.51 W
Auburn, N.Y., U.S.	38	42.56 N	76.34 W
Auckland	29	36.52 S	174.46 E
Audubon	46	41.43 N	94.55 W
Augsburg	7	48.23 N	10.53 E
Augusta, Austl.	27	34.19 S	115.10 E
Augusta, It.	10	37.13 N	15.13 E
Augusta, Ga., U.S.	43	33.29 N	81.57 W
Augusta, Maine, U.S.	38	44.19 N	69.47 W
Aurillac	8	44.56 N	2.26 E
Aurora, Ont., Can.	42	44.00 N	79.28 W
Aurora, S. Afr.	16	32.42 S	18.29 E
Aurora, Colo., U.S.	47	39.44 N	104.52 W
Aurora, Ill., U.S.	42	42.46 N	88.19 W
Aurora, Mo., U.S.	44	36.58 N	93.43 W
Austin, Minn., U.S.	42	43.40 N	92.59 W
Austin, Tex., U.S.	45	30.16 N	97.45 W
Australia □¹	27	25.00 S	135.00 E
Austria □¹	4	47.20 N	13.20 E
Autlán de Navarro	31	19.46 N	104.22 W
Auvergne □⁹	8	45.25 N	2.30 E
Aveiro	9	40.38 N	8.39 W
Avellino	10	40.54 N	14.47 E
Avery Island	44	29.55 N	91.55 W
Avesta	6	60.09 N	16.12 E
Avezzano	10	42.02 N	13.25 E
Avignon	8	43.57 N	4.49 E
Avila	9	40.39 N	4.42 W
Avilés	9	43.33 N	5.55 W
Avola	10	36.54 N	15.09 E
Avon Park	43	27.36 N	81.31 W
Ayden	43	35.25 N	77.20 W
Aydın	11	37.51 N	27.51 E
'Ayoûn el 'Atroûs	14	16.40 N	9.37 W
Ayr, Ont., Can.	42	43.17 N	80.27 W
Ayr, Scot., U.K.	5	55.28 N	4.38 W
Ayvalık	11	39.18 N	26.41 E
Azogues	33	2.44 S	78.50 W
Azovskoje More ᴥ²	4	46.00 N	36.00 E
Azua	32	18.27 N	70.44 W
Azuero, Península de ⅄¹	32	7.40 N	80.35 W
Azul	34	36.47 S	59.51 W
Az-Zaqāzīq	14	30.35 N	31.31 E
Az-Zarqā'	18	32.05 N	36.06 E
B			
Babaeski	11	41.26 N	27.06 E
Babbitt	42	47.43 N	91.57 W
Babuyan Islands II	25	19.10 N	121.40 E
Bacău	11	46.34 N	26.55 E
Bac-lieu (Vinh-loi)	26	9.17 N	105.44 E
Bacolod	25	10.40 N	122.57 E
Badajoz	9	38.53 N	6.58 W
Badalona	9	41.27 N	2.15 E
Baden-Baden	7	48.46 N	8.14 E
Badlands ᴧ²	46	43.30 N	102.20 W
Baffin Bay ᴄ	36	73.00 N	66.00 W
Baffin Island I	36	68.00 N	70.00 W
Bāgalkot	20	16.11 N	75.42 E
Bagdad			
→ Baghdād, 'Irāq	17	33.21 N	44.25 E
Bagdad, Ariz., U.S	47	34.34 N	113.11 W

Name	Map No.	Lat ° '	Long ° '
Bagdarin	13	54.26 N	113.36 E
Bagé	34	31.20 S	54.06 W
Baghdād	17	33.21 N	44.25 E
Bagheria	10	38.05 N	13.30 E
Baghlān	21	36.13 N	68.46 E
Baguio	25	16.25 N	120.36 E
Bahamas □¹	32	24.15 N	76.00 W
Bahāwalnagar	21	29.59 N	73.16 E
Bahāwalpur	19	29.24 N	71.41 E
Bahia, Islas de la II	32	16.20 N	86.30 W
Bahia Blanca	34	38.43 S	62.17 W
Bahrain □¹	17	26.00 N	50.30 E
Baia-Mare	11	47.40 N	23.35 E
Baidoa	17	3.04 N	43.48 E
Baie-Comeau	41	49.13 N	68.10 W
Baie-Saint-Paul	41	47.27 N	70.30 W
Băileşti	11	44.02 N	23.21 E
Bainbridge	43	30.54 N	84.34 W
Baja	7	46.11 N	18.57 E
Baja California ≻¹	31	28.00 N	113.30 W
Bajkal, Ozero (Lake Baikal) 🗗	13	53.00 N	107.40 E
Baker, Mount ∧	48	48.47 N	121.49 W
Baker Lake	36	64.15 N	96.00 W
Bakersfield	39	35.23 N	119.01 W
Baku	4	40.23 N	49.51 E
Balašicha	12	55.49 N	37.58 E
Balaton 🗗	7	46.50 N	17.45 E
Balchaš	13	46.49 N	74.59 E
Balchaš, Ozero 🗗	13	46.00 N	74.00 E
Balcones Escarpment •⁴	45	29.30 N	99.15 W
Baldwin	42	43.54 N	85.51 W
Baleares, Islas (Balearic Islands) II	9	39.30 N	3.00 E
Balearic Islands → Baleares, Islas II	9	39.30 N	3.00 E
Balfour, S. Afr.	16	26.44 S	28.45 E
Balfour, N.C., U.S.	43	35.21 N	82.28 W
Bali I	25	8.20 S	115.00 E
Balıkesir	11	39.39 N	27.53 E
Balikpapan	25	1.17 S	116.50 E
Balkan Mountains → Stara Planina ⚭	11	43.15 N	25.00 E
Ballinger	45	31.44 N	99.57 W
Balmoral Castle ✦	5	57.02 N	3.15 W
Balsas ≃	31	17.55 N	102.10 W
Baltic Sea ⲧ²	6	57.00 N	19.00 E
Baltimore	38	39.17 N	76.37 W
Baluchistan □⁹	19	28.00 N	63.00 E
Balygyčan	13	63.56 N	154.12 E
Bamako	14	12.39 N	8.00 W
Bambari	14	5.45 N	20.40 E
Bamberg	7	49.53 N	10.53 E
Bamenda	14	5.56 N	10.10 E
Banbury	5	52.04 N	1.20 W
Banda, Laut (Banda Sea) ⲧ²	25	5.00 S	128.00 E
Banda Aceh	25	5.34 N	95.20 E
Bandar Seri Begawan	25	4.56 N	114.55 E
Bandırma	11	40.20 N	27.58 E
Bandundu	15	3.18 S	17.20 E
Bandung	25	6.54 S	107.36 E
Banes	32	20.58 N	75.43 W
Bangalore	20	12.59 N	77.35 E
Bangbu	24	32.58 N	117.24 E
Banggai, Kepulauan II	25	1.30 S	123.15 E
Banghāzī	14	32.07 N	20.04 E
Bangkok → Krung Thep	26	13.45 N	100.31 E
Bangladesh □¹	19	24.00 N	90.00 E
Bangor, N. Ire., U.K.	5	54.40 N	5.40 W
Bangor, Wales, U.K.	5	53.13 N	4.08 W
Bangor, Maine, U.S.	38	44.49 N	68.47 W
Bangui	14	4.22 N	18.35 E
Bani ≃	14	14.30 N	4.12 W
Banī Suwayf	14	29.05 N	31.05 E
Banja Luka	10	44.46 N	17.11 E
Banjarmasin	25	3.20 S	114.35 E
Banjul	13	13.28 N	16.39 W
Banks Island I	36	73.15 N	121.30 W
Banks Peninsula ≻¹	29	43.45 S	173.00 E
Ban Na San	26	8.48 N	99.22 E
Bannu	21	32.59 N	70.36 E
Ban Pak Phraek	26	8.13 N	100.12 E
Banská Bystrica	7	48.44 N	19.07 E
Baoding	22	38.52 N	115.29 E
Baoji	22	34.22 N	107.14 E
Baotou	22	40.40 N	109.59 E
Baraga	42	46.47 N	88.30 W
Barbacena	35	21.14 S	43.46 W
Barbados □¹	32	13.10 N	59.32 W
Barbaros	11	40.54 N	27.27 E
Barbourville	43	36.52 N	83.53 W
Barcelona, Esp.	9	41.23 N	2.11 E
Barcelona, Méx.	31	26.12 N	103.25 W
Bardufoss	6	69.04 N	18.30 E
Bareilly	21	28.21 N	79.25 E
Barents Sea ⲧ²	2	74.00 N	36.00 E
Bargarh	21	21.20 N	83.37 E
Bar Harbor	38	44.23 N	68.13 W
Bari	10	41.07 N	16.52 E
Barisāl	21	22.42 N	90.22 E
Barkley, Lake 🗗¹	44	36.40 N	87.55 W
Barkly East	16	30.58 S	27.33 E
Barletta	10	41.19 N	16.17 E
Barmouth	5	52.43 N	4.03 W
Barnaul	13	53.22 N	83.45 E
Barnesville	46	46.39 N	96.25 W
Baroda	21	22.18 N	73.12 E
Barqah (Cyrenaica) ⊷¹	14	31.00 N	22.30 E
Barquisimeto	33	10.04 N	69.19 W
Barranquilla	33	10.59 N	74.48 W
Barre	38	44.12 N	72.30 W
Barre des Écrins ∧	8	44.55 N	6.22 E
Barreiro	9	38.40 N	9.04 W
Barretos	33	20.33 S	48.33 W
Barrie	42	44.24 N	79.40 W
Barrow, Point ≻	40	71.23 N	156.30 W
Barrow Creek	27	21.33 S	133.53 E
Barrys Bay	42	45.29 N	77.41 W
Barstow	39	34.54 N	117.01 W
Bartlesville	45	36.45 N	95.59 W
Bartow	43	27.54 N	81.50 W
Barú, Volcán ∧¹	32	8.48 N	82.33 W
Basel (Bâle)	8	47.33 N	7.35 E
Basile	44	30.29 N	92.36 W
Bassein	26	16.47 N	94.44 E
Basseterre	32	17.18 N	62.43 W
Basse-Terre I	32	16.10 N	61.40 W
Bassett	46	42.35 N	99.32 W
Bass Harbor	41	44.16 N	68.19 W
Bass Strait ⳩	28	39.20 S	145.30 E
Bastia	8	42.42 N	9.27 E
Bastrop	44	32.47 N	91.55 W
Batabanó, Golfo de C	32	22.15 N	82.30 W
Batamaj	13	63.31 N	129.27 E
Batan Islands II	25	20.30 N	121.50 E
Batatais	38	20.53 S	47.37 W
Batavia	38	43.00 N	78.11 W
Bătdâmbâng	26	13.06 N	103.12 E
Batesville, Ark., U.S.	44	35.46 N	91.39 W
Batesville, Miss., U.S.	44	34.18 N	90.00 W
Bath, Eng., U.K.	5	51.23 N	2.22 W
Bath, Maine, U.S.	38	43.55 N	69.49 W
Bath, N.Y., U.S.	38	42.20 N	77.19 W
Bathurst	41	47.36 N	65.39 W
Bathurst Island I	36	76.00 N	100.30 W
Batna	14	35.34 N	6.11 E
Baton Rouge	44	30.23 N	91.11 W
Batouri	14	4.26 N	14.22 E
Battle Creek	42	42.19 N	85.11 W
Battle Mountain	39	40.38 N	116.56 W
Batumi	4	41.38 N	41.38 E
Baubau	25	5.28 S	122.38 E
Baudette	42	48.43 N	94.36 W
Bauru	33	22.19 S	49.04 W
Bautzen	7	51.11 N	14.26 E
Bayamo	32	20.23 N	76.39 W
Bay City, Mich., U.S.	42	43.36 N	83.53 W
Bay City, Tex., U.S.	45	28.59 N	95.58 W
Bayerisch Alpen ⚭	7	47.30 N	11.00 E
Bayonne	8	43.29 N	1.29 W
Bay Port	42	43.51 N	83.23 W
Bayreuth	7	49.57 N	11.35 E
Bayrūt (Beirut)	18	33.53 N	35.30 E
Bay Shore	38	40.44 N	73.15 W
Baytown	45	29.44 N	94.58 W
Bear Lake 🗗	47	42.00 N	111.20 W
Bear Tooth Pass)(	48	44.58 N	109.28 W
Beatrice	46	40.16 N	96.44 W
Beatty	39	36.54 N	116.46 W
Beaufort Sea ⲧ²	2	73.00 N	140.00 W
Beaumont, N.Z.	29	45.49 S	169.32 E
Beaumont, Tex., U.S.	44	30.05 N	94.06 W
Beauvais	8	49.26 N	2.05 E
Beaver, Okla., U.S.	45	36.49 N	100.31 W

Name	Map No.	Lat ° '	Long ° '
Beaver, Utah, U.S.	47	38.17 N	112.38 W
Beaver ☲	47	39.10 N	112.57 W
Beaver Dam	42	43.28 N	88.50 W
Beaver Falls	38	40.46 N	80.19 W
Beaverhead Mountains ⋏	48	45.00 N	113.20 W
Bečej	11	45.37 N	20.03 E
Béchar	14	31.37 N	2.13 W
Beckley	38	37.46 N	81.13 W
Bedford	44	38.52 N	86.29 W
Be'er Sheva'	18	31.14 N	34.47 E
Beeville	45	28.24 N	97.45 W
Beian	22	48.15 N	126.30 E
Beihai	22	21.29 N	109.05 E
Beijing (Peking)	22	39.55 N	116.25 E
Beira	15	19.49 S	34.52 E
Beirut			
→ Bayrūt	18	33.53 N	35.30 E
Beja, Port.	9	38.01 N	7.52 W
Béja, Tun.	14	36.44 N	9.11 E
Bejaïa	14	36.45 N	5.05 E
Bekdaš	4	41.34 N	52.32 E
Békéscsaba	7	46.41 N	21.06 E
Belcher Islands ‖	36	56.20 N	79.30 W
Belding	42	43.06 N	85.14 W
Beled Weyne	17	4.47 N	45.12 E
Belém	33	1.27 S	48.29 W
Belen	47	34.40 N	106.46 W
Belfast	5	54.35 N	5.55 W
Belfield	46	46.53 N	103.12 W
Belgaum	20	15.52 N	74.30 E
Belgium □¹	4	50.50 N	4.00 E
Belgorod	4	50.36 N	36.35 E
Belgrade			
→ Beograd	11	44.50 N	20.30 E
Belitung ‖	25	2.50 S	107.55 E
Belize	32	17.30 N	88.12 W
Belize □²	32	17.15 N	88.45 W
Bella Coola	36	52.22 N	126.46 W
Bellavista	33	7.04 S	76.35 W
Belle Fourche	46	44.40 N	103.51 W
Belle Glade	43	26.41 N	80.40 W
Belle Plaine	42	44.37 N	93.46 W
Belleville	38	44.10 N	77.23 W
Bellevue, Iowa, U.S.	42	42.16 N	90.26 W
Bellevue, Wash., U.S.	48	47.37 N	122.12 W
Bellingham	48	48.49 N	122.29 W
Bellingshausen Sea ▼²	3	71.00 S	85.00 W
Belmont	16	29.28 S	24.22 E
Belmopan	32	17.15 N	88.46 W
Belo Horizonte	33	19.55 S	43.56 W
Beloit	42	42.31 N	89.02 W
Beloje More (White Sea) ▼²	13	65.30 N	38.00 E
Belovo	13	54.25 N	86.18 E
Bemidji	42	47.29 N	94.53 W
Bend	48	44.03 N	121.19 W
Bendigo	27	36.46 S	144.17 E
Benevento	10	41.08 N	14.45 E
Bengal, Bay !Of ⊂	1	15.00 N	90.00 E
Benghazi			
→ Banghāzī	14	32.07 N	20.04 E
Bengkalis	26	1.28 N	102.07 E
Bengkayang	26	0.50 N	109.29 E
Bengkulu	25	3.48 S	102.16 E
Beni ☲	33	10.23 S	65.24 W
Benin □¹	14	9.30 N	2.15 E
Benin, Bight of ⊂³	14	5.30 N	3.00 E
Benin City	14	6.19 N	5.41 E
Benkelman	46	40.03 N	101.32 W
Bennington	38	42.53 N	73.12 W
Benson	46	45.19 N	95.36 W
Benton Harbor	42	42.06 N	86.27 W
Bentonville	44	36.22 N	94.13 W
Benue (Bénoué) ☲	14	7.48 N	6.46 E
Benxi	22	41.18 N	123.45 E
Beograd (Belgrade)	11	44.50 N	20.30 E
Beppu	23	33.17 N	131.30 E
Berat	11	40.42 N	19.57 E
Berbera	17	10.25 N	45.02 E
Berens River	36	52.22 N	97.02 W
Beresford	46	43.05 N	96.47 W
Berg	6	69.26 N	17.15 E
Bergama	11	39.07 N	27.11 E
Bergamo	10	45.41 N	9.43 E
Bergen	6	60.23 N	5.20 E
Bergerac	8	44.51 N	0.29 E
Bergland	42	46.35 N	89.34 W
Bering Sea ▼²	1	59.00 N	174.00 W

Name	Map No.	Lat ° '	Long ° '
Berkåk	6	62.50 N	10.00 E
Berkeley	39	37.57 N	122.18 W
Berlevåg	6	70.51 N	29.06 E
Berlin (West), B.R.D.	7	52.31 N	13.24 E
Berlin (Ost), D.D.R.	7	52.30 N	13.25 E
Berlin, N.H., U.S.	38	44.29 N	71.10 W
Bermuda □²	37	32.20 N	64.45 W
Bern (Berne)	8	46.57 N	7.26 E
Bernburg	7	51.48 N	11.44 E
Berner Alpen ⋏	8	46.30 N	7.30 E
Ber'ozovo	13	63.56 N	65.02 E
Berryessa, Lake ⊜¹	39	38.35 N	122.14 W
Besançon	8	47.15 N	6.02 E
Bethal	16	26.27 S	29.28 E
Bethel, Alaska, U.S.	40	60.48 N	161.46 W
Bethel, Maine, U.S.	41	44.25 N	70.48 W
Bethlehem, S. Afr.	16	28.15 S	28.15 E
Bethlehem, Pa., U.S.	38	40.37 N	75.25 W
Betsy Layne	43	37.33 N	82.38 W
Bette ⋀	14	22.00 N	19.12 E
Bettendorf	42	41.32 N	90.30 W
Beulah	46	47.16 N	101.47 W
Béziers	8	43.21 N	3.15 E
Bhāgalpur	21	25.15 N	87.00 E
Bhaunagar	21	21.46 N	72.09 E
Bhopāl	21	23.16 N	77.24 E
Bhutan □¹	19	27.30 N	90.30 E
Biafra, Bight of ⊂³	14	4.00 N	8.00 E
Białystok	7	53.09 N	23.09 E
Biarritz	8	43.29 N	1.34 W
Bicaz	11	46.54 N	26.05 E
Biddeford	38	43.30 N	70.26 W
Biel (Bienne)	8	47.10 N	7.12 E
Bielefeld	7	52.01 N	8.31 E
Biella	10	45.34 N	8.03 E
Bielsko-Biała	7	49.49 N	19.02 E
Bien-hoa	26	10.57 N	106.49 E
Big Bay	42	46.49 N	87.44 W
Big Bend National Park ♠	45	29.22 N	103.12 W
Big Blue ☲	46	39.11 N	96.32 W
Biggar	36	52.04 N	108.00 W
Bighorn ☲	48	46.09 N	107.28 W
Bighorn Mountains ⋏	48	44.00 N	107.30 W
Big Lake	45	31.12 N	101.28 W
Big Spring	45	32.15 N	101.28 W
Big Stone Gap	43	36.52 N	82.47 W
Big Timber	48	45.50 N	109.57 W
Bijsk	13	52.34 N	85.15 E
Bīkaner	21	28.01 N	73.18 E
Bikin	13	46.48 N	134.16 E
Bilbao	9	43.15 N	2.58 W
Billings	48	45.47 N	118.27 W
Biloxi	44	30.24 N	88.53 W
Bimini Islands ‖	43	25.42 N	79.15 W
Binghamton	38	42.08 N	75.54 W
Binzert (Bizerte)	14	37.17 N	9.52 E
Bioko ‖	14	3.30 N	8.40 E
Birātnagar	21	26.29 N	87.17 E
Birch Run	42	43.15 N	83.48 W
Bird City	46	39.45 N	101.32 W
Birdum	27	15.39 S	133.13 E
Bīrganj	21	27.00 N	84.52 E
Birlad	11	46.14 N	27.40 E
Birmingham, Eng., U.K.	5	52.30 N	1.50 W
Birmingham, Ala., U.S.	44	33.31 N	86.49 W
Birobidžan	13	48.48 N	132.57 E
Bisbee	47	31.27 N	109.55 W
Biscay, Bay of ⊂	4	44.00 N	4.00 W
Biskra	14	34.51 N	5.44 E
Bismarck	46	46.48 N	100.47 W
Bissau	14	11.51 N	15.35 W
Bistrița	11	47.08 N	24.30 E
Bitola	11	41.01 N	21.20 E
Bitterfeld	7	51.37 N	12.20 E
Bitterroot Range ⋏	48	47.06 N	115.10 W
Biwa-ko ⊜	23	35.15 N	136.05 E
Blackall	27	24.25 S	145.28 E
Blackburn	5	53.45 N	2.29 W
Black Canyon of the Gunnison National Monument ♠	47	38.32 N	107.42 W
Black Eagle	48	47.31 N	111.17 W
Blackfoot	48	43.11 N	112.20 W
Black Hills ⋏	46	44.00 N	104.00 W
Blackpool	5	53.50 N	3.03 W
Black Rock Desert ⬌²	39	41.10 N	119.00 W
Black Sea ▼²	4	43.00 N	35.00 E
Blagoevgrad	11	42.01 N	23.06 E

Name	Map No.	Lat ° '	Long ° '
Blagoveščensk	13	50.17 N	127.32 E
Blaine	42	45.11 N	93.14 W
Blanc, Mont (Monte Bianco) ⋀	8	45.50 N	6.52 E
Blantyre	15	15.47 S	35.00 E
Blenheim	29	41.31 S	173.57 E
Bloemfontein	16	29.12 S	26.07 E
Bloemhof	16	27.38 S	25.32 E
Blois	8	47.35 N	1.20 E
Bloomfield	42	40.45 N	92.25 W
Bloomington, Ill., U.S.	42	40.29 N	88.60 W
Bloomington, Ind., U.S.	44	39.10 N	86.32 W
Bloomington, Minn., U.S.	42	44.50 N	93.17 W
Bluefield	43	37.16 N	81.13 W
Blue Mountains ⋏	36	44.35 N	118.25 W
Blue Nile (Al-Bahr al-Azraq) ≃	17	15.38 N	32.31 E
Blue Ridge ⋏	43	37.00 N	82.00 W
Bluff	29	46.36 S	168.20 E
Blumenau	34	26.56 S	49.03 W
Blyth	5	55.07 N	1.30 W
Blythe	39	33.37 N	114.36 W
Blytheville	44	35.56 N	89.55 W
Boa Vista	33	2.49 N	60.40 W
Bobcaygeon	42	44.33 N	78.33 W
Bobo Dioulasso	14	11.12 N	4.18 W
Bobrujsk	12	53.09 N	29.14 E
Bocas del Toro	32	9.20 N	82.15 W
Bocholt	7	51.50 N	6.36 E
Bochum	7	51.28 N	7.13 E
Bodajbo	13	57.51 N	114.10 E
Boden	6	65.50 N	21.42 E
Bodensee 🅖	7	47.35 N	9.25 E
Bodø	6	67.17 N	14.23 E
Bogale	26	16.17 N	95.24 E
Bogalusa	44	30.47 N	89.52 W
Bogor	25	6.35 S	106.47 E
Bogotá	33	4.36 N	74.05 W
Bogučany	13	58.23 N	97.29 E
Bohai ⊂	22	38.30 N	120.00 E
Bohemian Forest ⋏	7	49.15 N	12.45 E
Boise	48	43.37 N	116.13 W
Bokhara	16	27.57 S	20.30 E
Bola	30a	9.37 S	160.39 E
Bolesławiec	7	51.16 N	15.34 E
Bolivar	44	37.37 N	93.25 W
Bolivar, Pico ⋀	33	8.30 N	71.02 W
Bolivia ☐¹	33	17.00 S	65.00 W
Bollnäs	6	61.21 N	16.25 E
Bologna	10	44.29 N	11.20 E
Bol'ševik, Ostrov ▮	13	78.40 N	102.30 E
Bol'šoj Kavkaz (Caucasus) ⋏	4	42.30 N	45.00 E
Bol'šoj L'achovskij, Ostrov ▮	13	73.35 N	142.00 E
Bolzano (Bozen)	8	46.31 N	11.22 E
Boma	15	5.51 S	13.03 E
Bombay	20	18.58 N	72.50 E
Bonaire ▮	32	12.10 N	68.15 W
Bonarbridge	5	57.53 N	4.21 W
Bonavista	36	48.39 N	53.07 W
Bonham	45	33.35 N	96.11 W
Bonn	7	50.44 N	7.05 E
Bonne Terre	44	37.55 N	90.33 W
Bonneville Salt Flats ≃	47	40.45 N	113.52 W
Bonnievale	16	33.57 S	20.06 E
Booneville, Ark., U.S.	44	35.08 N	93.55 W
Booneville, Miss., U.S.	44	34.39 N	88.34 W
Boothia, Gulf of ⊂	36	71.00 N	91.00 W
Bora-Bora ▮	30d	16.30 S	151.95 W
Borah Peak ⋀	48	44.08 N	113.48 W
Borås	6	57.43 N	12.55 E
Bordeaux	8	44.50 N	0.34 W
Bordertown	27	36.19 S	140.47 E
Borger	45	35.39 N	101.24 W
Borlänge	6	60.29 N	15.25 E
Borneo (Kalimantan) ▮	25	0.30 N	114.00 E
Bornholm ▮	6	55.10 N	15.00 E
Borz'a	13	50.38 N	115.38 E
Boshan	22	36.29 N	117.50 E
Boshoek	16	25.30 S	27.09 E
Boshof	16	28.34 S	25.04 E
Bosporus → İstanbul Boğazı ⥮	11	41.06 N	29.04 E
Bossier City	44	32.31 N	93.43 W
Boston	38	42.21 N	71.04 W
Boston Mountains ⋏	44	35.50 N	93.20 W
Bothnia, Gulf of ⊂	6	63.00 N	20.00 E
Botoşani	11	47.45 N	26.40 E
Botswana ☐¹	16	22.00 S	24.00 E
Bottineau	46	48.50 N	100.27 W
Botucatu	35	22.52 S	48.26 W
Botwood	36	49.09 N	55.21 W
Bouaké	14	7.41 N	5.02 W
Bouar	14	5.57 N	15.36 E
Bougainville ▮	30a	6.00 S	155.00 E
Boulder, Colo., U.S.	46	40.01 N	105.17 W
Boulder, Mont., U.S.	48	46.14 N	112.07 W
Boulogne-sur-Mer	8	50.43 N	1.37 E
Bouloupari	30b	21.52 S	166.04 E
Boundary Peak ⋀	39	37.51 N	118.21 W
Bountiful	47	40.53 N	111.53 W
Bourail	30b	21.34 S	165.30 E
Bourg-en-Bresse	8	46.12 N	5.13 E
Bourges	8	47.05 N	2.24 E
Bourgogne ☐⁹	8	47.00 N	4.30 E
Bourke	27	30.05 S	145.56 E
Bournemouth	5	50.43 N	1.54 W
Bøvågen	6	60.40 N	4.58 E
Bøverdal	6	61.43 N	8.21 E
Bowie	38	39.00 N	76.47 W
Bowling Green, Ky., U.S.	44	37.00 N	86.27 W
Bowling Green, Mo., U.S.	44	39.20 N	91.12 W
Bowling Green, Ohio, U.S.	38	41.22 N	83.39 W
Bowling Green, Va., U.S.	43	38.03 N	77.21 W
Bozeman	48	45.41 N	111.02 W
Brač, Otok ▮	10	43.20 N	16.40 E
Bracebridge	42	45.02 N	79.19 W
Brad	11	46.08 N	22.47 E
Bradenton	43	27.29 N	82.34 W
Bradford	38	41.58 N	78.39 W
Brady	45	31.08 N	99.20 W
Braga	9	41.33 N	8.26 W
Bragança	9	41.49 N	6.45 W
Brāhmanbāria	21	23.59 N	91.07 E
Brahmaputra (Yaluzangbujiang) ≃	21	24.02 N	90.59 E
Brăila	11	45.16 N	27.58 E
Brainerd	42	46.21 N	94.12 W
Brampton	42	43.41 N	79.46 W
Branco ≃	33	1.24 S	61.51 W
Brandberg ⋀	15	21.10 S	14.33 E
Brandenburg	7	52.24 N	12.32 E
Brandenburg ☐⁹	7	52.00 N	13.30 E
Brandvlei	16	30.25 S	20.30 E
Br'ansk	12	53.15 N	34.22 E
Brantford	42	43.08 N	80.16 W
Brasília	33	15.47 S	47.55 W
Braşov	11	45.39 N	25.37 E
Bratislava	7	48.09 N	17.07 E
Bratsk	16	56.05 N	101.48 E
Bratskoje Vodochranilišče 🅖¹	13	56.10 N	102.10 E
Brattleboro	38	42.51 N	72.34 W
Braunschweig	7	52.16 N	10.31 E
Bravo del Norte (Rio Grande) ≃	37	25.55 N	97.09 W
Brawley	39	32.59 N	115.31 W
Brazil ☐¹	33	10.00 S	55.00 W
Brazos ≃	45	28.53 N	95.23 W
Brazzaville	15	4.16 S	15.17 E
Breckenridge	45	32.45 N	98.54 W
Breda	7	51.35 N	4.46 E
Bredasdorp	16	34.32 S	20.02 E
Bremen	7	53.04 N	8.49 E
Bremerhaven	7	53.33 N	8.34 E
Bremerton	48	47.34 N	122.38 W
Brenner Pass)(	8	47.00 N	11.30 E
Brescia	10	45.33 N	13.15 E
Brest	8	48.24 N	4.29 W
Bretagne ☐⁹	8	48.00 N	3.00 W
Brevard	43	35.09 N	82.44 W
Brewster	48	48.06 N	119.47 W
Bridgeport, Conn., U.S.	38	41.11 N	73.11 W
Bridgeport, Nebr., U.S.	46	41.40 N	103.06 W
Bridgeton	38	39.26 N	75.14 W
Bridgetown	32	13.06 N	59.37 W
Bridgewater	41	44.23 N	64.31 W
Brigham City	47	41.31 N	112.01 W
Brighton	5	50.50 N	0.08 W
Brindisi	10	40.38 N	17.56 E
Brinkley	44	34.53 N	91.12 W
Brisbane	27	27.28 S	153.02 E
Bristol, Eng., U.K.	5	51.27 N	2.35 W
Bristol, Conn., U.S.	38	41.41 N	72.57 W
Bristol, Tenn., U.S.	43	36.36 N	82.11 W
Bristol Bay ⊂	40	58.00 N	159.00 W
British Columbia ☐⁴	36	54.00 N	125.00 W
Britstown	16	30.37 S	23.30 E
Britton	46	45.48 N	97.45 W

Name	Map No.	Lat° '	Long° '
Brive-la-Gaillarde	8	45.10 N	1.32 E
Brno	7	49.12 N	16.37 E
Brochet	36	57.53 N	101.40 W
Brockville	38	44.35 N	75.41 W
Broken Arrow	45	36.03 N	95.48 W
Broken Bow	46	41.24 N	99.38 W
Broken Hill	27	31.57 S	141.27 E
Brokopondo	33	5.04 N	54.58 W
Brookfield	44	39.47 N	93.04 W
Brookhaven	44	31.35 N	90.26 W
Brookings	46	44.19 N	96.48 W
Brooks Range ⩕	40	68.00 N	154.00 W
Broome	27	17.58 S	122.14 E
Brownfield	45	33.11 N	102.16 W
Brownsburg	44	39.51 N	86.24 W
Brownsville, Tenn., U.S.	44	35.36 N	89.15 W
Brownsville, Tex., U.S.	45	25.54 N	97.30 W
Brownville Junction	38	45.21 N	69.03 W
Brownwood	45	31.43 N	98.59 W
Bruce, Mount ⩕	27	22.36 S	118.08 E
Bruce Peninsula �	42	44.50 N	81.20 W
Brugge	7	51.13 N	3.14 E
Bruneau ⩶	39	42.57 N	115.58 W
Brunei ☐[1]	25	4.30 N	114.40 E
Brunswick	43	31.10 N	81.29 W
Brush	46	40.15 N	103.37 W
Brus Laguna	32	15.47 N	84.35 W
Brussel			
→ Bruxelles	7	50.50 N	4.20 E
Bruxelles (Brussel)	7	50.50 N	4.20 E
Bryce Canyon National Park ⧫	47	37.29 N	112.12 W
Brzeg	7	50.52 N	17.27 E
Bucaramanga	33	7.08 N	73.09 W
Buchanan	14	5.57 N	10.02 W
Bucharest			
→ București	11	44.26 N	26.06 E
Buckeye	47	33.22 N	112.35 W
Buckingham	38	45.35 N	75.25 W
Buctouche	41	46.28 N	64.43 W
București (Bucharest)	11	44.26 N	26.06 E
Budapest	7	47.30 N	19.05 E
Buenaventura, Col.	33	3.53 N	77.04 W
Buenos Aires	34	34.36 S	58.27 W
Buffalo	38	42.54 N	78.53 W
Buffalo National River ⧫	44	35.58 N	92.53 W
Bug ⩶	4	52.31 N	21.05 E
Buhuși	11	46.43 N	26.41 E
Bujumbura	15	3.23 S	29.22 E
Bukavu	15	2.30 S	28.52 E
Bukovina ☐[9]	11	48.00 N	25.30 E
Buldan	11	38.03 N	28.51 E
Bulawayo	15	20.09 S	28.36 E
Bulgaria ☐[1]	4	43.00 N	25.00 E
Bultfontein	16	28.20 S	26.05 E
Bunbury	27	33.19 S	115.38 E
Bundaberg	27	24.52 S	152.21 E
Bunguran Utara, Kepulauan II	25	4.40 N	108.00 E
Bunia	15	1.34 N	30.15 E
Bunkie	44	30.57 N	92.11 W
Buras	44	29.21 N	89.32 W
Burgas	11	42.30 N	27.28 E
Burgos	9	42.21 N	3.42 W
Buriram	26	15.00 N	103.07 E
Burlington, Colo., U.S.	46	39.18 N	102.16 W
Burlington, Iowa, U.S.	42	40.49 N	91.14 W
Burlington, N.C., U.S.	43	36.04 N	79.26 W
Burlington, Vt., U.S.	38	44.29 N	73.13 W
Burma ☐[1]	25	22.00 N	98.00 E
Burnie	27	41.04 S	145.54 E
Burns Lake	36	54.14 N	125.46 W
Bursa	11	40.11 N	29.04 E
Būr Saʿ Īd (Port Said)	14	31.16 N	32.18 E
Būr Sūdān (Port Sudan)	14	19.37 N	37.14 E
Burt Lake ⬭	42	45.27 N	84.40 W
Burton	42	43.02 N	83.36 W
Buru I	25	3.24 S	126.40 E
Burundi ☐[1]	15	3.15 S	30.00 E
Burwell	46	41.47 N	99.08 W
Burwick	5	58.44 N	2.57 W
Buta	14	2.48 N	24.44 E
Butler, Mo., U.S.	44	38.16 N	94.20 W
Butler, Pa., U.S.	38	40.52 N	79.54 W
Butte	48	46.00 N	112.32 W
Butterworth	26	5.25 N	100.24 E
Butung, Pulau I	25	5.00 S	122.55 E
Buxton	16	27.38 S	24.42 E

Name	Map No.	Lat° '	Long° '
Büyük Ağrı Dağı (Mount Ararat)			
⩕	4	39.42 N	44.18 E
Büyükmenderes ⩶	11	37.27 N	27.11 E
Buzău	11	45.09 N	26.49 E
Bydgoszcz	7	53.08 N	18.00 E
Bytom (Beuthen)	7	50.22 N	18.54 E
C			
Cabimas	33	10.23 N	71.28 W
Cáceres	9	39.29 N	6.22 W
Cachoeira	35	12.36 S	38.58 W
Cachoeiro de Itapemirim	33	20.51 S	41.06 W
Cadillac	42	44.15 N	85.24 W
Cádiz	9	36.32 N	6.18 W
Caen	8	49.11 N	0.21 W
Çaernarvon	5	53.08 N	4.16 W
Çagda	13	58.45 N	130.37 E
Cagliari	10	39.20 N	9.00 E
Caguas	32	18.14 N	66.02 W
Caicos Islands II	32	21.56 N	71.58 W
Cairns	27	16.55 S	145.46 E
Cairo			
→ Al-Qāhirah, Mişr	14	30.03 N	31.15 E
Cairo, Ga., U.S.	43	30.53 N	84.12 W
Cairo, Ill., U.S.	44	37.00 N	89.11 W
Cajamarca	33	7.10 S	78.31 W
Calabozo	33	8.56 N	67.26 W
Calais, Fr.	8	50.57 N	1.50 E
Calais, Maine, U.S.	38	45.11 N	67.17 W
Calamian Group II	25	12.00 N	120.00 E
Călărași	11	44.11 N	27.20 E
Calcutta	21	22.32 N	88.22 E
Caldas da Rainha	9	39.24 N	9.08 W
Caldwell	48	43.40 N	116.41 W
Caledon	16	34.12 S	19.23 E
Caledonia	42	43.38 N	91.29 W
Calexico	39	32.40 N	115.30 W
Calgary	36	51.03 N	114.05 W
Cali	33	3.27 N	76.31 W
Calicut	20	11.15 N	75.46 E
Caliente	39	37.37 N	114.31 W
California	44	38.38 N	92.34 W
California ☐[3]	37	37.30 N	119.30 W
California, Golfo de C	31	28.00 N	112.00 W
Calitzdorp	16	33.33 S	21.42 E
Callao	33	12.04 S	77.09 W
Caltagirone	10	37.14 N	14.31 E
Caltanissetta	10	37.29 N	14.04 E
Calvinia	16	31.25 S	19.45 E
Camacho	31	24.25 N	102.18 W
Camagüey	32	21.23 N	77.55 W
Ca-mau, Mui ⟩	26	8.38 N	104.44 E
Cambrai	8	50.10 N	3.14 E
Cambrian Mountains ⩕	5	52.35 N	3.35 W
Cambridge, Ont., Can.	38	43.22 N	80.19 W
Cambridge, Eng., U.K.	5	52.13 N	0.08 E
Cambridge, Md., U.S.	38	38.34 N	76.04 W
Cambridge, Minn., U.S.	42	45.31 N	93.14 W
Cambridge, Ohio, U.S.	38	40.02 N	81.35 W
Cambridge Bay	36	69.03 N	105.05 W
Camden, Ark., U.S.	44	33.35 N	92.50 W
Camden, Maine, U.S.	38	44.12 N	69.04 W
Cameron	45	30.51 N	96.59 W
Cameroon ☐[1]	14	6.00 N	12.00 E
Cameroun, Mont ⩕	14	4.12 N	9.11 E
Campbell River	36	50.01 N	125.15 W
Campbellsville	44	37.21 N	85.20 W
Campbeltown	5	55.26 N	5.36 W
Campeche	31	19.51 N	90.32 W
Campeche, Bahia de C	31	20.00 N	94.00 W
Campina Grande	33	7.13 S	35.53 W
Campinas	33	22.54 S	47.05 W
Campobasso	10	41.34 N	14.39 E
Campobello Island I	41	44.53 N	66.55 W
Campo Grande	33	20.27 S	54.37 W
Campos	33	21.45 S	41.18 W
Cam-ranh	26	11.54 N	109.09 E
Cam-ranh, Vinh C	26	11.53 N	109.10 E
Canada ☐[1]	36	60.00 N	95.00 W
Canadian ⩶	45	35.27 N	95.03 W
Çanakkale Boğazı (Dardanelles)			
⊍	11	40.15 N	26.25 E
Cananea	31	30.57 N	110.18 W
Canarias, Islas (Canary Islands)			
II	14	28.00 N	15.30 W

Name	Map No.	Lat ° ′	Long ° ′
Canaveral, Cape ⌘	37	28.27 N	80.32 W
Canavieiras	35	15.39 S	38.57 W
Canberra	27	35.17 S	149.08 E
Cando	46	48.32 N	99.12 W
Candover	16	27.28 S	31.57 E
Cannes	8	43.33 N	7.01 E
Canon City	47	38.27 N	105.14 W
Cantábrica, Cordillera ⋏	9	43.00 N	5.00 W
Canterbury Bight C³	29	44.15 S	171.38 E
Canton, Ill., U.S.	42	40.33 N	90.02 W
Canton, Miss., U.S.	44	32.37 N	90.02 W
Canton, N.C., U.S.	43	35.32 N	82.50 W
Canton, Ohio, U.S.	38	40.48 N	81.22 W
Canton, S. Dak., U.S.	46	43.18 N	96.35 W
Canton			
→ Guangzhou, Zhg.	24	23.06 N	113.16 E
Canyon Ferry Lake ⊜¹	48	46.33 N	111.37 W
Canyonlands National Park ♦	47	38.10 N	110.00 W
Canyonville	48	42.56 N	123.17 W
Cap-Chat	41	49.06 N	66.42 W
Cape Breton Island I	36	46.00 N	60.30 W
Cape Charles	43	37.16 N	76.01 W
Cape Fear ≃	43	33.53 N	78.00 W
Cape Girardeau	44	37.19 N	89.32 W
Cape Town (Kaapstad)	16	33.55 S	18.22 E
Cape York Peninsula ⌘¹	27	14.00 S	142.30 E
Cap-Haïtien	32	19.45 N	72.12 W
Capitol Reef National Park ♦	47	38.11 N	111.20 W
Caprivi Strip ☐⁹	15	17.59 S	23.00 E
Caracal	11	44.07 N	24.21 E
Caracas	33	10.30 N	66.56 W
Carangola	35	20.44 S	42.02 W
Caraquet	41	47.48 N	64.57 W
Caratinga	35	19.47 S	42.08 W
Carbó	31	29.42 N	110.58 W
Carbondale, Ill., U.S.	44	37.44 N	89.13 W
Carbondale, Pa., U.S.	38	41.35 N	75.30 W
Carbonia	10	39.11 N	8.32 E
Carcassonne	8	43.13 N	2.21 E
Cárdenas	32	23.02 N	81.12 W
Cardiff	5	51.29 N	3.13 W
Cardigan	5	52.06 N	4.40 W
Caribbean Sea ⲧ²	32	15.00 N	73.00 W
Caribou	41	46.52 N	68.01 W
Carleton, Mount ⋀	41	47.23 N	66.53 W
Carletonville	16	26.23 S	27.22 E
Carlisle	38	40.12 N	77.12 W
Carlsbad	45	32.25 N	104.14 W
Carlsbad Caverns National Park ♦	45	32.08 N	104.35 W
Carmacks	36	62.05 N	136.18 W
Carmarthen	5	51.52 N	4.19 W
Carnarvon	16	30.56 S	22.08 E
Carolina	26	26.05 S	30.06 E
Caroline Islands II	25	8.00 N	140.00 E
Carpathian Mountains ⋏	4	48.00 N	24.00 E
Carpaţii Meridionali ⋏	11	45.30 N	24.15 E
Carpentaria, Gulf of C	27	14.00 S	139.00 E
Carrara	10	44.05 N	10.06 E
Carrauntoohill ⋀	5	52.00 N	9.45 W
Carrington	46	47.27 N	99.08 W
Carrizo Springs	45	28.31 N	99.52 W
Carroll	46	42.04 N	94.52 W
Carsk	13	49.35 N	81.05 E
Carson City	39	39.10 N	119.46 W
Cartagena, Col.	33	10.25 N	75.32 W
Cartagena, Esp.	9	37.36 N	0.59 W
Cartago	32	9.52 N	83.55 W
Cartersville	43	34.10 N	84.48 W
Carthage	44	32.46 N	89.32 W
Caruaru	33	8.17 S	35.58 W
Casablanca (Dar-el-Beida)	14	33.39 N	7.35 W
Casa Grande	47	32.53 N	111.45 W
Casale Monferrato	10	45.08 N	8.27 E
Cascade Range ⋏, N.A.	37	49.00 N	120.00 W
Cascade Range ⋏, U.S.	39	45.00 N	121.30 W
Cascais	9	38.42 N	9.25 W
Casper	48	42.51 N	106.19 W
Caspian Sea ⲧ²	4	42.00 N	50.30 E
Castellón de la Plana	9	39.59 N	0.02 W
Castelo Branco	9	39.49 N	7.30 W
Castletown	5	54.04 N	4.40 W
Castres	8	43.36 N	2.15 E
Castries	32	14.01 N	61.00 W
Catalão	35	18.10 S	47.57 W
Cataluña ☐⁹	9	42.00 N	2.00 E
Catamarca	34	28.28 S	65.47 W
Catanduanes Island I	25	13.45 N	124.15 E
Catanduva	35	21.08 S	48.58 W
Catania	10	37.30 N	15.06 E
Catanzaro	10	38.54 N	16.36 E
Cat Island I	32	24.27 N	75.30 W
Catoche, Cabo ⌘	31	21.35 N	87.05 W
Catskill Mountains ⋏	38	42.10 N	74.30 W
Caucasus			
→ Bol'šoj Kavkaz ⋏	4	42.30 N	45.00 E
Causapscal	41	48.22 N	67.14 W
Cavalier	46	48.48 N	97.37 W
Caxambu	35	21.59 S	44.56 W
Caxias do Sul	34	29.10 S	51.11 W
Cayenne	33	4.56 N	52.20 W
Cayman Islands ☐²	32	19.30 N	80.40 W
Cayuga Lake ⊜	38	42.45 N	76.45 W
Čeboksary	4	56.09 N	47.15 E
Cebu	25	10.18 N	123.54 E
Čečerleg	22	48.52 N	101.14 E
Čechy ☐⁹	7	49.50 N	14.00 E
Cedar City	47	37.41 N	113.04 W
Cedar Falls	42	42.32 N	92.27 W
Cedar Lake	44	41.22 N	87.26 W
Cedar Rapids	42	41.59 N	91.40 W
Cedar Springs	42	43.13 N	85.33 W
Cedartown	43	34.01 N	85.15 W
Cegléd	7	47.10 N	19.48 E
Čel'abinsk	4	55.10 N	61.24 E
Celaya	31	20.31 N	100.49 W
Celebes			
→ Sulawesi I	25	2.00 S	121.00 E
Celebes Sea ⲧ²	25	3.00 N	122.00 E
Čelestún	31	20.52 N	90.24 W
Čelkar	4	47.50 N	59.36 E
Celle	7	52.37 N	10.05 E
Čel'uskin, Mys ⌘	13	77.45 N	104.20 E
Cenderawasih, Teluk C	25	2.30 S	135.20 E
Central, Massif ⋏	8	45.00 N	3.10 E
Central African Republic ☐¹	14	7.00 N	21.00 E
Centralia, Ill., U.S.	44	38.31 N	89.08 W
Centralia, Wash., U.S.	48	46.43 N	122.58 W
Čeremchovo	13	53.09 N	103.05 E
Čerepovec	12	59.08 N	37.54 E
Čerignola	10	41.16 N	15.54 E
Černigov	4	51.30 N	31.18 E
Černogorsk	13	53.49 N	91.18 E
Černovcy	11	48.18 N	25.56 E
Cerritos	31	22.26 N	100.17 W
Cerro de Pasco	33	10.41 S	76.16 W
Čerskogo, Chrebet ⋏	13	65.00 N	144.00 E
Cesena	10	44.08 N	12.15 E
České Budějovice	7	48.59 N	14.28 E
Ceuta	14	35.53 N	5.19 W
Chabarovsk	13	48.27 N	135.06 E
Chad ☐¹	14	15.00 N	19.00 E
Chad, Lake (Lac Tchad) ⊜	14	13.20 N	14.00 E
Chadron	37	42.50 N	102.60 W
Chaffee	44	37.11 N	89.40 W
Chaidamupendi ⌣¹	21	37.00 N	95.00 E
Châlons-sur-Marne	8	48.57 N	4.22 E
Chalon-sur-Saône	8	46.47 N	4.51 E
Chambal ≃	19	26.30 N	79.15 E
Chamberlain	46	43.49 N	99.20 W
Chambéry	8	45.34 N	5.56 E
Chambi, Djebel ⋀	4	35.11 N	8.42 E
Champagne ☐⁹	8	49.00 N	4.30 E
Champaign	44	40.07 N	88.14 W
Champasak	26	14.53 N	105.52 E
Champlain, Lake ⊜	38	44.45 N	73.15 W
Chandeleur Sound ⋓	44	29.55 N	89.10 W
Chandler, Qué., Can.	41	48.21 N	64.41 W
Chandler, Ariz., U.S.	47	33.18 N	111.50 W
Chandyga	13	62.40 N	135.36 E
Changchun	22	43.53 N	125.19 E
Changjiang (Yangtze) ≃	22	31.48 N	121.10 E
Changsha	24	28.11 N	113.01 E
Changshu	24	31.39 N	120.45 E
Changzhi	22	36.11 N	113.08 E
Changzhou (Changchow)	24	31.47 N	119.57 E
Chanka, Ozero (Xingkathu) ⊜	22	45.00 N	132.24 E
Channel Islands II, Eur.	8	49.20 N	2.20 W
Channel Islands II, Calif., U.S.	39	34.00 N	120.00 W
Channel-Port-aux-Basques	36	47.34 N	59.09 W
Chanthaburi	26	12.36 N	102.09 E
Chanty-Mansijsk	13	60.59 N	69.06 E
Chanute	46	37.41 N	95.27 W
Chaoan	24	23.41 N	116.38 E

Name	Map No.	Lat ° ′	Long ° ′
Chao Phraya ≃	26	13.32 N	100.36 E
Chapala, Lago de ⊜	31	20.15 N	103.00 W
Chappell	46	41.06 N	102.28 W
Charcas	31	23.08 N	101.07 W
Chariton	42	41.01 N	93.19 W
Char'kov	4	50.00 N	36.15 E
Charleroi	7	50.25 N	4.26 E
Charleston, Ill., U.S.	44	39.30 N	88.10 W
Charleston, S.C., U.S.	43	32.48 N	79.57 W
Charleston, W. Va., U.S.	38	38.21 N	81.38 W
Charleston Peak ᐱ	39	36.16 N	115.42 W
Charleville	27	26.24 S	146.15 E
Charleville-Mézières	8	49.46 N	4.43 E
Charlevoix	42	45.19 N	85.16 W
Charlotte	43	35.14 N	80.50 W
Charlotte Amalie	32	18.21 N	64.56 W
Charlottesville	43	38.02 N	78.29 W
Charlottetown	36	46.14 N	63.08 W
Chārsadda	21	34.09 N	71.44 E
Chartres	8	48.27 N	1.30 E
Chatanga	13	71.58 N	102.30 E
Châteauroux	8	46.49 N	1.42 E
Châtellerault	8	46.49 N	0.33 E
Chatham	42	42.24 N	82.11 W
Chattahoochee	43	30.42 N	84.51 W
Chattahoochee ≃	37	30.52 N	84.57 W
Chattanooga	44	35.03 N	85.19 W
Chauk	26	20.54 N	94.50 E
Chau-phu	26	10.42 N	105.07 E
Chaves	9	41.44 N	7.28 W
Cheb	7	50.01 N	12.25 E
Cheboygan	42	45.39 N	84.29 W
Checotah	45	35.28 N	95.31 W
Cheju-do ❙	22	33.20 N	126.30 E
Chelan, Lake ⊜	48	48.05 N	120.30 W
Chełm	7	51.10 N	23.28 E
Chelyabinsk			
→ Čel'abinsk	4	55.10 N	61.24 E
Chengde	22	40.58 N	117.53 E
Chengdu	22	30.39 N	104.04 E
Chengtu			
→ Chengdu	22	30.39 N	104.04 E
Cherbourg	8	49.39 N	1.39 W
Cherson	4	46.38 N	32.35 E
Chesapeake	43	36.43 N	76.15 W
Chesapeake Bay C	38	38.40 N	76.25 W
Chesapeake Beach	38	38.41 N	76.32 W
Chester, Mont., U.S.	48	48.31 N	110.58 W
Chester, Pa., U.S.	38	39.51 N	75.21 W
Chesuncook Lake ⊜	41	46.00 N	69.20 W
Cheyenne	46	41.08 N	104.49 W
Cheyenne ≃	46	44.40 N	101.15 W
Cheyenne Wells	46	38.51 N	102.11 W
Chiai	24	23.29 N	120.27 E
Chiang Mai	26	18.47 N	98.59 E
Chiang Rai	26	19.54 N	99.50 E
Chiautla de Tapia	31	18.17 N	98.36 W
Chiba	23	35.36 N	140.07 E
Chibougamau	36	49.55 N	74.22 W
Chicago	42	41.53 N	87.38 W
Chicago Heights	42	41.30 N	87.38 W
Chichagof Island ❙	40	57.30 N	135.30 W
Chichén Itzá	31	20.40 N	88.34 W
Chichén Itzá ⊥	31	20.40 N	88.35 W
Chickasha	45	35.02 N	97.58 W
Chiclayo	33	6.46 S	79.51 W
Chico	39	39.44 N	121.50 W
Chicoutimi	41	48.26 N	71.04 W
Chidley, Cape ➤	36	60.23 N	64.26 W
Chieti	10	42.21 N	14.10 E
Chigasaki	23	35.19 N	139.24 E
Chihuahua	31	28.38 N	106.05 W
Childress	45	34.25 N	100.13 W
Chile ❑¹	34	30.00 S	71.00 W
Chillicothe, Mo., U.S.	44	39.48 N	93.33 W
Chillicothe, Ohio, U.S.	38	39.20 N	82.59 W
Chiloé, Isla de ❙	34	42.30 S	73.55 W
Chilpancingo [de los Bravos]	31	17.33 N	99.30 W
Chilung	24	25.08 N	121.44 E
Chimborazo ᐱ¹	33	1.28 S	78.48 W
Chimbote	33	9.05 S	78.36 W
China ❑¹	21	34.00 N	88.00 E
Chinandega	32	12.37 N	87.09 W
Chindwin ≃	26	21.26 N	95.15 E
Chingtao			
→ Qingdao	22	36.06 N	120.19 E
Chinmen Tao ❙	24	24.27 N	118.23 E
Chinook	48	48.35 N	109.14 W
Chioggia	10	45.13 N	12.17 E
Chipman	41	46.11 N	65.53 W
Chippewa Falls	42	44.56 N	91.24 W
Chīrāla	20	15.49 N	80.21 E
Chiricahua Peak ᐱ	47	31.52 N	109.20 W
Chiriquí, Golfo C	32	8.00 N	82.20 W
Chirripó, Cerro ᐱ	32	9.29 N	83.30 W
Chittagong	21	22.20 N	91.50 E
Choapan	31	17.20 N	95.57 W
Choiseul ❙	30a	7.05 S	157.00 E
Chomutov	7	50.28 N	13.26 E
Chon Buri	26	13.22 N	100.59 E
Ch'ŏngjin	22	41.47 N	129.50 E
Chongqing	22	29.39 N	106.34 E
Chŏnju	22	35.49 N	127.08 E
Chonos, Archipiélago de los ❙❙	34	45.00 S	74.00 W
Chōshi	23	35.44 N	140.50 E
Chovd	22	48.01 N	91.38 E
Christchurch	29	43.32 S	172.38 E
Christmas Island ❑²	25	10.30 S	105.40 E
Chukchi Sea ⊤²	2	69.00 N	171.00 W
Chula Vista	39	32.39 N	117.05 W
Chumphon	26	10.30 N	99.10 E
Chum Saeng	26	15.54 N	100.19 E
Chungking			
→ Chongqing	22	29.39 N	106.34 E
Churchill	36	58.46 N	94.10 W
Churchill ≃	36	58.47 N	94.12 W
Chužir	13	53.11 N	107.20 E
Cibecue	47	34.03 N	110.29 W
Ciego de Avila	32	21.51 N	78.46 W
Cienfuegos	32	22.09 N	80.27 W
Cimarron ≃	45	36.10 N	96.17 W
Ciml'anskoje Vodochranilišče ⊜¹	4	48.00 N	43.00 E
Cincinnati	38	39.06 N	84.31 W
Çisco	45	32.23 N	98.59 W
Čita	13	52.03 N	113.30 E
Citlaltépetl, Volcán (Pico de Orizaba) ᐱ¹	31	19.01 N	97.16 W
Citronelle	44	31.06 N	88.14 W
Citrusdal	16	32.36 S	19.00 E
Citrus Heights	39	38.42 N	121.17 W
Ciudad Acuña	31	29.18 N	100.55 W
Ciudad Anáhuac	31	27.14 N	100.09 W
Ciudad Bolívar	33	8.08 N	63.33 W
Ciudad Camargo	31	26.19 N	98.50 W
Ciudad Chetumal	31	18.30 N	88.18 W
Ciudad del Carmen	31	18.38 N	91.50 W
Ciudad de México (Mexico City)	31	19.24 N	99.09 W
Ciudad de Valles	31	21.59 N	99.01 W
Ciudad de Villaldama	31	26.30 N	100.26 W
Ciudad Guayana	33	8.22 N	62.40 W
Ciudad Guzmán	31	19.41 N	103.29 W
Ciudad Ixtepec	31	16.34 N	95.06 W
Ciudad Jiménez	31	27.08 N	104.55 W
Ciudad Juárez	31	31.44 N	106.29 W
Ciudad Madero	31	22.16 N	97.50 W
Ciudad Mante	31	22.44 N	98.57 W
Ciudad Melchor Múzquiz	31	27.53 N	101.31 W
Ciudad Obregón	31	27.29 N	109.56 W
Ciudad Ojeda	32	10.12 N	71.19 W
Ciudad Victoria	31	23.44 N	99.08 W
Claremont	38	43.23 N	72.20 W
Clark Fork ≃	48	48.09 N	116.15 W
Clarksdale	44	34.12 N	90.34 W
Clarksville, Ark., U.S.	44	35.28 N	93.28 W
Clarksville, Tenn., U.S.	44	36.32 N	87.21 W
Clayton	45	36.27 N	103.11 W
Clearfield	38	41.02 N	78.27 W
Clear Lake ⊜¹	39	39.02 N	122.50 W
Clearwater	43	27.58 N	82.48 W
Clearwater Mountains ᐠ	48	46.00 N	115.30 W
Cleburne	45	32.21 N	97.23 W
Clermont-Ferrand	8	45.47 N	3.05 E
Cleveland, Ohio, U.S.	38	41.30 N	81.41 W
Cleveland, Tenn., U.S.	43	35.10 N	84.53 W
Cleveland, Tex., U.S.	45	30.21 N	95.05 W
Clifton, Ariz., U.S.	47	33.03 N	109.18 W
Clifton, Tex., U.S.	45	31.47 N	97.35 W
Clifton Forge	43	37.49 N	79.49 W
Clinton, Ont., Can.	42	43.37 N	81.32 W
Clinton, Iowa, U.S.	42	41.51 N	90.12 W
Clinton, Miss., U.S.	44	32.20 N	90.20 W
Clinton, Mo., U.S.	44	38.22 N	93.46 W
Cloncurry	27	20.42 S	140.30 E
Clonmel	5	52.21 N	7.42 W

Name	Map No.	Lat °'	Long °'
Crystal City, Tex., U.S.	45	28.41 N	99.50 W
Crystal Lake	42	42.14 N	88.19 W
Crystal Springs	44	31.59 N	90.21 W
Cuba □¹	32	21.30 N	80.00 W
Cubango (Okavango) ≃	15	18.50 S	22.25 E
Cúcuta	33	7.54 N	72.31 W
Čudskoje Ozero (Peipsi Järv) 𝕖	12	58.45 N	27.30 E
Cuenca, Ec.	33	2.53 S	78.59 W
Cuenca, Esp.	9	40.04 N	2.08 W
Cuernavaca	31	18.55 N	99.15 W
Cuero	45	29.06 N	97.18 W
Cuiabá	33	15.35 S	56.05 W
Culiacán	31	24.48 N	107.24 W
Cullman	44	34.11 N	86.51 W
Cumaná	33	10.28 N	64.10 W
Cumberland, Ky., U.S.	43	36.59 N	82.59 W
Cumberland, Md., U.S.	38	39.39 N	78.46 W
Cumberland Gap)(	43	36.36 N	83.41 W
Cuneo	10	44.23 N	7.32 E
Curaçao I	32	12.11 N	69.00 W
Curitiba	34	25.25 S	49.15 W
Curvelo	35	18.45 S	44.25 W
Cut Bank	48	48.38 N	112.20 W
Cuttack	21	20.30 N	85.50 E
Cuxhaven	7	53.52 N	8.42 E
Cuzco	33	13.31 S	71.59 W
Cyclades			
→ Kikládhes II	11	37.30 N	25.00 E
Cyprus (Kípros) □¹	18	35.00 N	33.00 E
Czechoslovakia □¹	4	49.30 N	17.00 E
Częstochowa	7	50.49 N	19.06 E
D			
Dacca	21	23.43 N	90.25 E
Dachau	7	48.15 N	11.27 E
Dahlak Archipelago II	17	15.45 N	40.30 E
Dakar	14	14.40 N	17.26 W
Dakhla	14	23.43 N	15.57 W
Dalälven ≃	6	60.38 N	17.27 E
Da-lat	26	11.56 N	108.25 E
Dalhart	45	36.04 N	102.31 W
Dallas	45	32.47 N	96.48 W
Dalmacija □⁹	10	43.00 N	17.00 E
Dalton	43	34.47 N	84.58 W
Dalwallinu	27	30.17 S	116.40 E
Damascus			
→ Dimashq	18	33.30 N	36.18 E
Damāvand, Qolleh-ye A	4	35.56 N	52.08 E
Da-nang	26	16.04 N	108.13 E
Danbury	38	41.23 N	73.27 W
Danforth	38	45.40 N	67.52 W
Danube ≃	4	45.20 N	29.40 E
Danville, Ill., U.S.	44	40.08 N	87.37 W
Danville, Ky., U.S.	44	37.39 N	84.46 W
Danville, Pa., U.S.	38	40.57 N	76.37 W
Danville, Va., U.S.	43	36.35 N	79.24 W
Danzig, Gulf of C	7	54.40 N	19.15 E
Darchan	22	49.29 N	105.55 E
Dardanelles			
→ Çanakkale Boğazı U	11	40.15 N	26.25 E
Dar-el-Beida			
→ Casablanca	14	33.39 N	7.35 W
Dar-es-Salaam	15	6.48 S	39.17 E
Dargaville	29	35.56 S	173.53 E
Darling ≃	28	34.07 S	141.55 E
Darling Range ʌ	27	32.00 S	116.30 E
Darmstadt	7	49.53 N	8.40 E
Dartmouth	41	44.40 N	63.34 W
Daru	25	9.04 S	143.21 E
Darwin	27	12.28 S	130.50 E
Datong	22	40.08 N	113.13 E
Daugava (Zapadnaja Dvina) ≃	12	57.04 N	24.03 E
Daugavpils	12	55.53 N	26.32 E
Dauphin	36	51.09 N	100.03 W
Davao	25	7.04 N	125.36 E
Davenport	42	41.32 N	90.41 W
David City	46	41.15 N	97.08 W
Davidson	43	35.30 N	80.51 W
Davis City	42	40.38 N	93.49 W
Davis Strait U	36	67.00 N	57.00 W
Dawson	36	64.04 N	139.25 W
Dayr az-Zawr	18	35.20 N	40.09 E
Dayton, Ohio, U.S.	38	39.45 N	84.15 W
Dayton, Tenn., U.S.	44	35.30 N	85.00 W
Dayton, Tex., U.S.	44		
	45	30.03 N	94.54 W
Daytona Beach	43	29.12 N	81.00 W
De Aar	16	30.39 S	24.00 E
Dead Sea 𝕖	18	31.30 N	35.30 E
Deadwood	46	44.23 N	103.44 W
Dearborn	42	42.18 N	83.10 W
Death Valley V	39	36.30 N	117.00 W
Debrecen	7	47.32 N	21.38 E
Decatur, Ala., U.S.	44	34.36 N	86.59 W
Decatur, Ga., U.S.	43	33.46 N	84.18 W
Decatur, Ill., U.S.	44	39.51 N	89.32 W
Decatur, Ind., U.S.	44	40.50 N	84.56 W
Deccan ʌ¹	19	17.00 N	78.00 E
Děčín	7	50.48 N	14.13 E
Deckerville	42	43.32 N	82.44 W
Decorah	42	43.18 N	91.48 W
Deep River	44	46.06 N	77.30 W
Defiance	38	41.17 N	84.22 W
De Funiak Springs	44	30.43 N	86.07 W
Dehiwala-Mount Lavinia	20	6.51 N	79.52 E
Dehra Dūn	21	30.19 N	78.02 E
Dej	11	47.09 N	23.52 E
De Kalb	42	41.59 N	88.41 W
De Land	43	29.02 N	81.18 W
Delano	39	35.41 N	119.15 W
Delaware □³	37	39.10 N	75.30 W
Delaware ≃	38	39.20 N	75.25 W
Delaware Bay C	38	39.05 N	75.15 W
De Leon	45	32.07 N	98.32 W
Delhi, Bhārat	21	28.40 N	77.13 E
Delhi, La., U.S.	44	32.27 N	91.30 W
Delicias	31	28.13 N	105.28 W
Delmenhorst	7	53.03 N	8.38 E
Delray Beach	43	26.28 N	80.04 W
Del Rio	45	29.22 N	100.54 W
Delta	47	38.44 N	108.04 W
Demirci	11	39.03 N	28.40 E
Demopolis	44	32.31 N	87.50 W
Denain	8	50.20 N	3.23 E
Denham Springs	44	30.29 N	90.57 W
Denison	45	33.45 N	96.33 W
Denizli	11	37.46 N	29.06 E
Denmark □¹	4	56.00 N	10.00 E
Denpasar	25	8.39 S	115.13 E
Denton	45	33.13 N	97.08 W
Denver	46	39.43 N	105.01 W
Denver City	45	32.58 N	102.50 W
Dera Ghāzi Khān	19	30.03 N	70.38 E
Dera Ismāīl Khān	21	31.50 N	70.54 E
Derby	5	52.55 N	1.29 W
De Ridder	44	30.51 N	93.17 W
Dermott	44	33.32 N	91.26 W
Deschutes ≃	48	45.38 N	120.54 W
Dese	17	11.05 N	39.41 E
Des Moines	42	41.35 N	93.37 W
Des Moines ≃	37	40.22 N	91.26 W
Des Plaines	42	42.02 N	87.54 W
Dessau	7	51.50 N	12.14 E
Detmold	7	51.56 N	8.52 E
Detroit	42	42.20 N	83.03 W
Detroit Lakes	46	46.49 N	95.51 W
Deutsche Bucht C	7	54.30 N	7.30 E
Deva	11	45.53 N	22.55 E
Devils Lake	46	48.07 N	98.59 W
Devine	45	29.08 N	98.54 W
Devon Island I	36	75.00 N	87.00 W
Devonport	29	36.49 S	174.48 E
De Witt	44	34.18 N	91.20 W
Dexter, Maine, U.S.	38	45.01 N	69.18 W
Dexter, Mo., U.S.	44	36.48 N	89.57 W
Dezfūl	17	32.23 N	48.24 E
Dhodhekánisos (Dodecanese) II	11	36.30 N	27.00 E
Dhorāji	21	21.44 N	70.27 E
Diable, Île du I	33	5.17 N	52.35 W
Diablo Range ʌ	39	37.00 N	121.20 W
Diamantina	33	18.15 S	43.36 W
Diboll	44	31.11 N	94.47 W
Dickinson	46	46.53 N	102.47 W
Diégo-Suarez	15	12.16 S	49.17 E
Dieppe, N.B., Can.	41	46.06 N	64.45 W
Dieppe, Fr.	8	49.56 N	1.05 E
Digby	41	44.37 N	65.46 W
Dijon	8	47.19 N	5.01 E
Dillingham	40	59.02 S	158.29 W
Dillon	48	45.13 N	112.38 W
Dimashq (Damascus)	18	33.30 N	36.18 E

Name	Map No.	Lat ° '	Long ° '
El Ferrol del Caudillo	9	43.29 N	8.14 W
Elgin, Scot., U.K.	5	57.39 N	3.20 W
Elgin, Ill., U.S.	42	42.02 N	88.17 W
Elizabeth City	43	36.18 N	76.14 W
Elizabethton	43	36.21 N	82.13 W
Elizabethtown	44	37.42 N	85.52 W
Eł k	7	53.50 N	22.22 E
Elkhart	44	41.41 N	85.58 W
Elkins	38	38.55 N	79.51 W
Elko	39	40.50 N	115.46 W
Elkton	38	39.36 N	75.50 W
Ellendale	46	46.06 N	98.32 W
Ellesmere Island **l**	2	81.00 N	80.00 W
Ellinwood	46	38.21 N	98.35 W
Elliotdale	16	31.55 S	28.38 E
Elliot Lake	42	46.23 N	82.39 W
Ellisras	16	23.40 S	27.46 E
Ellisville	44	31.36 N	89.12 W
Ellsworth	38	44.33 N	68.26 W
Elmhurst	42	41.53 N	87.56 W
Elmira	38	42.06 N	76.49 W
Elmore	28	36.30 S	144.37 E
Elmshorn	7	53.45 N	9.39 E
Eloy	47	32.45 N	111.33 W
El Paso	47	31.45 N	106.29 W
El Progreso	32	15.21 N	87.49 W
El Puerto de Santa Maria	9	36.36 N	6.13 W
El Reno	45	35.32 N	97.57 W
El Salvador ◻[1]	32	13.50 N	88.55 W
El Sauce	32	12.53 N	86.32 W
El Tigre	33	8.55 N	64.15 W
Elvas	9	38.53 N	7.10 W
Elwood	44	40.17 N	85.50 W
Ely, Minn., U.S.	42	47.54 N	91.51 W
Ely, Nev., U.S.	39	39.15 N	114.53 W
Emba	4	48.50 N	58.08 E
Emden	7	53.22 N	7.12 E
Emerald	27	23.32 S	148.10 E
Emery	47	38.55 N	111.15 W
Empangeni	16	28.50 S	31.48 E
Empoli	10	43.43 N	10.57 E
Emporia, Kans., U.S.	46	38.24 N	96.11 W
Emporia, Va., U.S.	43	36.41 N	77.32 W
Emporium	38	41.31 N	78.14 W
Encarnación	34	27.20 S	55.54 W
Endicott	38	42.06 N	76.03 W
Engel's	4	51.30 N	46.07 E
England ◻[8]	5	52.30 N	1.30 W
Englewood	43	26.58 N	82.21 W
English Channel (La Manche) **ʊ**	8	50.20 N	1.00 W
Enid	45	36.19 N	97.48 W
Ennis	45	32.20 N	96.38 W
Enniskillen	5	54.21 N	7.38 W
Ensenada	31	31.52 N	116.37 W
Entebbe	15	0.04 N	32.28 E
Enterprise	44	31.19 N	85.51 W
Enugu	14	6.27 N	7.27 E
Épinal	8	48.11 N	6.27 E
Equatorial Guinea ◻[1]	14	2.00 N	9.00 E
Erdek	11	40.24 N	27.48 E
Erechim	34	27.38 S	52.17 W
Erfurt	7	50.58 N	11.01 E
Erie	38	42.08 N	80.04 W
Erie, Lake ⊛	42	42.15 N	81.00 W
Eritrea ◻[9]	17	15.20 N	39.00 E
Erlangen	7	49.36 N	11.01 E
Ermelo	16	26.34 S	29.58 E
Erode	20	11.21 N	77.44 E
Esbjerg	6	55.28 N	8.27 E
Escanaba	42	45.45 N	87.04 W
Esch-sur-Alzette	7	49.30 N	5.59 E
Escondido	39	33.07 N	117.05 W
Eşfahān	17	32.40 N	51.38 E
Eskilstuna	6	59.22 N	16.30 E
Esmeraldas	33	0.59 N	79.42 W
Espanola	47	36.06 N	106.02 W
Esperance	27	33.51 S	121.53 E
Espiritu Santo **l**	30b	15.50 S	166.50 E
Espoo (Esbo)	6	60.13 N	24.40 E
Esquel	34	42.54 S	71.19 W
Essen	7	51.28 N	7.01 E
Estacado, Llano ⨆	45	33.30 N	102.40 W
Esteli	32	13.05 N	86.23 W
Estherville	46	43.24 N	94.50 W
Estrela ⋀	9	40.19 N	7.37 W
Ethiopia ◻[1]	17	9.00 N	39.00 E
Etna, Monte ⋀[1]	10	37.46 N	15.00 E
Etowah	43	35.20 N	84.32 W
Ettelbruck	7	49.52 N	6.05 E
Eucla	27	31.43 S	128.52 E
Eufaula	45	35.17 N	95.35 W
Eugene	48	44.02 N	123.05 W
Eugenia, Punta **⟩**	37	27.50 N	115.05 W
Eunice, La., U.S.	44	30.30 N	92.25 W
Eunice, N. Mex., U.S.	45	32.26 N	103.09 W
Euphrates (Al-Furāt) ≈	17	31.00 N	47.25 E
Eureka, Calif., U.S.	39	40.47 N	124.09 W
Eureka, Nev., U.S.	39	39.31 N	115.58 W
Eureka, Utah, U.S.	47	39.57 N	112.07 W
Europe **●**[1]	1	50.00 N	20.00 E
Eustis	43	28.51 N	81.41 W
Evanston, Ill., U.S.	42	42.03 N	87.42 W
Evanston, Wyo., U.S.	48	41.16 N	110.58 W
Evansville	44	37.58 N	87.35 W
Evart	42	43.54 N	85.08 W
Everest, Mount (Zhumulangmafeng) ⋀	21	27.59 N	86.56 E
Everett	48	47.59 N	122.31 W
Everglades National Park **♠**	43	25.27 N	80.53 W
Évora	9	38.34 N	7.54 W
Évreux	8	49.01 N	1.09 E
Évvoia **l**	11	38.34 N	23.50 E
Excelsior Springs	44	39.20 N	94.13 W
Exeter	5	50.43 N	3.31 W
Eyre North, Lake ⊛	28	28.40 S	137.10 E
Eyre Peninsula **⟩**[1]	28	34.00 S	135.45 E
Eyre South, Lake ⊛	28	29.30 S	137.20 E
F			
Fabens	47	31.30 N	106.10 W
Faenza	10	44.17 N	11.53 E
Faeroe Islands ◻[2]	4	62.00 N	7.00 W
Fairbanks	40	64.51 N	147.43 W
Fairbury	46	40.08 N	97.11 W
Fairfield, Calif., U.S.	39	38.15 N	122.03 W
Fairfield, Iowa, U.S.	42	40.56 N	91.57 W
Fairfield, Ohio, U.S.	38	39.20 N	84.33 W
Fairlie	29	44.06 S	170.50 E
Fairmont, Minn., U.S.	46	43.39 N	94.28 W
Fairmont, W. Va., U.S.	38	39.29 N	80.09 W
Fairview	46	39.50 N	95.44 W
Falam	26	22.55 N	93.40 E
Falevai	30e	13.55 S	171.59 W
Falfurrias	45	27.14 N	98.09 W
Falkland Islands ◻[2]	34	51.45 S	59.00 W
Falköping	6	58.10 N	13.31 E
Fallon	39	39.28 N	118.47 W
Fall River	38	41.43 N	71.08 W
Falls City	46	40.03 N	95.36 W
Falun	6	60.36 N	15.38 E
Fan-si-pan ⋀	26	22.15 N	103.46 E
Farāh	19	32.22 N	62.07 E
Farewell, Cape **⟩**	29	40.30 S	172.41 E
Fargo	46	46.52 N	96.48 W
Faribault	42	44.18 N	93.16 W
Farmington, Mo., U.S.	44	37.47 N	90.25 W
Farmington, N. Mex., U.S.	47	36.44 N	108.12 W
Farmville	43	35.36 N	77.35 W
Faro	9	37.01 N	7.56 W
Farvel, Kap **⟩**	36	59.45 N	44.00 W
Fayette	44	33.42 N	87.50 W
Fayetteville, Ark., U.S.	44	36.04 N	94.10 W
Fayetteville, N.C., U.S.	43	35.03 N	78.54 W
Fazzān (Fezzan) ➴[1]	14	26.00 N	14.00 E
Fear, Cape **⟩**	43	33.50 N	77.58 W
Feira de Santana	33	12.15 S	38.57 W
Fenton	42	42.48 N	83.42 W
Fergus Falls	46	46.17 N	96.04 W
Fernando de Noronha, Ilha **l**	33	3.51 S	32.25 W
Fernandópolis	35	20.16 S	50.14 W
Ferrara	10	44.50 N	11.35 E
Fès	14	34.05 N	4.57 W
Fethiye	11	36.37 N	29.07 E
Feyzābād, Afg.	19	35.01 N	58.46 E
Feyzābād, Afg.	21	37.06 N	70.34 E
Fianarantsoa	15	21.26 S	47.05 E
Fichtelberg ⋀	7	50.26 N	12.57 E
Ficksburg	16	28.57 S	27.50 E
Figueira da Foz	9	40.09 N	8.52 W
Fiji ◻[1]	1	18.00 S	175.00 W
Findlay	38	41.02 N	83.39 W
Finland ◻[1]	4	64.00 N	26.00 E

Name	Map No.	Lat ° '	Long ° '
Finland, Gulf of **C**	6	60.00 N	27.00 E
Firenze (Florence)	10	43.46 N	11.15 E
Fish ≏	16	28.07 S	17.45 E
Fitchburg	38	42.35 N	71.48 W
Flagler	46	39.18 N	103.04 W
Flagstaff	47	35.12 N	111.39 W
Flaming Gorge Reservoir **☒**¹	47	41.15 N	109.30 W
Flathead Lake **☒**	48	47.52 N	114.08 W
Flensburg	7	54.47 N	9.26 E
Flinders Island **I**	28	40.00 S	148.00 E
Flinders Range **⋌**	27	31.00 S	139.00 E
Flin Flon	36	54.46 N	101.53 W
Flint	42	43.01 N	83.41 W
Florence			
→ Firenze, It.	10	43.46 N	11.15 E
Florence, Ala., U.S.	44	34.49 N	87.40 W
Florence, S.C., U.S.	43	34.12 N	79.46 W
Florencia	33	1.36 N	75.36 W
Flores **I**	25	8.30 S	121.00 E
Flores, Laut (Flores Sea) **⊤**²	25	8.00 S	120.00 E
Floresville	45	29.08 N	98.10 W
Florianópolis	34	27.35 S	48.34 W
Florida	32	21.32 N	78.14 W
Florida **☐**³	37	28.00 N	82.00 W
Florida, Straits of **U**	32	25.00 N	79.45 W
Florida Keys **II**	43	24.45 N	81.00 W
Floydada	45	33.59 N	101.20 W
Fly ≏	25	8.30 S	143.41 E
Focşani	11	45.41 N	27.11 E
Foggia	10	41.27 N	15.34 E
Foligno	10	42.57 N	12.42 E
Fond du Lac, Sask., Can.	36	59.19 N	107.10 W
Fond du Lac, Wis., U.S.	42	43.47 N	88.27 W
Foochow			
→ Fuzhou	24	26.06 N	119.17 E
Forbach	8	49.11 N	6.54 E
Forest Park	43	33.37 N	84.22 W
Forestville	41	48.45 N	69.06 W
Forman	46	46.07 N	97.38 W
Formiga	35	20.27 S	45.25 W
Formosa	34	26.11 S	58.11 W
Formosa Strait **U**	24	24.00 N	119.00 E
Forrest	27	30.51 S	128.06 E
Forrest City	44	35.01 N	90.47 W
Forst	7	51.44 N	14.39 E
Forsyth	48	46.16 N	106.41 W
Fortaleza	33	3.43 S	38.30 W
Fort Beaufort	16	32.46 S	26.40 E
Fort Benton	48	47.49 N	110.40 W
Fort Bridger	48	41.19 N	110.23 W
Fort Collins	46	40.35 N	105.05 W
Fort-de-France	32	14.36 N	61.05 W
Fort Dodge	42	42.30 N	94.10 W
Fort Frances	42	48.36 N	93.24 W
Forth, Firth of **C**¹	5	56.05 N	2.55 W
Fort-Lamy			
→ Ndjamena	14	12.07 N	15.03 E
Fort Laramie	46	42.13 N	104.31 W
Fort Lauderdale	43	26.07 N	80.08 W
Fort Macleod	36	49.43 N	113.25 W
Fort Madison	42	40.38 N	91.27 W
Fort McMurray	36	56.44 N	111.23 W
Fort Myers	43	26.37 N	81.54 W
Fort Nelson	36	58.49 N	122.39 W
Fort Payne	43	34.27 N	85.43 W
Fort Peck Lake **☒**¹	48	47.45 N	106.50 W
Fort Pierce	43	27.27 N	80.20 W
Fort Pierre	46	44.21 N	100.22 W
Fort Resolution	36	61.10 N	113.40 W
Fort Saint John	36	56.15 N	120.51 W
Fort Scott	46	37.50 N	94.42 W
Fort Simpson	36	61.52 N	121.23 W
Fort Smith	44	35.23 N	94.25 W
Fort Stockton	45	30.53 N	102.53 W
Fort Victoria	15	20.05 S	30.50 E
Fort Walton Beach	44	30.25 N	86.36 W
Fort Wayne	44	41.04 N	85.09 W
Fort Worth	45	32.45 N	97.20 W
Fort Yates	46	46.05 N	100.38 W
Fort Yukon	40	66.34 N	145.17 W
Foshan	24	23.03 N	113.09 E
Fostoria	38	41.09 N	83.25 W
Fowler	46	38.08 N	104.01 W
Foxe Basin **C**	36	68.25 N	77.00 W
Fox Islands **II**	40	54.00 N	168.00 W
Framingham	38	42.17 N	71.25 W
France **☐**¹	4	46.00 N	2.00 E
Francis Case, Lake **☒**¹	46	43.15 N	99.00 W
Francs Peak **⋀**	48	43.58 N	109.20 W
Frankfort, Ind., U.S.	44	40.17 N	86.31 W
Frankfort, Ky., U.S.	38	38.12 N	84.52 W
Frankfort, Mich., U.S.	42	44.38 N	86.14 W
Frankfurt am Main	7	50.07 N	8.40 E
Frankfurt an der Oder	7	52.20 N	14.33 E
Franklin Delano Roosevelt Lake **☒**¹	48	48.20 N	118.10 W
Fraser ≏	36	49.09 N	123.12 W
Fraserburgh	5	57.42 N	2.00 W
Fraser Island **I**	28	25.15 S	153.10 E
Frederick	38	39.25 N	77.25 W
Fredericksburg, Tex., U.S.	45	30.17 N	98.52 W
Fredericksburg, Va., U.S.	38	38.18 N	77.29 W
Fredericktown	44	37.33 N	90.18 W
Fredericton	41	45.58 N	66.39 W
Fredonia	46	37.32 N	95.49 W
Fredrikstad	6	59.13 N	10.57 E
Freeport, Ill., U.S.	42	42.17 N	89.36 W
Freeport, N.Y., U.S.	38	43.09 N	73.35 W
Freeport, Tex., U.S.	45	28.58 N	95.22 W
Freer	45	27.53 N	98.37 W
Freetown	14	8.30 N	13.15 W
Freiberg	7	50.54 N	13.20 E
Freiburg [im Breisgau]	7	47.59 N	7.51 E
Fréjus	8	43.26 N	6.44 E
Fremont, Mich., U.S.	42	43.26 N	85.57 W
Fremont, Nebr., U.S.	46	41.26 N	96.30 W
French Guiana **☐**²	33	4.00 N	53.00 W
French Polynesia **☐**²	1	15.00 S	140.00 W
Fresnillo	31	23.10 N	102.53 W
Fresno	39	36.45 N	119.45 W
Friesland **☐**⁹	7	53.00 N	5.40 E
Frobisher Bay	36	63.44 N	68.28 W
Frome, Lake **☒**	28	30.48 S	139.48 E
Front Range **⋌**	47	39.45 N	105.45 W
Fujinomiya	23	35.12 N	138.38 E
Fuji-san **⋀**¹	22	35.22 N	138.44 E
Fukui	23	36.04 N	136.13 E
Fukuoka	23	33.35 N	130.24 E
Fukushima	23	37.45 N	140.28 E
Fukuyama	23	34.29 N	133.22 E
Fulda	7	50.33 N	9.41 E
Fullerton	46	41.22 N	97.58 W
Fulton	44	38.52 N	91.57 W
Fundy, Bay of **C**	41	45.00 N	66.00 W
Fürstenwalde	7	52.21 N	14.04 E
Fürth	7	49.28 N	10.59 E
Fushun	22	41.52 N	123.53 E
Fuzhou (Foochow)	24	26.06 N	119.17 E
Fyn **I**	6	55.20 N	10.30 E

G

Gabbs	39	38.52 N	117.55 W
Gabon **☐**¹	15	1.00 S	11.45 E
Gaborone	15	24.45 S	25.55 E
Gabrovo	11	42.52 N	25.19 E
Gadsden	44	34.02 N	86.02 W
Gagnon	36	51.53 N	68.10 W
Gainesville, Fla., U.S.	43	29.40 N	82.20 W
Gainesville, Ga., U.S.	43	34.18 N	83.50 W
Gainesville, Tex., U.S.	45	33.37 N	97.08 W
Gairdner, Lake **☒**	27	31.35 S	136.00 E
Galashiels	5	55.37 N	2.49 W
Galaţi	11	45.26 N	28.03 E
Galesburg	42	40.57 N	90.22 W
Galicia **☐**⁹	7	49.50 N	21.00 E
Galka'yo	17	6.49 N	47.23 E
Gallarate	10	45.40 N	8.47 E
Gallatin	44	36.24 N	86.27 W
Galle	20	6.02 N	80.13 E
Gallipolis	38	38.49 N	82.12 W
Gällivare	6	67.07 N	20.45 E
Gallup	47	35.32 N	108.44 W
Galveston	45	29.18 N	94.48 W
Galveston Island **I**	45	29.13 N	94.55 W
Galway	5	53.16 N	9.03 W
Gambia **☐**¹	14	13.30 N	15.30 W
Ganado	47	35.43 N	109.33 W
Ganges (Ganga) (Padma) ≏	21	23.22 N	90.32 E
Gannett Peak **⋀**	48	43.11 N	109.39 W
Ganzhou	24	25.54 N	114.55 E
Gao	14	16.16 N	0.03 W
Garda, Lago di **☒**	10	45.40 N	10.41 E

Name	Map No.	Lat	Long
Garden City	46	37.58 N	100.53 W
Garden Grove	42	40.50 N	93.36 W
Gardēz	21	33.37 N	69.07 E
Gardner	38	42.34 N	71.60 W
Gardnerville	39	38.56 N	119.45 W
Garnett	46	38.17 N	95.14 W
Garonne ≃	8	45.02 N	0.36 W
Gary	44	41.36 N	87.20 W
Gaspé, Péninsule de ↘[1]	41	48.30 N	65.00 W
Gastonia	43	35.16 N	81.11 W
Gatesville	45	31.26 N	97.45 W
Gävle	6	60.40 N	17.10 E
Gaya	21	24.47 N	85.00 E
Gaylord	42	45.02 N	84.40 W
Gdańsk (Danzig)	7	54.23 N	18.40 E
Gdynia	7	54.32 N	18.33 E
Geelong	27	38.08 S	144.21 E
Gejiu (Kokiu)	22	23.22 N	103.06 E
Gelibolu	11	40.24 N	26.40 E
Gelibolu Yarımadası (Gallipoli Peninsula) ↘[1]	11	40.20 N	26.30 E
Gemlik	11	40.26 N	29.09 E
General Roca	34	39.02 S	67.35 W
Geneseo	46	38.31 N	98.09 W
Geneva	38	42.52 N	77.00 W
Geneva, Lake ⊜	8	46.25 N	6.30 E
Genève	8	46.12 N	6.09 E
Genk	7	50.58 N	5.30 E
Genova (Genoa)	10	44.25 N	8.57 E
George	16	33.58 S	22.24 E
George, Lake ⊜	43	29.17 N	81.36 W
Georgetown, Ont., Can.	38	43.39 N	79.55 W
Georgetown, P.E.I., Can.	41	46.11 N	62.32 W
Georgetown, Cay. Is.	32	19.18 N	81.23 W
Georgetown, Gam.	14	13.30 N	14.47 W
Georgetown, Guy.	33	6.48 N	58.10 W
George Town (Pinang), Malay.	26	5.25 N	100.20 E
Georgetown, Tex., U.S.	45	30.38 N	97.41 W
George West	45	28.20 N	98.07 W
Georgia □[3]	37	32.50 N	83.15 W
Georgia, Strait of ⋃	48	49.20 N	124.00 W
Georgian Bay C	42	45.15 N	80.50 W
Gera	7	50.52 N	12.04 E
Geraldton, Austl.	27	28.46 S	114.36 E
Geraldton, Ont., Can.	36	49.44 N	86.57 W
Gerlachovský štit ∧	7	49.12 N	20.08 E
German Democratic Republic (East Germany) □[1]	4	52.00 N	12.30 E
Germany, Federal Republic of (West Germany) □[1]	4	51.00 N	9.00 E
Germiston	16	26.15 S	28.05 E
Gerona	9	41.59 N	2.49 E
Getafe	9	40.18 N	3.43 W
Gettysburg	46	45.01 N	99.57 W
Ghana □[1]	14	8.00 N	2.00 W
Ghardaïa	14	32.31 N	3.37 E
Ghazāl, Baḥr al- ≃	14	9.31 N	30.25 E
Ghaznī	21	33.33 N	68.26 E
Ghazzah (Gaza)	18	31.30 N	34.28 E
Gia-dinh	26	10.48 N	106.42 E
Gibbon	46	40.45 N	98.51 W
Gibraltar	9	36.09 N	5.21 W
Gibraltar □[2]	4	36.11 N	5.22 W
Gibraltar, Strait of (Estrecho de Gibraltar) ⋃	9	35.57 N	5.36 W
Giessen	7	50.35 N	8.40 E
Gifu	23	35.25 N	136.45 E
Gijón	9	43.32 N	5.40 W
Gila ≃	47	32.43 N	114.33 W
Gila Bend	47	32.57 N	112.43 W
Gillette	46	44.18 N	105.30 W
Gilman	42	45.10 N	90.48 W
Gimli	36	50.38 N	96.59 W
Girard	46	37.31 N	94.51 W
Gironde C[1]	8	45.20 N	0.45 W
Gisborne	29	38.40 S	178.01 E
Gizo	30a	8.06 S	156.51 E
Gjirokastër	11	40.05 N	20.10 E
Glace Bay	36	46.12 N	59.57 W
Glacier Bay National Monument ◆	40	58.45 N	136.30 W
Glåma ≃	6	59.12 N	10.57 E
Glasgow, Scot., U.K.	5	55.53 N	4.15 W
Glasgow, Ky., U.S.	43	37.00 N	85.55 W
Glasgow, Mont., U.S.	48	48.12 N	106.38 W
Glen Canyon V	47	37.10 N	110.50 W
Glencoe, Ala., U.S.	44	33.57 N	85.56 W
Glencoe, Minn., U.S.	42	44.46 N	94.09 W
Glendale	47	33.32 N	112.11 W
Glen Rose	45	32.14 N	97.45 W
Glens Falls	38	43.19 N	73.39 W
Glen Ullin	46	46.49 N	101.50 W
Glenwood Springs	47	39.33 N	107.19 W
Glittertinden ∧	6	61.39 N	8.33 E
Globe	47	33.24 N	110.47 W
Gloucester, Eng., U.K.	5	51.53 N	2.14 W
Gloucester, Mass., U.S.	38	42.41 N	70.39 W
Gloversville	38	43.03 N	74.20 W
Gniezno	7	52.31 N	17.37 E
Gobabis	16	22.30 S	18.58 E
Gobi ◆[2]	22	43.00 N	105.00 E
Godāvari ≃	20	17.00 N	81.45 E
Godthåb	1	64.11 N	51.44 W
Godwin Austen (K2) ∧	21	35.53 N	76.30 E
Goiânia	33	16.40 S	49.16 W
Gökçeada I	11	40.10 N	25.50 E
Golden Meadow	44	29.23 N	90.16 W
Goldsboro	43	35.23 N	77.59 W
Gómez Palacio	31	25.34 N	103.30 W
Gonaïves	32	19.27 N	72.41 W
Gonâve, Golfe de la C	32	19.00 N	73.30 W
Gonâve, Île de la I	32	18.51 N	73.03 W
Gonder	17	12.40 N	37.30 E
Gönen	11	40.06 N	27.39 E
Good Hope, Cape of ↘	16	34.24 S	18.30 E
Good Hope Mountain ∧	36	51.09 N	124.10 W
Gooding	48	42.56 N	114.43 W
Goodland	46	39.21 N	101.43 W
Gorakhpur	21	26.45 N	83.22 E
Gordon	46	42.48 N	102.12 W
Gore, N.Z.	29	46.06 S	168.58 E
Gore, Yai.	17	8.08 N	35.33 E
Gorizia	10	45.57 N	13.38 E
Gor'kij (Gorky)	12	56.20 N	44.00 E
Gorkovskoje Vodochranilišče ⊜[1]	12	57.00 N	43.10 E
Gorky → Gor'kij	12	56.20 N	44.20 E
Gorontalo	25	0.33 N	123.03 E
Goshen	44	41.35 N	85.50 W
Göteborg (Gothenburg)	6	57.43 N	11.58 E
Gothenburg	46	40.56 N	100.09 W
Gotland I	6	57.30 N	18.33 E
Göttingen	7	51.32 N	9.55 E
Gottwaldov	7	49.13 N	17.41 E
Gouin, Réservoir ⊜[1]	36	48.38 N	74.54 W
Governador Valadares	33	18.51 S	41.56 W
Goya	34	29.08 S	59.16 W
Graaff-Reinet	16	32.14 S	24.32 E
Gracias a Dios, Cabo ↘	32	15.00 N	83.10 W
Grafton	27	29.41 S	152.56 E
Grahamstown	16	33.19 S	26.31 E
Grainfield	46	39.07 N	100.28 W
Grampian Mountains ↗	5	56.45 N	4.00 W
Granada, Esp.	9	37.13 N	3.41 W
Granada, Nic.	32	11.56 N	85.57 W
Granada, Colo., U.S.	45	38.04 N	102.19 W
Granby	38	45.24 N	72.44 W
Gran Chaco ≃	34	23.00 S	60.00 W
Grand ≃	44	39.23 N	93.06 W
Grand Bahama I	32	26.38 N	78.25 W
Grand Bank	36	47.06 N	55.46 W
Grand Canal → Yunhe ☲	24	32.12 N	119.31 E
Grand Canyon V	47	36.10 N	112.45 W
Grand Canyon National Park ✦	47	36.15 N	112.58 W
Grand Coulee	47	47.56 N	119.00 W
Grand Coulee V	48	47.45 N	119.15 W
Grande, Bahia C[3]	34	50.45 S	68.45 W
Grande, Rio (Bravo del Norte) ≃	37	25.55 N	97.09 W
Grande Comore I	15	11.35 S	43.20 E
Grand Erg Occidental ◆[1]	14	30.30 N	0.30 E
Grand Erg Oriental ◆[2]	14	30.30 N	7.00 E
Grande-Terre I	32	16.20 N	61.25 W
Grand Forks, B.C., Can.	36	49.02 N	118.27 W
Grand Forks, N. Dak., U.S.	46	47.55 N	97.03 W
Grand Island	46	40.55 N	98.21 W
Grand Junction	47	39.05 N	108.33 W
Grand Manan Island I	41	44.40 N	66.50 W
Grand Rapids, Man., Can.	36	53.08 N	99.20 W
Grand Rapids, Mich., U.S.	42	42.58 N	85.40 W
Grand Rapids, Minn., U.S.	42	47.14 N	93.31 W
Grand-Saint-Bernard, Tunnel du ◆[5]	8	45.51 N	7.11 E
Grand Teton ∧	48	43.44 N	110.48 W

Name	Map No.	Lat ° ′	Long ° ′
Grand Traverse Bay **C**	42	45.02 N	85.30 W
Grand Turk	32	21.28 N	71.08 W
Grandview	44	38.53 N	94.32 W
Granger	48	41.35 N	109.58 W
Grangeville	48	45.56 N	116.07 W
Granite Falls	46	44.49 N	95.33 W
Granite Peak **∧**	48	45.10 N	109.48 W
Grant	46	40.50 N	101.56 W
Grants	47	35.09 N	107.52 W
Grants Pass	48	42.26 N	123.19 W
Graskop	16	24.58 S	30.49 E
Graz	7	47.05 N	15.27 E
Great Abaco **I**	43	26.28 N	77.05 W
Great Artesian Basin **≌**[1]	28	25.00 S	143.00 E
Great Australian Bight **C**[3]	27	35.00 S	130.00 E
Great Barrier Island **I**	29	36.10 S	175.25 E
Great Barrier Reef **⊹**[2]	27	18.00 S	145.50 E
Great Basin **≌**[1]	39	40.00 N	117.00 W
Great Bear Lake **⊜**	36	66.00 N	120.00 W
Great Bend	46	38.22 N	98.46 W
Great Channel **⋓**	26	6.25 N	94.20 E
Great Dismal Swamp **☷**	43	36.30 N	76.30 W
Great Divide Basin **≌**[1]	48	42.00 N	108.10 W
Great Dividing Range **∧**	27	25.00 S	147.00 E
Greater Antilles **II**	32	20.00 N	74.00 W
Greater Sunda Islands **II**	25	2.00 S	110.00 E
Great Falls	48	47.30 N	111.17 W
Great Inagua **I**	32	21.05 N	73.18 W
Great Indian Desert (Thar Desert) **⇴**[2]	21	28.00 N	72.00 E
Great Karroo **∧**[1]	16	32.25 S	22.40 E
Great Salt Lake **⊜**	47	41.10 N	112.30 W
Great Salt Lake Desert **⇴**[2]	47	40.40 N	113.30 W
Great Sand Dunes National Monument **⧆**	47	37.43 N	105.36 W
Great Sandy Desert **⇴**[2]	27	21.30 S	125.00 E
Great Slave Lake **⊜**	36	61.30 N	114.00 W
Great Smoky Mountains **∧**	43	35.35 N	83.30 W
Great Victoria Desert **⇴**[2]	27	28.30 S	127.45 E
Greece **□**[1]	4	39.00 N	22.00 E
Greeley	47	40.25 N	104.42 W
Green **≃**	47	38.11 N	109.53 W
Green Bay	42	44.30 N	88.01 W
Green Bay **C**	42	45.00 N	87.30 W
Green Cove Springs	43	30.00 N	81.41 W
Greenfield	43	36.10 N	82.50 W
Greenfield	38	42.36 N	72.36 W
Greenland **□**[2]	1	70.00 N	40.00 W
Greenland Sea **⊽**[2]	2	77.00 N	1.00 W
Green Mountains **∧**	38	43.45 N	72.45 W
Greenock	5	55.57 N	4.45 W
Green River	48	41.32 N	109.28 W
Greensboro	43	36.04 N	79.47 W
Greensburg	38	40.18 N	79.33 W
Greenville, Miss., U.S.	44	33.25 N	91.05 W
Greenville, N.C., U.S.	43	35.37 N	77.23 W
Greenville, S.C., U.S.	43	34.51 N	82.23 W
Greenville, Tex., U.S.	45	33.08 N	96.07 W
Greenwood, Miss., U.S.	44	33.31 N	90.11 W
Greenwood, S.C., U.S.	43	34.12 N	82.10 W
Greifswald	7	54.05 N	13.23 E
Grenada	44	33.47 N	89.55 W
Grenada **□**[1]	32	12.07 N	61.40 W
Grenoble	8	45.10 N	5.43 E
Gretna	44	29.55 N	90.03 W
Greymouth	29	42.28 S	171.12 E
Grey Range **∧**	28	27.00 S	143.35 E
Griffin	43	33.15 N	84.16 W
Grimsby	5	53.35 N	0.05 W
Grodno	12	53.41 N	23.50 E
Groningen	7	53.13 N	6.33 E
Groote Eylandt **I**	27	14.00 S	136.40 E
Grosseto	10	42.46 N	11.08 E
Grossglockner **∧**	7	47.04 N	12.42 E
Groton	46	45.27 N	98.06 W
Grouse Creek	47	41.42 N	113.53 W
Grove City	38	41.10 N	80.05 W
Groznyj	4	43.20 N	45.42 E
Grudziądz	7	53.29 N	18.45 E
Guadalajara, Esp.	9	40.38 N	3.10 W
Guadalajara, Méx.	31	20.40 N	103.20 W
Guadalcanal **I**	30a	9.32 S	160.12 E
Guadalquivir **≃**	9	36.47 N	6.22 W
Guadalupe	31	25.41 N	100.15 W
Guadalupe Peak **∧**	45	31.50 N	104.52 W
Guadeloupe **□**[2]	32	16.15 N	61.35 W
Guadiana **≃**	9	37.14 N	7.22 W
Guam **□**[2]	25	13.28 N	144.47 E
Guanajuato	31	21.01 N	101.15 W
Guangzhou (Canton)	24	23.06 N	113.16 E
Guantánamo	32	20.08 N	75.12 W
Guaratinguetá	35	22.49 S	45.13 W
Guatemala	32	14.38 N	90.31 W
Guatemala **□**[1]	32	15.30 N	90.15 W
Guayaquil	33	2.10 S	79.50 W
Guayaquil, Golfo de **C**	33	3.00 S	80.30 W
Guaymas	31	27.56 N	110.54 W
Guelph	42	43.33 N	80.15 W
Guernsey **□**[2]	8	49.28 N	2.35 W
Guildford	5	51.14 N	0.35 W
Guilin	22	25.11 N	110.09 E
Guinea **□**[1]	14	11.00 N	10.00 W
Guinea, Gulf **≻ C**	14	2.00 N	2.30 E
Guinea-Bissau **□**[1]	14	12.00 N	15.00 W
Güines	32	22.50 N	82.02 W
Guiyang	22	26.35 N	106.43 E
Gujrānwāla	19	32.26 N	74.33 E
Gujrāt	19	32.34 N	74.05 E
Gulfport	44	30.22 N	89.06 W
Gunnison	47	38.33 N	106.56 W
Guntakal	20	15.10 N	77.23 E
Guntersville	44	34.21 N	86.18 W
Guntūr	20	16.18 N	80.27 E
Gurjev	4	47.07 N	51.56 E
Gurupi	45	35.53 N	97.25 W
Guyana **□**[1]	33	5.00 N	59.00 W
Guymon	45	36.41 N	101.29 W
Gwalior	21	26.13 N	78.10 E
Gwelo	15	19.27 S	29.49 E
Gyöngyös	7	47.47 N	19.56 E
Györ	7	47.42 N	17.38 E

H

Name	Map No.	Lat ° ′	Long ° ′
Haast	29	43.53 S	169.03 E
Hachinohe	23	40.30 N	141.29 E
Hachiōji	23	35.39 N	139.20 E
Hackberry	44	29.59 N	93.21 W
Hadera	18	32.26 N	34.55 E
Ha-dong	26	20.58 N	105.46 E
Ḥaḑūr Shuʿayb **∧**	17	15.18 N	43.59 E
Haenertsburg	16	24.00 S	29.50 E
Haerbin	22	45.45 N	126.41 E
Hagerman	45	33.07 N	104.20 W
Hagerstown	38	39.39 N	77.43 W
Ha-giang	26	22.50 N	104.59 E
Haikou	22	20.06 N	110.21 E
Haileybury	42	47.27 N	79.38 W
Hainandao **I**	26	19.00 N	109.30 E
Hai-phong	26	20.52 N	106.41 E
Haiti (Haïti) **□**[1]	32	19.00 N	72.25 W
Hakodate	23a	41.45 N	140.43 E
Halab (Aleppo)	18	36.12 N	37.10 E
Haleakala Crater **●**[6]	39a	20.43 N	156.13 W
Haleyville	44	34.14 N	87.37 W
Halifax	41	44.39 N	63.36 W
Halle	7	51.29 N	11.58 E
Hallettsville	45	29.27 N	96.56 W
Hallowell	38	44.17 N	69.48 W
Halls Creek	27	18.16 S	127.46 E
Halmahera **I**	25	1.00 N	128.00 E
Halmstad	6	56.39 N	12.50 E
Haltiatunturi **∧**	6	69.18 N	21.16 E
Hamadān	17	34.48 N	48.30 E
Hamāh	18	35.08 N	36.45 E
Hamamatsu	23	34.42 N	137.44 E
Hamar	6	60.48 N	11.06 E
Hamburg	7	53.33 N	9.59 E
Hämeenlinna	6	61.00 N	24.27 E
Hamhŭng	22	39.54 N	127.32 E
Hamilton, Ber.	37	32.17 N	64.46 W
Hamilton, Ont., Can.	42	43.15 N	79.51 W
Hamilton, N.Z.	29	37.47 S	175.17 E
Hamilton, Mont., U.S.	48	46.15 N	114.09 W
Hamilton, Ohio, U.S.	38	39.26 N	84.30 W
Hamilton, Tex., U.S.	45	31.42 N	98.07 W
Hamlin	45	32.53 N	100.08 W
Hammerfest	6	70.40 N	23.42 E
Hammond	44	30.30 N	90.28 W
Hampton	48	37.01 N	76.22 W
Hancock	42	47.07 N	88.35 W
Handan	22	36.37 N	114.29 E
Hangzhou (Hangchow)	24	30.15 N	120.10 E

Name	Map No.	Lat ° ′	Long ° ′
Hankinson	46	46.04 N	96.54 W
Hannibal	44	39.42 N	91.22 W
Hannover	7	52.24 N	9.44 E
Ha-noi	26	21.02 N	105.51 E
Hanover	38	39.48 N	76.59 W
Hanzhong	22	32.59 N	107.11 E
Harbin			
→ Haerbin	22	45.45 N	126.41 E
Harbor Beach	42	43.51 N	82.39 W
Hardangerfjorden **C**²	6	60.10 N	6.00 E
Hardin	48	45.44 N	107.37 W
Harer	17	9.18 N	42.08 E
Hargeysa	17	9.30 N	44.03 E
Harlem	48	48.32 N	108.47 W
Harlingen	45	26.11 N	97.42 W
Harlowton	48	46.26 N	109.50 W
Harney Lake **⊜**	48	43.14 N	119.07 W
Härnösand	6	62.38 N	17.56 E
Harriman	43	35.56 N	84.33 W
Harrisburg	38	40.16 N	76.52 W
Harrison	44	36.14 N	93.07 W
Harrisonburg	38	36.34 N	78.58 W
Harrisonville	44	38.39 N	94.21 W
Harstad	6	68.46 N	16.30 E
Hartford	38	41.46 N	72.41 W
Harts **≃**	16	28.24 S	24.17 E
Hartsville	43	34.23 N	80.04 W
Harvey, Ill., U.S.	42	41.37 N	87.39 W
Harvey, N. Dak., U.S.	46	47.47 N	99.56 W
Haskovo	11	41.56 N	25.33 E
Hastings, N.Z.	29	39.38 S	176.51 E
Hastings, Eng., U.K.	5	50.51 N	0.36 E
Hastings, Nebr., U.S.	46	40.35 N	98.23 W
Hatteras, Cape **⊁**	43	35.13 N	75.32 W
Hattiesburg	44	31.19 N	89.16 W
Hatton	46	47.38 N	97.27 W
Hat Yai	26	7.01 N	100.28 E
Haugesund	6	59.25 N	5.18 E
Hauterive	41	49.12 N	68.16 W
Havana			
→ La Habana	32	23.08 N	82.22 W
Haverhill	38	42.47 N	71.05 W
Havre	48	48.33 N	109.41 W
Hawaii **□**³	39a	20.00 N	157.45 W
Hawaii **I**	39a	19.30 N	155.30 W
Hawera	29	39.35 S	174.17 E
Hawick	5	55.25 N	2.47 W
Hawke Bay **C**	29	39.20 S	177.30 E
Haw Knob **∧**	43	35.19 N	84.02 W
Hawthorne	39	38.32 N	118.38 W
Hay	27	34.30 S	144.51 E
Hayden Peak **∧**	48	42.59 N	116.39 W
Hayrabolu	11	41.12 N	27.06 E
Hay River	36	60.51 N	115.40 W
Hays	46	38.53 N	99.20 W
Haysville	46	37.34 N	97.21 W
Hayward	42	46.01 N	91.29 W
Hazard	43	37.15 N	83.12 W
Hazlehurst	44	31.52 N	90.24 W
Hazleton	38	40.58 N	75.59 W
Headland	44	31.21 N	85.20 W
Healdton	45	34.14 N	97.29 W
Healy	46	38.36 N	100.37 W
Hearst	36	49.41 N	83.40 W
Hebbronville	45	27.18 N	98.41 W
Hebrides **II**	4	57.00 N	6.30 W
Hebron	46	46.54 N	102.03 W
Hecate Strait **U**	36	53.00 N	131.00 W
Hefa (Haifa)	18	32.50 N	35.00 E
Hefei	24	31.51 N	117.17 E
Hegang	22	47.24 N	130.17 E
Heidelberg, B.R.D.	7	49.25 N	8.43 E
Heidelberg, S. Afr.	16	34.06 S	20.59 E
Heidenheim	7	49.01 N	10.44 E
Heilbron	16	27.21 S	27.58 E
Heilbronn	7	49.08 N	9.13 E
Helena	48	46.36 N	112.01 W
Helmand **≃**	19	31.12 N	61.34 E
Helmsdale	5	58.07 N	3.40 W
Helsingborg	6	56.03 N	12.42 E
Helsingfors			
→ Helsinki	6	60.10 N	24.58 E
Helsinki (Helsingfors)	6	60.10 N	24.58 E
Henderson, Ky., U.S.	44	37.50 N	87.35 W
Henderson, N.C., U.S.	43	36.20 N	78.25 W
Henderson, Tex., U.S.	44	32.09 N	94.48 W
Hengyang	22	26.51 N	112.30 E
Hennessey	45	36.06 N	97.54 W
Henzada	26	17.38 N	95.28 E
Herāt	19	34.20 N	62.07 E
Hereford	45	34.49 N	102.24 W
Herford	7	52.06 N	8.40 E
Hermiston	48	45.51 N	119.17 W
Hermosillo	31	29.04 N	110.58 W
Hesston	46	38.08 N	97.26 W
Hialeah	43	25.49 N	80.17 W
Hibbing	42	47.25 N	92.56 W
Hickory	43	35.44 N	81.21 W
Hidalgo del Parral	31	26.56 N	105.40 W
Highland Park	42	42.11 N	87.48 W
Highmore	46	44.31 N	99.27 W
Hiiumaa **I**	12	58.52 N	22.40 E
Hikone	23	35.15 N	136.15 E
Hillsboro, N. Dak., U.S.	46	47.26 N	97.03 W
Hillsboro, Tex., U.S.	45	32.01 N	97.08 W
Hilo	39a	19.43 N	155.05 W
Hilton Head Island **I**	43	32.12 N	80.45 W
Himalayas **∧**	21	28.00 N	84.00 E
Himeji	23	34.49 N	134.42 E
Hims (Homs)	18	34.44 N	36.43 E
Hindu Kush **∧**	21	36.00 N	71.30 E
Hinganghāt	20	20.34 N	78.50 E
Hinnøya **I**	6	68.30 N	16.00 E
Hinton	36	53.25 N	117.34 W
Hirosaki	23	40.35 N	140.28 E
Hiroshima	23	34.24 N	132.27 E
Hispaniola **I**	32	19.00 N	71.00 W
Hitachi	23	36.36 N	140.39 E
Hobart, Austl.	27	42.53 S	147.19 E
Hobart, Okla., U.S.	45	35.01 N	99.06 W
Hobbs	45	32.42 N	103.08 W
Hódmezővásárhely	7	46.25 N	20.20 E
Hof	7	50.18 N	11.55 E
Hofmeyr	16	31.39 S	25.50 E
Höfu	23	34.03 N	131.34 E
Hohe Tauern **∧**	7	47.10 N	12.30 E
Hokitika	29	42.43 S	170.58 E
Hokkaidō **I**	23a	44.00 N	143.00 E
Holden	38	37.50 N	82.04 W
Holguin	32	20.53 N	76.15 W
Holladay	47	40.40 N	111.49 W
Holland	42	42.47 N	86.07 W
Hollandale	44	33.10 N	90.58 W
Hollister	39	36.51 N	121.24 W
Holly Springs	44	34.41 N	89.26 W
Hollywood	43	26.00 N	80.09 W
Holt	44	33.15 N	87.29 W
Holy Cross	40	62.12 N	159.47 W
Holyhead	5	53.19 N	4.38 W
Holyoke, Colo., U.S.	46	40.35 N	102.18 W
Holyoke, Mass., U.S.	38	42.12 N	72.37 W
Homer	40	59.39 N	151.33 W
Homestead	43	25.29 N	80.29 W
Honduras **□**¹	15	15.00 N	88.00 W
Honduras, Gulf of **C**	32	16.10 N	87.50 W
Honesdale	38	41.34 N	75.16 W
Hon-gay	26	20.57 N	107.05 E
Hong Kong **□**²	22	22.15 N	114.10 E
Honguedo, Détroit d' **U**	41	49.15 N	64.00 W
Hongzehu **⊜**	24	33.16 N	118.34 E
Honiara	30a	9.26 S	159.57 E
Honolulu	39a	21.19 N	157.52 W
Honshū **I**	23	36.00 N	138.00 E
Hood, Mount **∧**	48	45.23 N	121.41 W
Hood River	48	45.43 N	121.31 W
Hooghly **≃**	21	21.56 N	88.04 E
Hoonah	40	58.07 N	135.26 W
Hooper Bay	40	61.31 N	166.06 W
Hoopstad	16	27.54 S	25.58 E
Hope	44	33.40 N	93.36 W
Hopewell	43	37.18 N	77.17 W
Hopi Indian Reservation **⊷**⁴	47	35.45 N	110.35 W
Hopkinsville	44	36.52 N	87.29 W
Hormuz, Strait of **U**	17	26.34 N	56.15 E
Hornell	38	42.19 N	77.40 W
Hornos, Cabo de (Cape Horn) **⊁**	34	55.59 S	67.16 W
Hospitalet	9	41.22 N	2.08 E
Hot Springs National Park	44	34.30 N	93.03 W
Houaïlou	30b	21.17 S	165.38 E
Houghton	42	47.06 N	88.34 W
Houma	44	29.36 N	90.43 W
Houston	45	29.46 N	95.22 W
Howe, Cape **⊁**	27	37.31 S	149.59 E
Howland	38	45.14 N	68.40 W

Name	Map No.	Lat ° '	Long ° '
Howrah	21	22.35 N	88.20 E
Hradec Králové	7	50.12 N	15.50 E
Hsinchu	24	24.48 N	120.58 E
Hsinkao Shan ▲	24	23.28 N	120.57 E
Hua Hin	26	12.34 N	99.58 E
Huainan	24	32.40 N	117.00 E
Huambo	15	12.44 S	15.47 E
Huancayo	33	12.04 S	75.14 W
Huanghe ≃	22	37.32 N	118.19 E
Huangshi	24	30.13 N	115.05 E
Huánuco	33	9.55 S	76.14 W
Huaras	33	9.32 S	77.32 W
Huascarán, Nevado ▲	33	9.07 S	77.37 W
Hubbard	45	31.51 N	96.48 W
Hubli	20	15.21 N	75.10 E
Hudiksvall	6	61.44 N	17.07 E
Hudson	38	42.15 N	73.47 W
Hudson ≃	38	40.42 N	74.02 W
Hudson Bay	36	52.52 N	102.25 W
Hudson Bay C	36	60.00 N	86.00 W
Hudson Strait ⋓	36	62.30 N	72.00 W
Hue	26	16.28 N	107.36 E
Huehuetenango	32	15.20 N	91.28 W
Huelva	9	37.16 N	6.57 W
Huesca	9	42.08 N	0.25 W
Hughenden	27	20.51 S	144.12 E
Hugoton	46	37.11 N	101.21 W
Huhehaote	22	40.51 N	111.40 E
Huixtla	31	15.09 N	92.28 W
Hulett	46	44.41 N	104.36 W
Hull	38	45.26 N	75.43 W
Humboldt	44	35.49 N	88.55 W
Humboldt ≃	39	40.02 N	118.31 W
Humphreys Peak ▲	37	35.20 N	111.40 W
Hunedoara	11	45.45 N	22.54 E
Hungary ◻¹	4	47.00 N	20.00 E
Huntington, Ind., U.S.	44	40.53 N	85.30 W
Huntington, W. Va., U.S.	38	38.25 N	82.26 W
Huntly	5	57.27 N	2.47 W
Huntsville, Ont., Can.	42	45.20 N	79.13 W
Huntsville, Ala., U.S.	44	34.44 N	86.35 W
Huntsville, Tex., U.S.	45	30.43 N	95.33 W
Huron	46	44.22 N	98.13 W
Huron, Lake ◓	42	44.30 N	82.15 W
Hutchinson	46	38.05 N	97.56 W
Hvannadalshnúkur ▲	4	64.01 N	16.41 W
Hwang Ho → Huanghe ≃	22	37.32 N	118.19 E
Hyden	43	37.10 N	83.22 W
Hyderābād, Bhārat	20	17.23 N	78.29 E
Hyderābād, Pāk.	19	25.22 N	68.22 E
Hyères	8	43.07 N	6.07 E
Hyvinkää	6	60.38 N	24.52 E

I			
Ialomiţa ≃	11	44.42 N	27.51 E
Ibadan	14	7.17 N	3.30 E
Ibagué	33	4.27 N	75.14 W
Ibapah Peak ▲	39	39.50 N	113.55 W
Iboundji, Mont ▲	15	1.08 S	11.48 E
Ica	33	14.04 S	75.42 W
Iceland ◻¹	4	65.00 N	18.00 W
Ida Grove	46	42.21 N	95.28 W
Idaho ◻³	37	45.00 N	115.00 W
Idaho Falls	48	43.30 N	112.02 W
Idalou	45	33.40 N	101.41 W
Igarka	13	67.28 N	86.35 E
Iglesias	36	39.19 N	8.32 E
Igloolik	31	18.21 N	99.32 W
Iguala	23	35.31 N	137.50 E
Iida	23	33.38 N	130.41 E
Iizuka	7	52.45 N	5.25 E
IJsselmeer (Zuiderzee) ▾²	33	14.49 S	39.02 W
Ilhéus	40	59.30 N	155.00 W
Iliamna Lake ◓	38	43.01 N	75.02 W
Ilion	33	16.39 S	67.48 W
Illimani, Nevado ▲	37	40.00 N	89.00 W
Illinois ◻³	44	38.58 N	90.27 W
Illinois ≃	25	10.42 N	122.34 E
Iloilo	23	34.03 N	133.00 E
Imabari	43	26.25 N	81.25 W
Immokalee	10	43.53 N	8.03 E
Imperia	39	32.50 N	115.30 W
Imperial Valley ⋁	22	37.28 N	126.38 E
Inch'ŏn			

Name	Map No.	Lat ° '	Long ° '
Independence, Kans., U.S.	46	37.13 N	95.42 W
Independence, Mo., U.S.	44	39.05 N	94.24 W
India ◻¹	19	20.00 N	77.00 E
Indiana	38	40.37 N	79.09 W
Indiana ◻³	37	40.00 N	86.15 W
Indianapolis	44	39.46 N	86.09 W
Indian Ocean ▾¹	1	10.00 S	70.00 E
Indianola	44	33.27 N	90.39 W
Indian Springs	39	36.34 N	115.40 W
Indigirka ≃	13	70.48 N	148.54 E
Indio	39	33.43 N	116.13 W
Indonesia ◻¹	25	5.00 S	120.00 E
Indore	21	22.43 N	75.50 E
Indus ≃	21	24.20 N	67.47 E
Inegöl	11	40.05 N	29.31 E
Inez	43	37.52 N	82.32 W
Infiernillo, Presa del ◓¹	31	18.35 N	101.45 W
Inhambane	15	23.51 S	35.29 E
Inharrime	15	24.29 S	35.01 E
Inn (En) ≃	7	48.35 N	13.28 E
Innsbruck	7	47.16 N	11.24 E
Inowrocław	7	52.48 N	18.15 E
International Falls	42	48.36 N	93.25 W
Inthanon, Doi ▲	26	18.35 N	98.29 E
Inuvik	36	68.25 N	133.30 W
Invercargill	29	46.24 S	168.21 E
Inverness	5	57.27 N	4.15 W
Inyangani ▲	15	18.20 S	32.50 E
Ioánnina	11	39.40 N	20.50 E
Iona	42	42.59 N	85.04 W
Ionian Islands → Iónioi Nísoi II	11	38.30 N	20.30 E
Ionian Sea ▾²	4	39.00 N	19.00 E
Iónioi Nísoi II	11	38.30 N	20.30 E
Iowa ◻³	37	42.15 N	93.15 W
Iowa ≃	42	41.10 N	91.02 W
Iowa City	42	41.40 N	91.32 W
Ipiaú	35	14.08 S	39.44 W
Ipoh	26	4.35 N	101.05 E
Ipswich, Austl.	27	27.36 S	152.46 E
Ipswich, Eng., U.K.	5	52.04 N	1.10 E
Iquique	33	20.13 S	70.10 W
Iquitos	33	3.46 S	73.15 W
Iraan	45	30.54 N	101.54 W
Iráklion	11	35.20 N	25.09 E
Iran ◻¹	1	32.00 N	53.00 E
Irapuato	31	20.41 N	101.21 W
Iraq ◻¹	17	33.00 N	44.00 E
Irbid	18	32.33 N	35.51 E
Ireland ◻¹	4	53.00 N	8.00 W
Iringa	15	7.46 S	35.42 E
Irish Sea ▾²	5	53.30 N	5.20 W
Irkutsk	13	52.16 N	104.20 E
Iron Gate Reservoir ◓¹	11	44.30 N	22.00 E
Iron Mountain	42	45.49 N	88.04 W
Ironwood	42	46.27 N	90.10 W
Irrawaddy ≃	26	15.50 N	95.06 E
Irtyš ≃	13	61.04 N	68.52 E
Irún	9	43.21 N	1.47 W
Isabelia, Cordillera ⋀	32	13.45 N	85.15 W
Ise	23	34.29 N	136.42 E
Ishinomaki	23	38.25 N	141.18 E
Ishpeming	42	46.30 N	87.40 W
Isim ≃	13	56.09 N	69.27 E
Islāmābād	19	33.42 N	73.10 E
Isle of Man ◻²	4	54.15 N	4.30 W
Isleta	47	34.55 N	106.42 W
Israel (Yisra'el) ◻¹	18	31.30 N	35.00 E
İstanbul	11	41.01 N	28.58 E
İstanbul Boğazı (Bosporus) ⋓	11	41.06 N	29.04 E
Itabira	35	19.37 S	43.13 W
Itabuna	33	14.48 S	39.16 W
Itajaí	34	26.53 S	48.39 W
Itajubá	35	22.26 S	45.27 W
Italy ◻¹	4	42.50 N	12.50 E
Itapetinga	35	15.15 S	40.15 W
Itapetininga	35	23.36 S	48.03 W
Itararé	35	24.07 S	49.20 W
Itasca	45	32.10 N	97.09 W
Itasca State Park ♠	46	47.18 N	95.18 W
Ithaca	38	42.27 N	76.30 W
Ituiutaba	33	18.58 S	49.28 W
Itumbiara	35	18.25 S	49.13 W
Itzehoe	7	53.55 N	9.31 E
Ivano-Frankovsk	11	48.55 N	24.43 E
Ivanovo	12	57.00 N	40.59 E
Ivdel'	13	60.42 N	60.24 E

Name	Map No.	Lat ° ′	Long ° ′
Ivory Coast □[1]	14	8.00 N	5.00 W
Iwaki (Taira)	23	37.03 N	140.55 E
Iwakuni	23	34.09 N	132.11 E
Iwo	14	7.38 N	4.11 E
Iževsk	4	56.51 N	53.14 E
İzmir	11	38.25 N	27.09 E

J

Name	Map No.	Lat ° ′	Long ° ′
Jabalpur	21	23.10 N	79.57 E
Jablonec nad Nisou	7	50.44 N	15.10 E
Jacarèzinho	35	23.09 S	49.59 W
Jacksboro	45	33.13 N	98.10 W
Jackson, Mich., U.S.	42	42.15 N	84.24 W
Jackson, Miss., U.S.	44	32.18 N	90.12 W
Jackson, Mo., U.S.	44	37.23 N	89.40 W
Jackson, Tenn., U.S.	44	35.37 N	88.49 W
Jackson Lake ⊜[1]	48	43.55 N	110.40 W
Jacksonville, Ark., U.S.	44	34.52 N	92.07 W
Jacksonville, Fla., U.S.	43	30.20 N	81.40 W
Jacksonville, Ill., U.S.	44	39.44 N	90.14 W
Jacksonville, N.C., U.S.	43	34.45 N	77.26 W
Jacksonville, Tex., U.S.	45	31.58 N	95.17 W
Jacobābād	21	28.17 N	68.26 E
Jacques-Cartier, Détroit de ⋓	41	50.00 N	63.30 W
Jacques-Cartier, Mont ∧	41	48.59 N	65.57 W
Jaén	9	37.46 N	3.47 W
Jaffna	20	9.40 N	80.00 E
Jaipur	21	26.55 N	75.49 E
Jakarta	25	6.10 S	106.48 E
Jakobstad (Pietarsaari)	6	63.40 N	22.42 E
Jakutsk	13	62.13 N	129.49 E
Jalālābād	21	34.26 N	70.28 E
Jalapa Enríquez	31	19.32 N	96.55 W
Jamaica □[1]	32	18.15 N	77.30 W
Jamal, Poluostrov ≻[1]	13	70.00 N	70.00 E
Jambi	25	1.36 S	103.37 E
Jambol	11	42.29 N	26.30 E
James ≃	46	42.52 N	97.18 W
James Bay C	36	53.30 N	80.30 W
Jamestown, Ky., U.S.	44	36.59 N	85.04 W
Jamestown, N. Dak., U.S.	46	46.54 N	98.42 W
Jamestown, N.Y., U.S.	38	42.06 N	79.14 W
Jammu and Kashmir □[2]	21	34.00 N	76.00 E
Jāmnagar	21	22.28 N	70.04 E
Jamshedpur	21	22.48 N	86.11 E
Jamuna ≃	21	23.51 N	89.45 E
Janesville	42	42.41 N	89.01 W
Japan □[1]	22	36.00 N	138.00 E
Japan, Sea of ▾[2]	22	40.00 N	135.00 E
Japurá (Caquetá) ≃	33	3.08 S	64.46 W
Jaroslavl'	12	57.37 N	39.52 E
Jarosław	7	50.02 N	22.42 E
Jasper, Ala., U.S.	44	33.50 N	87.17 W
Jasper, Tex., U.S.	44	30.55 N	94.01 W
Jataí	35	17.53 S	51.43 W
Java Sea → Jawa, laut ▾[2]	25	5.00 S	110.00 E
Jawa (Java) I	25	7.30 S	110.00 E
Jawa, Laut (Java Sea) ▾[2]	25	5.00 S	110.00 E
Jay	45	36.25 N	94.48 W
Jaya, Puncak ∧	25	4.05 S	137.11 E
Jayapura (Sukarnapura)	25	2.32 S	140.42 E
Jefferson	44	32.46 N	94.21 W
Jefferson City	44	38.34 N	92.10 W
Jelenia Góra (Hirschberg)	7	50.55 N	15.46 E
Jena	7	50.56 N	11.35 E
Jenisej ≃	13	71.50 N	82.40 E
Jenisejsk	13	58.27 N	92.10 E
Jennings	44	30.13 N	92.39 W
Jequié	33	13.51 S	40.05 W
Jérémie	32	18.39 N	74.07 W
Jerez de la Frontera	9	36.41 N	6.08 W
Jerome	48	42.43 N	114.31 W
Jersey □[2]	8	49.15 N	2.10 W
Jersey City	38	40.44 N	74.02 W
Jerusalem → Yerushalayim	18	31.46 N	35.14 E
Jessore	21	23.10 N	89.13 E
Jetmore	46	38.03 N	99.54 W
Jhang Maghiāna	19	31.16 N	72.19 E
Jhānsi	21	25.26 N	78.35 E
Jhelum	21	32.56 N	73.44 E
Jiddah	17	21.30 N	39.12 E
Jilin	22	43.51 N	126.33 E
Jima	17	7.36 N	36.50 E
Jinan (Tsinan)	22	36.40 N	116.57 E
Jinshajiang (Yangtze) ≃	26	26.40 N	102.55 E
Jinzhou	22	41.07 N	121.08 E
Jirjā	14	26.20 N	31.53 E
Jixi	22	45.17 N	130.59 E
João Pessoa	33	7.07 S	34.52 W
Jodhpur	21	26.17 N	73.02 E
Joensuu	6	62.36 N	29.46 E
Johannesburg	16	26.15 S	28.00 E
John Day	48	44.25 N	118.57 W
John Day ≃	48	45.44 N	120.39 W
Johnson City	43	36.19 N	82.21 W
Johnstown	38	40.20 N	78.55 W
Johor Baharu	26	1.28 N	103.45 E
Joinvile	34	26.18 S	48.50 W
Joliet	42	41.32 N	88.05 W
Joliette	38	46.01 N	73.27 W
Jolo Island I	25	5.58 N	121.06 E
Jonesboro	44	35.50 N	90.42 W
Jonesport	41	44.32 N	67.36 W
Jönköping	6	57.47 N	14.11 E
Jonquière	41	48.24 N	71.15 W
Joplin	44	37.06 N	94.31 W
Jordan □[1]	18	31.00 N	36.00 E
Jos	14	9.55 N	8.53 E
Joškar-Ola	4	56.38 N	47.52 E
Juan de Fuca, Strait of ⋓	48	48.18 N	124.00 W
Juàzeiro do Norte	33	7.12 S	39.20 W
Jūbā	14	4.51 N	31.37 E
Juba ≃	17	0.12 N	42.40 E
Juiz de Fora	33	21.45 S	43.20 W
Juliaca	33	15.30 S	70.08 W
Juliana Top ∧	33	3.41 N	56.32 W
Julianehåb	36	60.43 N	46.01 W
Jullundur	21	31.19 N	75.34 E
Junction	45	30.29 N	99.46 W
Juneau	40	58.20 N	134.27 W
Jungfrau ∧	8	46.32 N	7.58 E
Juniata ≃	42	40.24 N	77.01 W
Jura ⋀⋀	8	46.45 N	6.30 E
Juticalpa	32	14.42 N	86.15 W
Juventud, Isla de la (Isla de Pinos) I	32	21.40 N	82.50 W
Južno-Sachalinsk	13	46.58 N	142.42 E
Jylland ≻[1]	6	56.00 N	9.15 E
Jyväskylä	6	62.14 N	25.44 E

K

Name	Map No.	Lat ° ′	Long ° ′
Kaap Plato ⋀⋀[1]	16	28.20 S	23.57 E
Kābul	21	34.31 N	69.12 E
Kabwe (Broken Hill)	15	14.27 S	28.27 E
Kaduna	14	10.33 N	7.27 E
Kadykčan	13	63.02 N	146.50 E
Kaédi	14	16.09 N	13.30 W
Kaesŏng	22	37.59 N	126.33 E
Kagoshima	23	31.36 N	130.33 E
Kahoolawe I	39a	20.33 N	156.37 W
Kaikoura	29	42.25 S	173.41 E
Kailua Kona	39a	19.39 N	155.59 W
Kaitangata	29	46.18 S	169.51 E
Kaiwi Channel ⋓	39a	21.15 N	157.30 W
Kajaani	6	64.14 N	27.41 E
Kalahari Desert ✦[2]	15	24.00 S	21.30 E
Kalakan	13	55.08 N	116.45 E
Kalámai	11	37.04 N	22.07 E
Kalamazoo	42	42.17 N	85.32 W
Kalasin	26	16.29 N	103.30 E
Kalemie (Albertville)	15	5.56 S	29.12 E
Kalgoorlie	27	30.45 S	121.28 E
Kalinin	12	56.52 N	35.55 E
Kaliningrad (Königsberg)	12	54.43 N	20.30 E
Kalispell	48	48.12 N	114.19 W
Kalmar	6	56.40 N	16.22 E
Kaluga	12	54.31 N	36.16 E
Kamaishi	23	39.16 N	141.53 E
Kamālia	21	30.44 N	72.39 E
Kamčatka, Poluostrov ≻[1]	13	56.00 N	160.00 E
Kamen'-na-Obi	13	53.47 N	81.20 E
Kamensk-Ural'skij	13	56.28 N	61.54 E
Kamina	15	8.44 S	25.00 E
Kamloops	36	50.40 N	120.20 W
Kampala	15	0.19 N	32.25 E
Kamphaeng Phet	26	16.28 N	99.30 E
Kâmpóng Cham	26	12.00 N	105.27 E
Kâmpóng Chhnăng	26	12.15 N	104.40 E

Name	Map No.	Lat ° '	Long ° '
Kiribati □[1]	1	4.00 S	175.00 E
Kirinia	18	35.20 N	33.19 E
Kirkcaldy	5	56.07 N	3.10 W
Kirkland Lake	42	48.09 N	80.02 W
Kırklareli	11	41.44 N	27.12 E
Kirksville	44	40.12 N	92.35 W
Kirkūk	17	35.28 N	44.28 E
Kirkwall	5	58.59 N	2.58 W
Kirovograd	4	48.30 N	32.18 E
Kiruna	6	67.51 N	20.16 E
Kiryū	23	36.24 N	139.20 E
Kisangani (Stanleyville)	15	0.30 N	25.12 E
Kishiwada	23	34.28 N	135.22 E
Kišin'ov	4	47.00 N	28.50 E
Kitakyūshū	23	33.53 N	130.50 E
Kitami	23a	43.48 N	143.54 E
Kitchener	42	43.27 N	80.29 W
Kithira I	11	36.20 N	22.58 E
Kitwe	15	12.49 S	28.13 E
Kıyıköy	11	41.38 N	28.05 E
Kjustendil	11	42.17 N	22.41 E
Kladno	7	50.08 N	14.05 E
Klagenfurt	7	46.38 N	14.18 E
Klamath ≃	39	41.33 N	124.04 W
Klamath Falls	48	42.13 N	121.46 W
Klamath Mountains ⋏	39	41.40 N	123.20 W
Klerksdorp	16	26.58 S	26.39 E
Klipdale	16	34.19 S	19.57 E
Kłodzko	7	50.27 N	16.39 E
Klondike □[9]	40	63.30 N	139.00 W
Kluane Lake ◎	36	61.15 N	138.40 W
Kl'učevskaja Sopka, Vulkan ⋏[1]	13	56.04 N	160.38 E
Knoxville	43	35.58 N	83.56 W
Knysna	16	34.02 S	23.02 E
Kōbe	23	34.41 N	135.10 E
København (Copenhagen)	6	55.40 N	12.35 E
Koblenz	7	50.21 N	7.35 E
Kobrin	12	52.13 N	24.21 E
Kōchi	23	33.33 N	133.33 E
Kodiak	40	57.48 N	152.23 W
Kodiak Island I	40	57.30 N	153.30 W
Kōfu	23	35.39 N	138.35 E
Kokomo	44	40.29 N	86.08 W
Kokstad	16	30.32 S	29.29 E
Kolhāpur	20	16.42 N	74.13 E
Koliganek	40	59.48 N	157.25 W
Köln (Cologne)	7	50.56 N	6.59 E
Kolpaševo	13	58.20 N	82.50 E
Kol'skij Poluostrov (Kola Peninsula) ≻[1]	13	67.30 N	37.00 E
Kolwezi	15	10.43 S	25.28 E
Kolyma ≃	13	69.30 N	161.00 E
Komárno	7	47.45 N	18.09 E
Komatsu	23	36.24 N	136.27 E
Kommunizma, Pik ⋏	19	38.57 N	72.01 E
Komotini	11	41.08 N	25.25 E
Komsomolec, Ostrov I	13	80.30 N	95.00 E
Komsomol'sk-na-Amure	13	50.35 N	137.02 E
Kona Coast •[2]	39a	19.25 N	155.55 W
Koné	30b	21.04 S	164.52 E
Konin	7	52.13 N	18.16 E
Konstanz	7	47.40 N	9.10 E
Koocanusa, Lake ◎[1]	48	49.00 N	115.10 W
Kootenai ≃	48	49.15 N	117.39 W
Kor'akskoje Nagorje ⋏	13	62.30 N	172.00 E
Korçë	11	40.37 N	20.46 E
Korea, North □[1]	22	40.00 N	127.00 E
Korea, South □[1]	22	36.30 N	128.00 E
Korf	13	60.19 N	165.50 E
Korinthiakós Kólpos C	11	38.19 N	22.04 E
Kōriyama	23	37.24 N	140.23 E
Korkino	4	54.54 N	61.23 E
Korolevu	30c	18.13 S	177.44 E
Koro Sea ▽[2]	30c	18.00 S	179.50 E
Kos I	11	36.50 N	27.10 E
Koš-Agač	13	50.00 N	88.40 E
Kosciusko, Mount ⋏	28	36.27 S	148.16 E
Košice	7	48.43 N	21.15 E
Kosovska Mitrovica	11	42.53 N	20.52 E
Kostroma	12	57.46 N	40.55 E
Koszalin (Köslin)	7	54.12 N	16.09 E
Kota Baharu	26	6.08 N	102.15 E
Kotel'nyj, Ostrov I	13	75.45 N	138.44 E
Kotka	6	60.28 N	26.55 E
Kotuj ≃	13	71.55 N	102.05 E
Kotzebue Sound ⋃	40	66.20 N	163.00 W
Koussi, Emi ⋏	14	19.50 N	18.30 E
Kouvola	6	60.52 N	26.42 E
Kowloon (Jiulong)	24	22.18 N	114.10 E
Koyukuk ≃	40	64.56 N	157.30 W
Koza	23b	26.20 N	127.50 E
Kra, Isthmus of ●[3]	26	10.20 N	99.00 E
Krāchèh	26	12.29 N	106.01 E
Kragujevac	11	44.01 N	20.55 E
Kraków	7	50.03 N	19.58 E
Kraljevo	11	43.43 N	20.41 E
Kranj	10	46.15 N	14.21 E
Krasnodar	4	45.02 N	39.00 E
Krasnojarsk	13	56.01 N	92.50 E
Krasnosel'kup	13	65.41 N	82.28 E
Krasnoural'sk	13	58.21 N	60.03 E
Krems an der Donau	7	48.25 N	15.36 E
Krishna ≃	20	15.57 N	80.59 E
Kristiansand	6	58.10 N	8.00 E
Kristiansund	6	63.07 N	7.45 E
Kríti I	11	35.29 N	24.42 E
Kritikòn Pélagos ▽[2]	11	35.46 N	23.54 E
Krivoj Rog	4	47.55 N	33.21 E
Kroonstad	16	27.46 S	27.12 E
Kropotkin	13	58.30 N	115.17 E
Kruidfontein	16	32.51 S	21.57 E
Krung Thep (Bangkok)	26	13.45 N	100.31 E
Kruševac	11	43.35 N	21.20 E
Kuala Lumpur	26	3.10 N	101.42 E
Kuala Terengganu	26	5.20 N	103.08 E
Kuching	26	1.33 N	110.20 E
Kuitan	24	23.05 N	115.58 E
Kuito	15	12.22 S	16.56 E
Kujbyšev, S.S.S.R.	4	53.12 N	50.09 E
Kujbyšev, S.S.S.R.	13	55.27 N	78.19 E
Kula Kangri ⋏	21	28.03 N	90.27 E
Kumagaya	23	36.08 N	139.23 E
Kumamoto	23	32.48 N	130.43 E
Kumanovo	11	42.08 N	21.43 E
Kumasi	14	6.41 N	1.35 W
Kumo	14	10.03 N	11.13 E
Kunlunshanmai ⋏	19	36.30 N	88.00 E
Kunming	22	25.05 N	102.40 E
Kupang	26	10.10 S	123.35 E
Kupino	13	54.22 N	77.18 E
Kurashiki	23	34.35 N	133.46 E
Kure	23	34.14 N	132.34 E
Kurgan	13	55.26 N	65.18 E
Kuril Islands → Kuril'skije Ostrova II	13	46.10 N	152.00 E
Kuril'skije Ostrova (Kuril Islands) **II**	13	46.10 N	152.00 E
Kursk	4	51.42 N	36.12 E
Kuruman	16	27.28 S	23.28 E
Kurume	23	33.19 N	130.31 E
Kurumkan	13	54.18 N	110.18 E
Kuskokwim ≃	40	60.17 N	162.27 W
Kustanaj	4	53.10 N	63.35 E
Kūstī	14	13.10 N	32.40 E
Kutaisi	4	42.15 N	42.40 E
Kutch, Gulf of C	21	22.36 N	69.30 E
Kutno	7	52.15 N	19.23 E
Kuwait □[1]	17	29.30 N	47.45 E
Kuybyshev → Kujbyšev	4	53.12 N	50.09 E
Kwangju	22	35.09 N	126.54 E
Kyaukpyu	26	19.05 N	93.52 E
Kyle of Lochalsh	5	57.17 N	5.43 W
Kyoga, Lake ◎	15	1.30 N	33.00 E
Kyōto	23	35.00 N	135.45 E
Kyštym	4	55.42 N	60.34 E
Kyūshū I	23	33.00 N	131.00 E
Kyzyl	13	51.42 N	94.27 E

L

Labrador ◆[1]	36	54.00 N	62.00 W
Labrador City	36	52.57 N	66.55 W
Labrador Sea ▽[2]	36	57.00 N	53.00 W
Labutta	26	16.09 N	94.46 E
Laccadive Islands II	20	10.00 N	73.00 E
La Ceiba	32	15.47 N	86.50 W
Lac-giao	26	12.40 N	108.03 E
Lachlan ≃	28	34.21 S	143.57 E
La Chorrera	32	8.53 N	79.47 W
Lac la Biche	36	54.46 N	111.58 W
Lac-Mégantic	41	45.36 N	70.53 W
Laconia	38	43.31 N	71.29 W

Name	Map No.	Lat ° ′	Long ° ′
La Coruña	9	43.22 N	8.23 W
La Crosse	42	43.49 N	91.15 W
Ladoga, Lake → Ladožskoje Ozero ⊜	6	61.00 N	31.30 E
Ladožskoje Ozero (Lake Ladoga) ⊜	6	61.00 N	31.30 E
Ladybrand	16	29.19 S	27.25 E
Ladysmith	16	28.34 S	29.45 E
Lafayette, Ala., U.S.	43	32.54 N	85.24 W
Lafayette, Ind., U.S.	44	40.25 N	86.53 W
Lafayette, La., U.S.	44	30.14 N	92.01 W
La Follette	43	36.23 N	84.07 W
Laghouat	14	33.50 N	2.59 E
Lagos	14	6.27 N	3.24 E
La Grange, Ga., U.S.	43	33.02 N	85.02 W
Lagrange, Ind., U.S.	44	41.39 N	85.25 W
La Grange, Tex., U.S.	45	29.54 N	96.52 W
La Guajira, Peninsula de ≻[1]	33	12.00 N	71.40 W
Laguna Beach	39	33.33 N	117.51 W
La Habana (Havana)	32	23.08 N	82.22 W
Lahaina	39a	20.52 N	156.41 W
Lahore	19	31.35 N	74.18 E
Lahti	6	60.58 N	25.40 E
La Junta	46	37.59 N	103.33 W
Lake Charles	44	30.13 N	93.12 W
Lake City, Fla., U.S.	43	30.12 N	82.38 W
Lake City, S.C., U.S.	43	33.52 N	79.45 W
Lake Geneva	42	42.36 N	88.26 W
Lake Havasu City	47	34.27 N	114.22 W
Lake Jackson	45	29.02 N	95.27 W
Lakeland	43	28.03 N	81.57 W
Lake Oswego	48	45.26 N	122.39 W
Lakewood Center	48	47.10 N	122.31 W
La Loche	36	56.29 N	109.27 W
La Mancha ◆[1]	9	39.05 N	3.00 W
Lamap	30b	16.26 S	167.43 E
Lamar, Colo., U.S.	46	38.05 N	102.37 W
Lamar, Mo., U.S.	44	37.29 N	94.17 W
La Marque	44	29.22 N	94.58 W
Lambaréné	15	0.42 S	10.13 E
Lambasa	30c	16.26 S	179.24 E
Lamesa	45	32.44 N	101.57 W
Lamont	39	35.15 N	118.55 W
Lampang	26	18.18 N	99.31 E
Lamphun	26	18.35 N	99.01 E
Lanai I	39a	20.50 N	156.55 W
Lanai City	39a	20.50 N	156.55 W
Lancaster, Eng., U.K.	5	54.03 N	2.48 W
Lancaster, Calif., U.S.	39	34.42 N	118.08 W
Lancaster, Ohio, U.S.	38	39.43 N	82.36 W
Lancaster, Pa., U.S.	38	40.02 N	76.19 W
Lancaster Sound ⩊	36	74.13 N	84.00 W
Lanchow → Lanzhou	22	36.03 N	103.41 E
Land Between the Lakes ◆	44	36.55 N	88.05 W
Lander	48	42.50 N	108.44 W
Land's End ≻	5	50.03 N	5.44 W
Langdon	46	48.46 N	98.22 W
Langenhagen	7	52.27 N	9.44 E
Langsa	26	4.28 N	97.58 E
L'Annonciation	38	46.25 N	74.52 W
Lansing	42	42.43 N	84.34 W
Lanzhou	22	36.03 N	103.41 E
Laoag	25	18.12 N	120.36 E
Laos □[1]	25	18.00 N	105.00 E
La Paz, Bol.	33	16.30 S	68.09 W
La Paz, Méx.	31	24.10 N	110.18 W
La Perouse Strait (Sōya-kaikyō) ⩊	23a	45.45 N	142.00 E
La Piedad [Cavadas]	31	20.21 N	102.00 W
Lapland ◆[1]	6	68.00 N	25.00 E
La Plata	34	34.55 S	57.57 W
La Pocatière	41	47.22 N	68.41 W
Lappeenranta	6	61.04 N	28.11 E
Laptev Sea → Laptevych, More ▾[2]	13	76.00 N	126.00 E
Laptevych, More (Laptev Sea) ▾[2]	13	76.00 N	126.00 E
L'Aquila	10	42.22 N	13.22 E
Laramie	46	41.19 N	105.35 W
Laramie Mountains ⋀	47	42.00 N	105.40 W
Laredo	45	27.31 N	99.30 W
La Rioja	34	29.26 S	66.51 W
Lárisa	11	39.38 N	22.25 E
Lārkāna	21	27.33 N	68.13 E
Larne	5	54.51 N	5.49 W
La Rochelle	8	46.10 N	1.10 W
La Roche-sur-Yon	8	46.40 N	1.26 W
La Ronge	36	55.06 N	105.17 W
Lasa (Lhasa)	22	29.40 N	91.09 E
La Salle	42	41.20 N	89.06 W
La Sarre	36	48.48 N	79.12 W
Las Cruces	47	32.23 N	106.29 W
Las Minas, Cerro Λ	32	14.33 N	88.39 W
Las Palmas de Gran Canaria	14	28.06 N	15.24 W
La Spezia	10	44.07 N	9.50 E
Lassen Peak Λ[1]	39	40.29 N	121.31 W
Las Vegas, Nev., U.S.	39	36.11 N	115.08 W
Las Vegas, N. Mex., U.S.	47	35.36 N	105.13 W
Latina	10	41.28 N	12.52 E
Latta	43	34.21 N	79.26 W
La Tuque	36	47.26 N	72.47 W
Lātūr	20	18.24 N	76.35 E
Lauchhammer	7	51.30 N	13.47 E
Launceston	27	41.26 S	147.08 E
La Union	32	13.20 N	87.57 W
Laurel, Miss., U.S.	44	31.42 N	89.08 W
Laurel, Mont., U.S.	48	45.40 N	108.46 W
Laurel Bay	43	32.27 N	80.48 W
Lausanne	8	46.31 N	6.38 E
Lautoka	30c	17.37 S	177.27 E
Laval, Qué., Can.	38	45.33 N	73.44 W
Laval, Fr.	8	48.04 N	0.46 W
Laverne	45	36.43 N	99.54 W
Lavras	35	21.14 S	45.00 W
Lawrence	46	38.58 N	95.14 W
Lawton	45	34.37 N	98.25 W
Layton	47	41.04 N	111.58 W
Leadville	47	39.15 N	106.20 W
Leamington	42	42.03 N	82.36 W
Leavenworth, Kans., U.S.	46	39.19 N	94.55 W
Leavenworth, Wash., U.S.	48	47.36 N	120.40 W
Lebanon, Mo., U.S.	44	37.41 N	92.40 W
Lebanon, Pa., U.S.	38	40.20 N	76.25 W
Lebanon, Tenn., U.S.	44	36.12 N	86.18 W
Lebanon, Va., U.S.	43	36.54 N	82.05 W
Lebanon □[1]	18	33.50 N	35.50 E
Lecce	10	40.23 N	18.11 E
Lecco	10	45.51 N	9.23 E
Lecompte	44	31.05 N	92.24 W
Leeds	5	53.50 N	1.35 W
Leesburg	43	28.49 N	81.53 W
Leeward Islands II	32	17.00 N	63.00 W
Legnica (Liegnitz)	7	51.13 N	16.09 E
Le Havre	8	49.30 N	0.08 E
Leicester	5	52.38 N	1.05 W
Leinster □[9]	5	53.05 N	7.00 W
Leipzig	7	51.19 N	12.20 E
Leitchfield	44	37.29 N	86.18 W
Le Mans	8	48.00 N	0.12 E
Leme	35	22.12 S	47.24 W
Lemesós (Limassol)	18	34.40 N	33.02 E
Lemhi Range ⋀	48	44.30 N	113.25 W
Lemmon	46	45.56 N	102.10 W
Lena ≃	13	72.25 N	126.40 E
Lenakel	30b	19.32 S	169.16 E
Leninakan	4	40.48 N	43.50 E
Leningrad	12	59.55 N	30.15 E
Leninsk-Kuzneckij	13	54.38 N	86.10 E
Lenoir	43	35.55 N	81.32 W
Lenoir City	43	35.48 N	84.16 W
Lenox	46	40.53 N	94.34 W
Lens	8	50.26 N	2.50 E
Lensk	13	61.00 N	114.50 E
Leoben	7	47.23 N	15.06 E
León, Esp.	9	42.36 N	5.34 W
León, Nic.	32	12.26 N	86.53 W
León [de los Aldamas]	31	21.07 N	101.40 W
Leonora	27	28.53 S	121.20 E
Leopoldina	35	21.32 S	42.38 W
Leoti	46	38.29 N	101.21 W
Lérida	9	41.37 N	0.37 E
Lerwick	5	60.09 N	1.09 W
Lesbos → Lésvos I	11	39.10 N	26.20 E
Les Cayes	32	18.12 N	73.45 W
Leskovac	11	42.59 N	21.57 E
Lesotho □[1]	15	29.30 S	28.30 E
Lesozavodsk	13	45.28 N	133.27 E
Lesser Antilles II	32	15.00 N	61.00 W
Lesser Sunda Islands II	25	9.00 S	120.00 E
Le Sueur	42	44.27 N	93.54 W
Lésvos I	11	39.10 N	26.20 E
Leszno	7	51.51 N	16.35 E
Lethbridge	36	49.42 N	112.50 W

Name	Map No.	Lat	Long
Levelland	45	33.35 N	102.23 W
Leverkusen	7	51.03 N	6.59 E
Levin	29	40.37 S	175.17 E
Lévis	41	46.48 N	71.11 W
Levittown	38	40.09 N	74.50 W
Levkás I	11	38.39 N	20.27 E
Levkosia (Nicosia)	18	35.10 N	33.22 E
Lewis, Isle of I	5	58.10 N	6.40 W
Lewisburg	44	35.27 N	86.48 W
Lewis Range ⩕	48	48.30 N	113.15 W
Lewiston, Idaho, U.S.	48	46.25 N	117.01 W
Lewiston, Maine, U.S.	38	44.06 N	70.13 W
Lewistown, Mont., U.S.	48	47.04 N	109.26 W
Lewistown, Pa., U.S.	38	40.36 N	77.31 W
Lexington, Ky., U.S.	43	38.03 N	84.30 W
Lexington, N.C., U.S.	43	35.49 N	80.15 W
Leyte I	25	10.50 N	124.50 E
Lhasa			
→ Lasa	22	29.40 N	91.09 E
Liaoyuan	22	42.54 N	125.07 E
Libby	48	48.23 N	115.33 W
Liberal	46	37.02 N	100.55 W
Liberec	7	50.46 N	15.03 E
Liberia	32	10.38 N	85.27 W
Liberia □¹	14	6.00 N	10.00 W
Libreville	15	0.23 N	9.27 E
Libya □¹	14	27.00 N	17.00 E
Licata	10	37.05 N	13.56 E
Lichtenburg	16	26.08 S	26.08 E
Liechtenstein □¹	4	47.09 N	9.35 E
Liège	7	50.38 N	5.34 E
Liepāja	12	56.31 N	21.01 E
Lier	7	51.08 N	4.34 E
Ligurian Sea ⲧ²	8	43.00 N	8.00 E
Lihue	39a	21.59 N	159.22 W
Likasi (Jadotville)	15	10.59 S	26.44 E
Lille	8	50.38 N	3.04 E
Lilongwe	15	13.59 S	33.44 E
Lima, Perú	33	12.03 S	77.03 W
Lima, Ohio, U.S.	38	40.46 N	84.06 W
Limeira	35	22.34 S	47.24 W
Limerick	5	52.40 N	8.38 W
Limnos I	11	39.54 N	25.21 E
Limoges	8	45.50 N	1.16 E
Limón, C.R.	32	10.00 N	83.02 W
Limón, Hond.	32	15.52 N	85.33 W
Limon, Colo., U.S.	46	39.16 N	103.41 W
Limpopo ⩳	16	25.15 S	33.30 E
Linares, Esp.	9	38.05 N	3.38 W
Lincoln, Eng., U.K.	5	53.14 N	0.33 W
Lincoln, Ill., U.S.	44	40.09 N	89.22 W
Lincoln, Kans., U.S.	46	39.02 N	98.09 W
Lincoln, Nebr., U.S.	46	40.48 N	96.42 W
Linden	44	32.18 N	87.47 W
Lindi	15	10.00 S	39.43 E
Lindsay	45	34.50 N	97.38 W
Lingga, Kepulauan II	25	0.05 S	104.35 E
Lingling	26	26.11 N	111.29 E
Linköping	6	58.25 N	15.37 E
Lins	35	21.40 S	49.45 W
Linton	46	46.16 N	100.14 W
Linz	7	48.18 N	14.18 E
Lion, Golfe du C	8	43.00 N	4.00 E
Lipeck	12	52.37 N	39.35 E
Lippstadt	7	51.40 N	8.19 E
Lisboa (Lisbon)	9	38.43 N	9.08 W
Lisbon			
→ Lisboa, Port.	9	38.43 N	9.08 W
Lisbon, N. Dak., U.S.	46	46.27 N	97.41 W
Lismore	27	28.48 S	153.17 E
Listowel	42	43.44 N	80.57 W
Litchfield	44	39.11 N	89.39 W
Little Missouri ⩳	36	47.30 N	102.25 W
Little Rock	44	34.44 N	92.15 W
Littleton	47	39.37 N	105.01 W
Liuzhou	22	24.22 N	109.32 E
Live Oak	43	30.18 N	82.59 W
Livermore Falls	38	44.28 N	70.11 W
Liverpool	5	53.25 N	2.55 W
Livingston, Mont., U.S.	48	45.40 N	110.34 W
Livingston, Tex., U.S.	44	30.43 N	94.56 W
Livingstone	15	17.50 S	25.53 E
Livonia	42	42.25 N	83.23 W
Livorno (Leghorn)	10	43.33 N	10.19 E
Ljubljana	10	46.03 N	14.31 E
Llanos ⪥	33	5.00 N	70.00 W
Lloydminster	36	53.17 N	110.00 W
Lobito	15	12.20 S	13.34 E
Lochgilphead	5	56.03 N	5.26 W
Lochinver	5	58.09 N	5.15 W
Lockhart	45	29.53 N	97.41 W
Lock Haven	38	41.08 N	77.27 W
Lockport	38	43.10 N	78.42 W
Lodi	39	38.08 N	121.16 W
Łódź	7	51.46 N	19.30 E
Lofoten II	6	68.30 N	15.00 E
Logan	47	41.44 N	111.50 W
Logan, Mount ⩕	40	60.34 N	140.24 W
Logansport	44	40.45 N	86.21 W
Logroño	9	42.28 N	2.27 W
Loire ⩳	8	47.16 N	2.11 W
Loja	33	4.00 S	79.13 W
Lolo Pass)(	48	46.38 N	114.35 W
Lom	11	43.49 N	23.14 E
Lombok I	25	8.45 S	116.30 E
Lomé	14	6.08 N	1.13 E
Lompoc	39	34.38 N	120.27 W
Łomża	7	53.11 N	22.05 E
London, Ont., Can.	42	42.59 N	81.14 W
London, Eng., U.K.	5	51.30 N	0.10 W
London, Ky., U.S.	43	37.08 N	84.05 W
Londonderry	5	55.00 N	7.19 W
Londrina	35	23.18 S	51.09 W
Long Beach	39	33.46 N	118.11 W
Long Branch	38	40.18 N	74.00 W
Long Island I, Ba.	32	23.15 N	75.07 W
Long Island I, N.Y., U.S.	38	40.50 N	73.00 W
Long Point ⳝ¹	42	42.34 N	80.15 W
Long Prairie	46	45.59 N	94.52 W
Longview, Tex., U.S.	44	32.30 N	94.44 W
Longview, Wash., U.S.	48	46.08 N	122.57 W
Long-xuyen	26	10.23 N	105.25 E
Lop Buri	26	14.48 N	100.37 E
Lorain	38	41.28 N	82.10 W
Lorca	9	37.40 N	1.42 W
Lord Howe Island I	27	31.33 S	159.05 E
Lordsburg	47	32.21 N	108.43 W
Lorient	8	47.45 N	3.22 W
Lorraine □⁹	8	49.00 N	6.00 E
Los Alamos	47	35.53 N	106.19 W
Los Angeles	39	34.03 N	118.15 W
Los Banos	39	37.04 N	120.51 W
Los Mochis	31	25.45 N	108.57 W
Lost River Range ⩕	48	44.10 N	113.35 W
Lost Trail Pass)(	48	45.41 N	113.57 W
Louang Namtha	26	20.57 N	101.25 E
Louangphrabang	26	19.52 N	102.08 E
Louisiana □³	37	31.15 N	92.15 W
Louis Trichardt	16	23.01 S	29.43 E
Louisville, Ky., U.S.	44	38.16 N	85.45 W
Louisville, Miss., U.S.	44	33.07 N	89.03 W
Loup City	46	41.17 N	98.58 W
Lourdes	8	43.06 N	0.03 W
Lourenço Marques			
→ Maputo	15	25.58 S	32.35 E
Lovec	11	43.08 N	24.43 E
Loveland	46	40.24 N	105.05 W
Lovelock	39	40.11 N	118.28 W
Lowell	38	42.39 N	71.18 W
Lower Hutt	29	41.13 S	174.55 E
Lower Red Lake ⬙	46	48.00 N	94.50 W
Loyalty Islands			
→ Loyauté,îles II	30b	21.00 S	167.00 E
Loyauté, Îles (Loyality Islands) II	30b	21.00 S	167.00 E
Lualaba ⩳	15	0.26 N	25.20 E
Luanda	15	8.48 S	13.14 E
Luanshya	15	13.08 S	28.24 E
Lubango	15	14.55 S	13.30 E
Lubbock	45	33.35 N	101.51 W
Lübeck	7	53.52 N	10.40 E
Lublin	7	51.15 N	22.35 E
Lubudi	15	6.51 S	21.18 E
Lubumbashi (Élisabethville)	15	11.40 S	27.28 E
Lucedale	44	30.55 N	88.35 W
Luchiang	24	24.03 N	120.25 E
Luckenwalde	7	52.05 N	13.10 E
Lucknow	21	26.51 N	80.55 E
Lüda (Dairen)	22	38.53 N	121.35 E
Lüderitz	16	26.38 S	15.10 E
Ludhiāna	21	30.54 N	75.51 E
Ludington	42	43.57 N	86.27 W
Ludlow	38	43.24 N	72.42 W
Ludwigsburg	7	48.53 N	9.11 E
Ludwigshafen	7	49.29 N	8.26 E

Name	Map No.	Lat °′	Long °′
Lufkin	44	31.20 N	94.44 W
Luganville	30b	15.32 S	167.08 E
Lugo	9	43.00 N	7.34 W
Lugoj	11	45.41 N	21.54 E
Luleå	6	65.34 N	22.10 E
Luleälven ≃	6	65.35 N	22.03 E
Lüleburgaz	11	41.24 N	27.21 E
Lumberton, Miss., U.S.	44	31.00 N	89.27 W
Lumberton, N.C., U.S.	43	34.37 N	79.00 W
Lund	6	55.42 N	13.11 E
Lüneburg	7	53.15 N	10.23 E
Lunenburg	41	44.23 N	64.19 W
Luoyang	22	34.41 N	112.28 E
Lupeni	11	45.22 N	23.13 E
Luray	38	38.40 N	78.28 W
Lusaka	15	15.25 S	28.17 E
Lushnje	11	40.56 N	19.42 E
Lūt, Dasht-e ⟿²	17	33.00 N	57.00 E
Luton	5	51.53 N	0.25 W
Lutzville	16	31.33 S	18.22 E
Luverne	44	31.43 N	86.16 W
Luxembourg	7	49.36 N	6.09 E
Luxembourg □¹	4	49.45 N	6.05 E
Luzhou	22	28.54 N	105.27 E
Luzon I	25	16.00 N	121.00 E
L'vov	4	49.50 N	24.00 E
Lyallpur	19	31.25 N	73.05 E
Lynchburg	43	37.24 N	79.10 W
Lynn	38	42.28 N	70.57 W
Lynn Lake	36	56.51 N	101.03 W
Lyon	8	45.45 N	4.51 E
M			
Ma'ān	18	30.12 N	35.44 E
Maastricht	7	50.52 N	5.43 E
Macaé	35	22.23 S	41.47 W
McAlester	45	34.56 N	95.46 W
McAllen	45	26.12 N	98.15 W
Macapá	33	0.02 N	51.03 W
Macau (Aomen)	24	22.14 N	113.35 E
Macau □²	25	22.10 N	113.33 E
McClusky	46	47.29 N	100.27 W
McComb	44	31.14 N	90.27 W
McConnellsburg	38	39.56 N	77.59 W
McCook	46	40.12 N	100.38 W
Macedonia □⁹	11	41.00 N	23.00 E
Maceió	33	9.40 S	35.43 W
Macerata	10	43.18 N	13.27 E
McGill	39	39.23 N	114.47 W
Mcgrath	40	62.58 N	155.38 W
Machačkala	4	42.58 N	47.30 E
Machias	38	44.43 N	67.28 W
Macina ⟿¹	14	14.30 N	5.00 W
Mackay	27	21.09 S	149.11 E
Mackenzie ≃	36	69.15 N	134.08 W
Mackenzie Mountains ⟑	36	64.00 N	130.00 W
Mackinac, Straits of ﬗ	37	45.49 N	84.42 W
Mackinac Island I	42	45.51 N	84.38 W
Mackinaw City	42	45.47 N	84.44 W
McKinley, Mount ⋀	40	63.30 N	151.00 W
McKinney	45	33.12 N	96.37 W
McMinnville, Oreg., U.S.	48	45.13 N	123.12 W
McMinnville, Tenn., U.S.	44	35.41 N	85.46 W
McNary	47	34.04 N	109.51 W
Macomb	42	40.27 N	90.40 W
Mâcon, Fr.	8	46.18 N	4.50 E
Macon, Ga., U.S.	43	32.50 N	83.38 W
Macon, Miss., U.S.	44	33.07 N	88.34 W
Macon, Mo., U.S.	44	39.44 N	92.28 W
McPherson	46	38.22 N	97.40 W
Madagascar □¹	15	19.00 S	46.00 E
Maddock	46	47.58 N	99.32 W
Madeira ≃	33	3.22 S	58.45 W
Madeira, Arquipélago da (Madeira Islands) II	14	32.40 N	16.45 W
Madera	39	36.57 N	120.03 W
Madison, Kans., U.S.	46	38.08 N	96.08 W
Madison, Minn., U.S.	46	45.01 N	96.11 W
Madison, S. Dak., U.S.	46	44.00 N	97.07 W
Madison, Wis., U.S.	42	43.05 N	89.22 W
Madisonville	44	37.20 N	87.30 W
Madras	20	13.05 N	80.17 E
Madre, Laguna ⊂, Méx.	31	25.00 N	97.40 W
Madre, Laguna ⊂, Tex., U.S.	45	27.00 N	97.35 W
Madre, Sierra ⟑	31	15.30 N	92.35 W
Madre del Sur, Sierra ⟑	31	17.00 N	100.00 W
Madre Occidental, Sierra ⟑	31	25.00 N	105.00 W
Madre Oriental, Sierra ⟑	31	22.00 N	99.30 W
Madrid	9	40.24 N	3.41 W
Madura I	25	7.00 S	113.20 E
Madurai	20	9.56 N	78.07 E
Madyan ⟿¹	18	27.40 N	35.35 E
Maebashi	23	36.23 N	139.04 E
Mafeking	16	25.53 S	25.39 E
Magadan	13	59.34 N	150.48 E
Magallanes, Estrecho de (Strait of Magellan) ﬗ	34	54.00 S	71.00 W
Maganguė	33	9.14 N	74.45 W
Magdalena ≃	33	11.06 N	74.51 W
Magdeburg	7	52.07 N	11.38 E
Magee	44	31.52 N	89.44 W
Magnitogorsk	4	53.27 N	59.04 E
Magnolia, Ark., U.S.	44	33.16 N	93.14 W
Magnolia, Miss., U.S.	44	31.09 N	90.28 W
Magog	38	45.16 N	72.09 W
Magwe	26	20.09 N	94.55 E
Mahón	9	39.53 N	4.15 E
Maiduguri	14	11.51 N	13.10 E
Mai-Ndombe, Lac ⊜	15	2.00 S	18.20 E
Maine □³	37	45.15 N	69.15 W
Mainland I, Scot., U.K.	5	60.20 N	1.22 W
Mainland I, Scot., U.K.	5	59.00 N	3.10 W
Mainz	7	50.01 N	8.16 E
Maipú	34	36.52 S	57.52 W
Maizuru	23	35.28 N	135.24 E
Majunga	15	15.43 S	46.19 E
Makasar, Selat (Makassar Strait) ﬗ	25	2.00 S	117.30 E
Makat	4	47.39 N	53.19 E
Makinsk	13	52.37 N	70.26 E
Makkah (Mecca)	17	21.27 N	39.49 E
Makó	7	46.13 N	20.29 E
Makurdi	14	7.45 N	8.32 E
Makwassie	16	27.26 S	26.00 E
Malabar Coast ●²	20	10.00 N	76.15 E
Malabo	14	3.45 N	8.47 E
Malacca, Strait of ﬗ	26	2.30 N	101.20 E
Malad City	48	42.12 N	112.15 W
Málaga	9	36.43 N	4.25 W
Malaita I	30a	9.00 S	161.00 E
Malakāl	14	9.31 N	31.39 E
Malang	25	7.59 S	112.37 E
Malanje	15	9.32 S	16.20 E
Malanville	14	11.52 N	3.23 E
Malawi □¹	15	13.30 S	34.00 E
Malaya □⁹	26	4.00 N	102.00 E
Malay Peninsula ⟩¹	26	6.00 N	101.00 E
Malaysia □¹	25	2.30 N	112.30 E
Malbork	7	54.02 N	19.01 E
Maldives □¹	20	3.15 N	73.00 E
Malekula I	30b	16.15 S	167.30 E
Malheur Lake ⊜	48	43.20 N	118.45 W
Mali □¹	14	17.00 N	4.00 W
Malkara	11	40.53 N	26.54 E
Mallaig	5	57.00 N	5.50 W
Mallawī	14	27.44 N	30.50 E
Mallorca I	9	39.30 N	3.00 E
Malmesbury	16	33.28 S	18.44 E
Malmö	6	55.36 N	13.00 E
Małopolska ⟿¹	7	50.10 N	21.30 E
Malta	48	48.21 N	107.52 W
Malta □¹	4	35.50 N	14.35 E
Maluku (Moluccas) II	25	2.00 S	128.00 E
Maluku, Laut (Molucca Sea) ⟿²	25	0.00 S	125.00 E
Malvern	44	34.22 N	92.49 W
Mamagota	30a	6.46 S	155.24 E
Mammoth Cave National Park ♦	44	37.08 N	86.13 W
Manado	25	1.29 N	124.51 E
Managua	32	12.09 N	86.17 W
Manakara	15	22.08 S	48.01 E
Manaus	33	3.08 S	60.01 W
Manawai	30a	9.05 S	161.11 E
Manchester, Eng., U.K.	5	53.30 N	2.15 W
Manchester, N.H., U.S.	38	42.59 N	71.28 W
Manchester, Vt., U.S.	38	43.10 N	73.05 W
Mandalay	22	22.00 N	96.05 E
Mandan	46	46.50 N	100.54 W
Mandeb, Bāb el- ﬗ	17	12.40 N	43.20 E
Manderson	48	44.16 N	107.58 W
Manfredonia	10	41.38 N	15.55 E
Mangalore	20	12.52 N	74.53 E
Mangham	44	32.19 N	91.47 W

Name	Map No.	Lat ° '	Long ° '
Mangum	45	34.53 N	99.30 W
Manhattan	46	39.11 N	96.35 W
Manhuaçu	35	20.15 S	42.02 W
Manicouagan ≏	41	49.11 N	68.13 W
Manicouagan, Réservoir ⏃[1]	41	51.30 N	68.19 W
Manila	25	14.35 N	121.00 E
Manisa	11	38.36 N	27.26 E
Manistee	42	44.15 N	86.19 W
Manitoba □[4]	36	54.00 N	97.00 W
Manitoba, Lake ⏃	36	51.00 N	98.45 W
Manitoulin Island I	42	45.45 N	82.30 W
Manitowoc	42	44.06 N	87.40 W
Maniwaki	42	46.23 N	75.58 W
Manizales	33	5.05 N	75.32 W
Mankato	42	44.10 N	94.01 W
Manly	42	43.17 N	93.12 W
Mannar, Gulf of C	20	8.30 N	79.00 E
Mannheim	7	49.29 N	8.29 E
Manono	15	7.18 S	27.25 E
Manresa	9	41.44 N	1.50 E
Mansfield	38	40.46 N	82.31 W
Mansfield, Mount ∧	38	44.33 N	72.49 W
Manta	33	0.57 S	80.44 W
Mantova	10	45.09 N	10.48 E
Many	44	31.34 N	93.29 W
Manzanillo	32	20.21 N	77.07 W
Maoke, Pegunungan ⋌	25	4.00 S	138.00 E
Maputo (Lourenço Marques)	15	25.58 S	32.35 E
Maracaibo	33	10.40 N	71.37 W
Maracay	33	10.15 N	67.36 W
Maragogipe	35	12.46 S	38.55 W
Marañón ≏	33	4.30 S	73.27 W
Maravovo	30a	9.17 S	159.38 E
Marble Canyon ⋎	47	36.30 N	111.50 W
Marburg an der Lahn	7	50.49 N	8.46 E
Marceline	44	39.43 N	92.57 W
Marcy, Mount ∧	38	44.07 N	73.56 W
Mardān	21	34.12 N	72.02 E
Mar del Plata	34	38.00 S	57.33 W
Marengo	42	41.48 N	92.04 W
Margate	43	26.18 N	80.12 W
Margherita Peak ∧	15	0.22 N	29.51 E
Mariana Islands II	25	16.00 N	145.30 E
Marianao	32	23.05 N	82.26 W
Marianna	43	30.47 N	85.14 W
Marías ≏	48	47.56 N	110.30 W
Marias, Islas II	31	21.25 N	106.28 W
Maribor	10	46.33 N	15.39 E
Mariental	16	24.36 S	17.59 E
Marietta, Ga., U.S.	43	33.57 N	84.33 W
Marietta, Ohio, U.S.	38	39.25 N	81.27 W
Marília	35	22.13 S	49.56 W
Marinette	42	45.06 N	87.38 W
Maringá	34	23.25 S	51.55 W
Marion, Ala., U.S.	44	32.38 N	87.26 W
Marion, Ill., U.S.	44	37.44 N	88.56 W
Marion, Ind., U.S.	44	40.33 N	85.40 W
Marion, Ohio, U.S.	38	40.35 N	83.08 W
Marion, Lake ⏃[1]	43	33.30 N	80.25 W
Maritime Alps ⋌	8	44.15 N	7.10 E
Marked Tree	44	35.32 N	90.25 W
Markham, Mount ∧	3	82.51 S	161.21 E
Marlborough	38	42.21 N	71.33 W
Marmara Denizi (Sea of Marmara) ⊽[2]	11	40.40 N	28.15 E
Marmara Gölü ⏃	11	38.37 N	28.02 E
Marmet	38	38.15 N	81.04 W
Marne ≏	8	48.49 N	2.24 E
Maromokotro ∧	15	14.01 S	48.59 E
Maroua	14	10.36 N	14.20 E
Marovoay	15	16.06 S	46.39 E
Marquette	42	46.33 N	87.24 W
Marrah, Jabal ∧	14	14.04 N	24.21 E
Marrakech	14	31.38 N	8.00 W
Marsala	10	37.48 N	12.26 E
Marseille	8	43.18 N	5.24 E
Marshall, Mo., U.S.	44	39.07 N	93.12 W
Marshall, Tex., U.S.	44	32.33 N	94.23 W
Marshalltown	42	42.03 N	92.55 W
Martaban, Gulf of C	26	16.30 N	97.00 E
Martha's Vineyard I	38	41.25 N	70.40 W
Martigues	8	43.24 N	5.03 E
Martin	46	43.10 N	101.44 W
Martinique □[2]	32	14.40 N	61.00 W
Martinsburg	38	39.27 N	77.58 W
Martinsville	43	36.41 N	79.52 W
Maryborough	27	25.32 S	152.42 E
Maryland □[3]	37	39.00 N	76.45 W
Marysville, N.B., Can.	41	45.59 N	66.35 W
Marysville, Calif., U.S.	39	39.09 N	121.35 W
Maryville	43	35.46 N	83.58 W
Masai Steppe ⋌[1]	15	4.45 S	37.00 E
Mascarene Islands II	15	21.00 S	57.00 E
Maseru	16	29.28 S	27.30 E
Mason	42	42.35 N	84.26 W
Mason City	42	43.09 N	93.12 W
Masqaţ (Muscat)	17	23.37 N	58.35 E
Massachusetts □[3]	37	42.15 N	71.50 W
Massachusetts Bay C	38	42.20 N	70.50 W
Massena	38	44.56 N	74.54 W
Massillon	38	40.48 N	81.32 W
Masterton	29	40.57 S	175.40 E
Matadi	15	5.49 S	13.27 E
Matagalpa	32	12.55 N	85.55 W
Matagorda Island I	45	28.15 N	96.30 W
Matamoros	31	25.53 N	97.30 W
Matane	41	48.51 N	67.32 W
Matanzas	32	23.03 N	81.35 W
Matera	10	40.40 N	16.37 E
Matias Romero	31	16.53 N	95.02 W
Matsudo	23	35.47 N	139.54 E
Matsue	23	35.28 N	133.04 E
Matsumoto	23	36.14 N	137.58 E
Matsuyama	23	33.50 N	132.45 E
Mattawamkeag	38	45.31 N	68.21 W
Matterhorn ∧	8	45.59 N	7.43 E
Matthew Town	32	20.57 N	73.40 W
Mattoon	44	39.29 N	88.22 W
Maturin	33	9.45 N	63.11 W
Maubeuge	8	50.17 N	3.58 E
Maui I	39a	20.45 N	156.15 W
Mauna Loa ∧[1]	39a	19.29 N	155.36 W
Maunath Bhanjan	21	25.57 N	83.33 E
Mauritania □[1]	14	20.00 N	12.00 W
Mauritius □[1]	15	20.17 S	57.33 E
Mawlaik	26	23.38 N	94.24 E
Maxwell	42	41.53 N	93.24 W
Mayagüez	32	18.12 N	67.09 W
Mayer	47	34.24 N	112.14 W
Mayfield	44	36.44 N	88.38 W
Maymyo	26	22.02 N	96.28 E
Mayotte □[2]	15	12.50 S	45.10 E
Mazara del Vallo	10	37.39 N	12.36 E
Mazār-e Sharīf	21	36.42 N	67.06 E
Mazatlán	31	23.13 N	106.25 W
Mazury ⋏[1]	7	53.45 N	21.00 E
Mbabane	16	26.18 S	31.06 E
Mbale	15	1.05 N	34.10 E
Mbandaka (Coquilhatville)	15	0.04 N	18.16 E
Mbua	30c	16.48 S	178.37 E
Mbuji-Mayi (Bakwanga)	15	6.09 S	23.38 E
M'Clintock Channel ⋃	36	71.00 N	101.00 W
Mead, Lake ⏃[1]	47	36.05 N	114.25 W
Meadville	38	41.38 N	80.09 W
Mecca			
→ Makkah	17	21.27 N	39.49 E
Mechelen	7	51.02 N	4.28 E
Mecklenburg □[9]	7	53.30 N	13.00 E
Medan	26	3.35 N	98.40 E
Medellín	33	6.15 N	75.35 W
Médenine	14	32.21 N	10.30 E
Medford	48	42.19 N	122.52 W
Medgidia	11	44.15 N	28.16 E
Medicine Hat	36	50.03 N	110.40 W
Medicine Lodge	46	37.17 N	98.35 W
Mediterranean Sea ⊽[2]	1	35.00 N	20.00 E
Meekatharra	27	26.36 S	118.29 E
Meeker	47	40.02 N	107.55 W
Meerut	21	28.59 N	77.42 E
Meiktila	26	20.52 N	95.52 E
Meiningen	7	50.34 N	10.25 E
Mekong ≏	26	10.33 N	105.24 E
Melaka	26	2.12 N	102.15 E
Melanesia II	1	13.00 S	164.00 E
Melbourne, Austl.	27	37.49 S	144.58 E
Melbourne, Fla., U.S.	43	28.05 N	80.37 W
Melby House	5	60.18 N	1.39 W
Melilla	14	35.19 N	2.58 W
Melita	36	49.16 N	101.00 W
Melitopol'	4	46.50 N	35.22 E
Melun	8	48.32 N	2.40 E
Melville Island I, Austl.	27	11.40 S	131.00 E
Melville Island I, N.W. Ter., Can.	36	75.15 N	110.00 W
Melville Peninsula ⋗[1]	36	68.00 N	84.00 W

Name	Map No.	Lat	Long
Memmingen	7	47.59 N	10.11 E
Memphis	44	35.08 N	90.03 W
Mendocino, Cape ➤	39	40.25 N	124.25 W
Mendota	42	41.33 N	89.07 W
Mendoza	34	32.53 S	68.49 W
Menemen	11	38.36 N	27.04 E
Menominee	42	45.06 N	87.37 W
Menomonee Falls	42	43.11 N	88.07 W
Menorca I	9	40.00 N	4.00 E
Mentawai, Kepulauan II	25	2.00 S	99.30 E
Merano (Meran)	10	46.40 N	11.09 E
Merced	39	37.18 N	120.29 W
Mercedes	34	33.40 S	65.28 W
Mergui (Myeik)	26	12.26 N	98.36 E
Mergui Archipelago II	26	12.00 N	98.00 E
Mérida, Esp.	9	38.55 N	6.20 W
Mérida, Méx.	31	20.58 N	89.37 W
Meriden	38	41.32 N	72.48 W
Meridian	44	32.22 N	88.42 W
Merritt Island	43	28.21 N	80.42 W
Merseburg	7	51.21 N	11.59 E
Merthyr Tydfil	5	51.46 N	3.23 W
Mesa	47	33.25 N	111.50 W
Mesabi Range ⋏²	42	47.30 N	92.50 W
Mesa Verde National Park ⋏	47	37.13 N	108.30 W
Mesewa (Massaua)	17	15.38 N	39.28 E
Mesopotamia ➙¹	17	34.00 N	44.00 E
Mesquite	39	36.48 N	114.04 W
Messina	10	38.11 N	15.33 E
Metairie	44	29.59 N	90.09 W
Metropolis	44	37.09 N	88.44 W
Metz	8	49.08 N	6.10 E
Meuse (Maas) ≈	7	51.49 N	5.01 E
Mexicali	31	32.40 N	115.29 W
Mexican Hat	47	37.09 N	109.52 W
Mexico	44	39.10 N	91.53 W
Mexico (México) □¹	31	23.00 N	102.00 W
Mexico, Gulf of C	31	24.00 N	93.00 W
Mexico City			
→ Ciudad de México	31	19.24 N	99.09 W
Meymaneh	21	35.55 N	64.47 E
Miami, Ariz., U.S.	47	33.24 N	110.52 W
Miami, Fla., U.S.	43	25.46 N	80.12 W
Miami, Okla., U.S.	45	36.53 N	94.53 W
Miami Beach	43	25.47 N	80.08 W
Miānwāli	21	32.35 N	71.33 E
Miass	4	54.59 N	60.06 E
Michigan □³	37	44.00 N	85.00 W
Michigan, Lake ⊜	42	44.00 N	87.00 W
Michigan City	44	41.43 N	86.54 W
Micronesia II	1	11.00 N	159.00 E
Mičurinsk	12	52.54 N	40.30 E
Middlebury	38	44.01 N	73.10 W
Middlesboro	43	36.36 N	83.43 W
Middleton	41	44.57 N	65.04 W
Middletown, N.Y., U.S.	38	41.27 N	74.25 W
Middletown, Ohio, U.S.	38	39.29 N	84.25 W
Midland, Ont., Can.	42	44.45 N	79.53 W
Midland, Mich., U.S.	42	43.37 N	84.14 W
Midland, Tex., U.S.	45	32.00 N	102.05 W
Midwest	48	43.25 N	106.16 W
Mielec	7	50.18 N	21.25 E
Miguel Alemán, Presa ⊜¹	31	18.13 N	96.32 W
Mihajlovgrad	11	43.25 N	23.13 E
Mikkeli	6	61.41 N	27.15 E
Milan			
→ Milano, It.	10	45.28 N	9.12 E
Milan, N. Mex., U.S.	47	35.09 N	107.54 W
Milano (Milan)	10	45.28 N	9.12 E
Milbank	46	45.13 N	96.38 W
Mildura	27	34.12 S	142.09 E
Miles City	48	46.25 N	105.51 W
Milford, Del., U.S.	38	38.55 N	75.25 W
Milford, Iowa, U.S.	46	43.20 N	95.09 W
Milford Haven	5	51.40 N	5.02 W
Milledgeville	43	33.04 N	83.14 W
Millington	44	35.21 N	89.54 W
Millinocket	38	45.39 N	68.43 W
Milparinka	27	29.44 S	141.53 E
Milton	44	30.38 N	87.03 W
Milwaukee	42	43.02 N	87.55 W
Minas	34	34.23 S	55.14 W
Minas, Sierra de las ⋏	32	15.10 N	89.40 W
Minatitlán	31	17.59 N	94.31 W
Mindanao I	25	8.00 N	125.00 E
Minden, La., U.S.	44	32.37 N	93.17 W
Minden, Nebr., U.S.	46	40.30 N	98.57 W
Mindoro I	25	12.50 N	121.05 E
Minjiang ≈	24	26.05 N	119.32 E
Minneapolis	42	44.59 N	93.13 W
Minneola	46	37.26 N	100.01 W
Minnesota □³	37	46.00 N	94.15 W
Minot	46	48.14 N	101.18 W
Minsk	12	53.54 N	27.34 E
Miskolc	7	48.06 N	20.47 E
Mississippi □³	37	32.50 N	89.30 W
Mississippi ≈	37	29.00 N	89.15 W
Mississippi Delta ≥²	44	29.10 N	89.15 W
Missoula	48	46.52 N	114.01 W
Missouri □³	37	38.30 N	93.30 W
Missouri ≈	37	38.50 N	90.08 W
Mistassini, Lac ⊜	36	51.00 N	73.37 W
Mitchell, Ont., Can.	42	43.28 N	81.12 W
Mitchell, S. Dak., U.S.	46	43.43 N	104.01 W
Mitchell, Mount ⋏	43	35.46 N	82.16 W
Mitilini	11	39.06 N	26.32 E
Mito	23	36.22 N	140.28 E
Miyakonojō	23	31.44 N	131.04 E
Miyazaki	23	31.54 N	131.26 E
Mladá Boleslav	7	50.23 N	14.59 E
Moab	47	38.35 N	109.33 W
Moberly	44	39.25 N	92.26 W
Mobile	44	30.42 N	88.05 W
Mobile Bay C	44	30.25 N	88.00 W
Mobridge	46	45.32 N	100.26 W
Moçambique	15	15.03 S	40.42 E
Moçâmedes	15	15.10 S	12.09 E
Mochudi	15	24.28 S	26.05 E
Mococa	35	21.28 S	47.01 W
Modena	10	44.40 N	10.55 E
Modesto	39	37.39 N	120.60 W
Modica	10	36.51 N	14.47 E
Moenkopi	47	36.07 N	111.13 W
Moffat	5	55.20 N	3.27 W
Moga	21	30.48 N	75.10 E
Mogadishu	17	2.01 N	45.20 E
Mogaung	26	25.18 N	96.56 E
Mogil'ov	12	53.54 N	30.21 E
Mogoča	13	53.44 N	119.44 E
Mogollon Rim ▲⁴	47	32.30 N	111.00 W
Mohall	46	48.46 N	101.31 W
Mohave, Lake ⊜¹	39	35.25 N	114.38 W
Mohawk ≈	38	42.47 N	73.42 W
Mojave Desert ➙²	39	35.00 N	117.00 W
Mokp'o	22	34.48 N	126.22 E
Moldavia □⁹	11	46.30 N	27.00 E
Moldoveanu ⋏	11	45.36 N	24.44 E
Molfetta	10	41.12 N	16.36 E
Moline	42	41.30 N	90.31 W
Mollendo	33	17.02 S	72.01 W
Molokai I	39a	21.07 N	157.00 W
Moluccas			
→ Maluku II	25	2.00 S	128.00 E
Mombasa	15	4.03 S	39.40 E
Momi	30c	17.55 S	177.17 E
Monaco □¹	4	43.45 N	7.25 E
Monarch Pass)(	47	38.30 N	106.19 W
Mönchengladbach	7	51.12 N	6.28 E
Monclova	31	26.54 N	101.25 W
Moncton	41	46.06 N	64.47 W
Mondovi	42	44.34 N	91.40 W
Monessen	38	40.09 N	79.53 W
Monfalcone	10	45.49 N	13.32 E
Mongolia □¹	22	46.00 N	105.00 E
Mono Lake ⊜	39	38.00 N	119.00 W
Monroe, La., U.S.	44	32.33 N	92.07 W
Monroe, Mich., U.S.	42	41.55 N	83.24 W
Monroeville	44	31.31 N	87.20 W
Monrovia	14	6.18 N	10.47 W
Montana □³	37	47.00 N	110.00 W
Montargis	8	48.00 N	2.45 E
Montauban	8	44.01 N	1.21 E
Montbéliard	8	47.31 N	6.48 E
Montceau [-les-Mines]	8	46.40 N	4.22 E
Montego Bay	32	18.28 N	77.55 W
Monterey	39	36.37 N	121.55 W
Monterey Bay C	39	36.45 N	121.55 W
Monteria	33	8.46 N	75.53 W
Monterrey	31	25.40 N	100.19 W
Montes Claros	33	16.43 S	43.52 W
Montevideo	34	34.53 S	56.11 W
Monte Vista	47	37.35 N	106.09 W
Montgomery	44	32.23 N	86.18 W
Monticello, Ark., U.S.	44	33.38 N	91.47 W

Name	Map No.	Lat	Long
Monticello, Ky., U.S.	44	36.50 N	84.51 W
Mont-Joli	41	48.35 N	68.11 W
Montluçon	8	46.21 N	2.36 E
Montmagny	41	46.59 N	70.33 W
Montpelier, Idaho, U.S.	48	42.19 N	111.18 W
Montpelier, Vt., U.S.	38	44.16 N	72.35 W
Montpellier	8	43.36 N	3.53 E
Montréal	38	45.31 N	73.34 W
Montrose, Colo., U.S.	47	38.29 N	107.53 W
Montrose, Pa., U.S.	38	41.50 N	75.53 W
Montserrat □[2]	32	16.45 N	62.12 W
Monywa	26	22.05 N	95.08 E
Monza	10	45.35 N	9.16 E
Moorea **I**	30d	17.32 S	149.50 W
Moorhead	46	46.53 N	96.45 W
Moosehead Lake ⊜	38	45.40 N	69.40 W
Moose Jaw	36	50.23 N	105.32 W
Mooselookmeguntic Lake ⊜	38	44.53 N	70.48 W
Mopti	14	14.30 N	4.12 W
Morādābād	21	28.50 N	78.47 E
Morava □[9]	7	49.20 N	17.00 E
Morden	36	49.11 N	98.05 W
Moreau ≌	46	45.18 N	100.43 W
Morehead City	43	34.43 N	76.43 W
Morelia	31	19.42 N	101.07 W
Morgan City	44	29.42 N	91.12 W
Morgantown	38	39.38 N	79.57 W
Moriah, Mount ᴧ	39	39.17 N	114.12 W
Morioka	23	39.42 N	141.09 E
Morocco □[1]	14	32.00 N	5.00 W
Morogoro	15	6.49 S	37.40 E
Moro Gulf **C**	25	6.51 N	123.00 E
Morondava	15	20.17 S	44.17 E
Morón de la Frontera	9	37.08 N	5.27 W
Moroni	15	11.41 S	43.16 E
Morrinsville	29	37.39 S	175.32 E
Morristown	43	36.13 N	83.18 W
Morton	42	40.37 N	89.28 W
Moscow			
→ Moskva, S.S.S.R.	12	55.45 N	37.35 E
Moscow, Idaho, U.S.	48	46.44 N	117.00 W
Moselle (Mosel) ≌	8	50.22 N	7.36 E
Moses Lake	48	47.08 N	119.17 W
Moskva (Moscow)	12	55.45 N	37.35 E
Mosquitos, Golfo de los **C**	32	9.00 N	81.15 W
Mossburn	29	45.40 S	168.15 E
Mosselbaai	16	34.11 S	22.08 E
Mossoró	33	5.11 S	37.20 W
Most	7	50.32 N	13.39 E
Mostar	10	43.20 N	17.49 E
Motherwell	5	55.48 N	4.00 W
Mou	30b	21.05 S	165.26 E
Moulins	8	46.34 N	3.20 E
Moulmein	26	16.30 N	97.38 E
Moultrie	43	31.11 N	83.47 W
Mound City	46	38.08 N	94.49 W
Moundou	14	8.34 N	16.05 E
Moundsville	38	39.55 N	80.44 W
Mountainair	47	34.31 N	106.15 W
Mountain Home, Ark., U.S.	44	36.20 N	92.23 W
Mountain Home, Idaho, U.S.	48	43.08 N	115.41 W
Mountain Nile (Baḩr al-Jabal) ≌	17	9.30 N	30.30 E
Mount Airy	43	36.31 N	80.37 W
Mount Ayliff	16	30.54 S	29.20 E
Mount Ayr	46	40.43 N	94.14 W
Mount Carmel	44	38.25 N	87.46 W
Mount Forest	42	43.59 N	80.44 W
Mount Gambier	27	37.50 S	140.46 E
Mount Isa	27	20.44 S	139.30 E
Mount Magnet	27	28.04 S	117.49 E
Mount McKinley National Park ♦	40	63.30 N	150.00 W
Mount Olivet	38	38.32 N	84.02 W
Mount Pleasant	42	43.35 N	84.47 W
Mount Union	38	40.23 N	77.53 W
Mount Vernon, Ill., U.S.	44	38.19 N	88.55 W
Mount Vernon, Ky., U.S.	43	37.21 N	84.20 W
Mount Vernon, Wash., U.S.	48	48.25 N	122.20 W
Mozambique □[1]	15	18.15 S	35.00 E
Mozambique Channel ⋃	15	19.00 S	41.00 E
Mtwara	15	10.16 S	40.11 E
Muang Khammouan	26	17.24 N	104.48 E
Muang Không	26	14.07 N	105.51 E
Muang Khôngxédôn	26	15.34 N	105.49 E
Muang Pakxan	26	18.22 N	103.39 E
Muang Xaignabouri	26	19.15 N	101.45 E
Muar (Bandar Maharani)	26	2.02 N	102.34 E
Mudanjiang	22	44.35 N	129.36 E
Mufulira	15	12.33 S	28.14 E
Mühlviertel ◢[1]	7	48.25 N	14.10 E
Mukden			
→ Shenyang	22	41.48 N	123.27 E
Mulhacén ᴧ	9	37.03 N	3.19 W
Mulhouse	8	47.45 N	7.20 E
Mull, Island of **I**	5	56.27 N	6.00 W
Mullins	43	34.12 N	79.15 W
Multān	19	30.11 N	71.29 E
München (Munich)	7	48.08 N	11.34 E
Muncie	44	40.11 N	85.23 W
Munfordville	44	37.16 N	85.54 W
Munich			
→ München	7	48.08 N	11.34 E
Münster	7	51.57 N	7.37 E
Munster □[9]	5	52.25 N	8.20 W
Murcia	9	37.59 N	1.07 W
Murfreesboro	44	35.51 N	86.23 W
Murmansk	4	68.58 N	33.05 E
Muroran	23a	42.18 N	140.59 E
Murray ≌	28	35.22 S	139.22 E
Murraysburg	16	31.58 S	23.47 E
Murrumbidgee ≌	28	34.43 S	143.12 E
Murupara	29	38.28 S	176.42 E
Mūsā, Jabal (Mount Sinai) ᴧ	18	28.32 N	33.59 E
Musala ᴧ	11	42.11 N	23.34 E
Muscat			
→ Masqaţ	17	23.37 N	58.35 E
Muscatine	42	41.25 N	91.03 W
Muscle Shoals	44	34.45 N	87.40 W
Muskegon	42	43.14 N	86.16 W
Muskogee	45	35.45 N	95.22 W
Musselshell ≌	48	47.21 N	107.58 W
Mustafakemalpaşa	11	40.02 N	28.24 E
Mwanza	15	2.31 S	32.54 E
Myanaung	26	18.17 N	95.19 E
Myingyan	26	21.28 N	95.23 E
Myitkyinā	26	25.23 N	97.24 E
Myrtle Beach	43	33.42 N	78.52 W
Myrtle Grove	44	30.25 N	87.18 W
Myrtle Point	48	43.04 N	124.08 W
Mysore	20	12.18 N	76.39 E
Mzuzu	15	11.27 S	33.55 E

N

Naalehu	39a	19.04 N	155.35 W
Naberežnyje Čelny	4	55.42 N	52.19 E
Nābulus	18	32.13 N	35.16 E
Nachodka	13	42.48 N	132.52 E
Nacogdoches	44	31.36 N	94.39 W
Naga	25	13.37 N	123.11 E
Nagano	23	36.39 N	138.11 E
Nagaoka	23	37.27 N	138.51 E
Nagasaki	23	32.48 N	129.55 E
Nagoya	23	35.10 N	136.55 E
Nāgpur	21	21.09 N	79.06 E
Naha	23b	26.13 N	127.40 E
Nairobi	15	1.17 S	36.49 E
Najin	22	42.15 N	130.18 E
Nakhon Pathom	26	13.49 N	100.03 E
Nakhon Ratchasima	26	14.58 N	102.07 E
Nakhon Sawan	26	15.41 N	100.07 E
Nakhon Si Thammarat	26	8.26 N	99.58 E
Nakuru	15	0.17 S	36.04 E
Nal'čik	4	43.29 N	43.37 E
Nam-dinh	26	20.25 N	106.10 E
Namib Desert ◢[2]	16	23.00 S	15.00 E
Namibia □[2]	15	22.00 S	17.00 E
Nampa	48	43.34 N	116.34 W
Namp'o	22	38.45 N	125.23 E
Nampula	15	15.07 S	39.15 E
Namsos	6	64.29 N	11.30 E
Nanchang	24	28.41 N	115.53 E
Nanchong	22	30.48 N	106.04 E
Nancy	8	48.41 N	6.12 E
Nanda Devi ᴧ	21	30.23 N	79.59 E
Nānga Parbat ᴧ	21	35.15 N	74.36 E
Nanjing (Nanking)	24	32.03 N	118.47 E
Nanking			
→ Nanjing	24	32.03 N	118.47 E
Nanling ⩘	22	25.00 N	112.00 E
Nanning	22	22.48 N	108.20 E
Nansei-shotō (Ryukyu Islands) **II**	22	26.30 N	128.00 E
Nantes	8	47.13 N	1.33 W
Nantong	24	32.02 N	120.53 E

Name	Map No.	Lat ° '	Long ° '
Nome	40	64.30 N	165.24 W
Noranda	42	48.15 N	79.02 W
Nordhausen	7	51.30 N	10.47 E
Nordhorn	7	52.27 N	7.05 E
Nordkapp ➤	6	71.11 N	25.48 E
Norfolk, Nebr., U.S.	46	42.02 N	97.25 W
Norfolk, Va., U.S.	43	36.40 N	76.14 W
Noril´sk	13	69.20 N	88.06 E
Normal	42	40.31 N	88.59 W
Norman	45	35.13 N	97.26 W
Normandie □[9]	8	49.00 N	0.05 W
Normanton	27	17.40 S	141.05 E
Norristown	38	40.07 N	75.21 W
Norseman	27	32.12 S	121.46 E
North Adams	38	42.42 N	73.07 W
Northam	27	31.39 S	116.40 E
North America ▲[1]	1	45.00 N	100.00 W
Northampton, Eng., U.K.	5	52.14 N	0.54 W
Northampton, Mass., U.S.	38	42.19 N	72.38 W
North Augusta	43	33.30 N	81.58 W
North Bay	42	46.19 N	79.28 W
North Cape			
→ Nordkapp ➤	6	71.11 N	25.48 E
North Carolina □[3]	37	35.30 N	80.00 W
North Cascades National Park ▲	48	48.30 N	121.00 W
North Channel ⨆, Ont., Can.	42	46.02 N	82.50 W
North Channel ⨆, U.K.	5	55.10 N	5.40 W
North Charleston	43	32.53 N	80.00 W
North Dakota □[3]	37	47.30 N	100.15 W
North East	38	42.13 N	79.50 W
Northern Ireland □[8]	5	54.40 N	6.45 W
Northfield	42	44.27 N	93.09 W
North Island ▮	29	39.00 S	176.00 E
North Little Rock	44	34.46 N	92.14 W
North Magnetic Pole �	2	76.16 N	99.55 W
North Platte	46	41.08 N	100.46 W
North Platte ⇌	37	41.15 N	100.45 W
North Pole �	2	90.00 N	0.00
North Sea ⇌[2]	4	55.20 N	3.00 E
Northumberland Strait ⨆	41	46.00 N	63.30 W
Northwest Territories □[4]	36	70.00 N	100.00 W
Norton Sound ⨆	40	63.50 N	164.00 W
Norwalk	38	41.15 N	82.37 W
Norway □[1]	4	62.00 N	10.00 E
Norwegian Sea ⇌[2]	2	70.00 N	2.00 E
Norwich, Eng., U.K.	5	52.38 N	1.18 E
Norwich, N.Y., U.S.	38	42.32 N	75.31 W
Noshiro	23	40.12 N	140.02 E
Notre Dame, Monts ⩗	41	48.10 N	68.00 W
Nottingham	5	52.58 N	1.10 W
Nouadhibou	14	20.54 N	17.04 W
Nouakchott	14	18.06 N	15.57 W
Nouméa	30b	22.16 S	166.27 E
Nouvelle-Calédonie ▮	30b	21.30 S	165.30 E
Nova Friburgo	35	22.16 S	42.32 W
Nova Iguaçu	35	22.45 S	43.27 W
Novaja Sibir´, Ostrov ▮	13	75.00 N	149.00 E
Novaja Zeml'a ▮▮	13	74.00 N	57.00 E
Nova Lima	35	19.59 S	43.51 W
Nova Scotia □[4]	36	45.00 N	63.00 W
Nové Zámky	7	47.59 N	18.11 E
Novgorod	12	58.31 N	31.17 E
Novi Pazar	11	43.08 N	20.31 E
Novi Sad	11	45.15 N	19.50 E
Novokuzneck	13	53.45 N	87.06 E
Novomoskovsk	12	54.05 N	38.13 E
Novorossijsk	4	44.45 N	37.45 E
Novosibirsk	13	55.02 N	82.55 E
Novosibirskije Ostrova ▮▮	13	75.00 N	142.00 E
Novyj Port	13	67.40 N	72.52 E
Nowa Sól (Neusalz)	7	51.48 N	15.44 E
Nowy Sacz	7	49.38 N	20.42 E
Nubian Desert ➣[2]	17	20.30 N	33.00 E
Nueces ⇌	45	27.50 N	97.30 W
Nueva Rosita	31	27.57 N	101.13 W
Nueva San Salvador	32	13.41 N	89.17 W
Nuevitas	32	21.33 N	77.16 W
Nuevo Laredo	31	27.30 N	99.31 W
Numazu	23	35.06 N	138.52 E
Nunivak Island ▮	40	60.00 N	166.30 W
N'urba	13	63.17 N	118.20 E
Nürnberg	7	49.27 N	11.04 E
Nyala	14	12.03 N	24.53 E
Nyasa, Lake ⊜	15	12.00 S	34.30 E
Nyaunglebin	26	17.57 N	96.44 E
Nyíregyháza	7	47.59 N	21.43 E
Nyngan	28	31.34 S	147.11 E

Name	Map No.	Lat ° '	Long ° '
Nysa	7	50.29 N	17.20 E
Nyssa	48	43.53 N	117.00 W
O			
Oahe, Lake ⊜[1]	36	45.30 N	100.40 W
Oahe Reservoir ⊜[1]	46	45.30 N	100.25 W
Oahu ▮	39a	21.30 N	158.00 W
Oakland	39	37.47 N	122.13 W
Oakridge, Oreg., U.S.	48	43.45 N	122.28 W
Oak Ridge, Tenn., U.S.	43	36.01 N	84.16 W
Oakville	42	43.27 N	79.41 W
Oamaru	29	45.06 S	170.58 E
Oaxaca [de Juárez]	31	17.03 N	96.43 W
Ob' ⇌	13	66.45 N	69.30 E
Obihiro	23a	42.55 N	143.12 E
Obskaja Guba ⊂	13	69.00 N	73.00 E
Ocala	43	29.11 N	82.07 W
Ocean City	38	39.16 N	74.36 W
Oceanside	39	33.12 N	117.23 W
Ocha	13	53.34 N	142.56 E
Ochotsk	13	59.23 N	143.18 E
Oconto	42	44.43 N	87.52 W
Ocotlán	31	20.21 N	102.46 W
Odawara	23	35.15 N	139.10 E
Ödemiş	11	38.13 N	27.59 E
Odendaalsrus	16	27.48 S	26.45 E
Odense	6	55.24 N	10.23 E
Oder (Odra) ⇌	7	53.32 N	14.38 E
Odessa, S.S.S.R.	4	46.28 N	30.44 E
Odessa, Tex., U.S.	45	31.51 N	102.22 W
Odessa, Wash., U.S.	48	47.20 N	118.41 W
Offenbach	7	50.08 N	8.47 E
Ōgaki	23	35.21 N	136.37 E
Ogallala	46	41.08 N	101.43 W
Ogbomosho	14	8.08 N	4.15 E
Ogden	47	41.14 N	111.58 W
Ogdensburg	38	44.42 N	75.29 W
Ogunquit	41	43.16 N	70.36 W
Ohio □[3]	37	40.15 N	82.45 W
Ohio ⇌	37	36.59 N	89.08 W
Ohrid, Lake ⊜	11	41.02 N	20.43 E
Oil City	38	41.26 N	79.42 W
Oildale	39	35.25 N	119.01 W
Ōita	23	33.14 N	131.36 E
Ojos del Salado, Nevado ⋀	34	27.06 S	68.32 W
Oka ⇌	12	56.20 N	43.59 E
Okaihau	29	35.19 S	173.47 E
Okavango (Cubango) ⇌	15	18.50 S	22.25 E
Okavango Swamp ⫩	15	18.45 S	22.45 E
Okaya	23	36.03 N	138.03 E
Okayama	23	34.39 N	133.55 E
Okazaki	23	34.57 N	137.10 E
Okeechobee, Lake ⊜	43	26.55 N	80.45 W
Okefenokee Swamp ⫩	43	30.42 N	82.20 W
Okhotsk, Sea of (Ochotskoje More) ⇌[2]	13	53.00 N	150.00 E
Oki-guntō ▮▮	23	36.15 N	133.15 E
Okinawa-jima ▮	23b	26.30 N	128.00 E
Oklahoma □[3]	37	35.30 N	98.00 W
Oklahoma City	45	35.28 N	97.32 W
Okmulgee	45	35.37 N	95.58 W
Okolona	44	34.00 N	88.45 W
Okt´abr´skoj Revol´ucii, Ostrov ▮	13	79.30 N	97.00 E
Öland ▮	6	56.45 N	16.38 E
Olathe	46	38.53 N	94.49 W
Old Crow	36	67.35 N	139.50 W
Oldenburg	7	53.08 N	8.13 E
Old Town	38	44.56 N	68.39 W
Olean	38	42.05 N	78.26 W
Ólimbos ⋀, Ellás	11	40.05 N	22.21 E
Ólimbos ⋀, Kípros	18	34.56 N	32.52 E
Olímpia	35	20.44 S	48.54 W
Olinda	33	8.01 S	34.51 W
Oliveira	35	20.41 S	44.49 W
Olney	44	38.44 N	88.05 W
Ol´okminsk	13	60.24 N	120.24 E
Olomouc	7	49.36 N	17.16 E
Olsztyn (Allenstein)	7	53.48 N	20.29 E
Olt ⇌	11	43.43 N	24.51 E
Oluan Pi ➤	24	21.54 N	120.51 E
Olympia	48	47.03 N	122.53 W
Olympic Mountains ⩗	48	47.50 N	123.45 W
Olympus, Mount ⋀			
→ Ólimbos ⋀, Ellás	11	40.05 N	22.21 E
Olympus, Mount ⋀, Wash., U.S.	48	47.48 N	123.43 W

Name	Map No.	Lat ° '	Long ° '
Omagh	5	54.36 N	7.18 W
Omaha	46	41.16 N	95.57 W
Oman ☐[1]	17	22.00 N	58.00 E
Oman, Gulf of C	17	24.30 N	58.30 E
Omar	43	37.46 N	82.00 W
Omarama	29	44.29 S	169.58 E
Ometepe, Isla de I	32	11.30 N	85.35 W
Ōmiya	23	35.54 N	139.38 E
Omsk	13	55.00 N	73.24 E
Ōmuta	23	33.02 N	130.27 E
Onawa	46	42.02 N	96.06 W
Oneida	38	43.06 N	75.39 W
Oneida Lake ⊜	38	43.13 N	76.00 W
O'Neill	46	42.27 N	98.39 W
Oneonta, Ala., U.S.	44	33.57 N	86.29 W
Oneonta, N.Y., U.S.	38	42.27 N	75.04 W
Ongole	20	15.31 N	80.04 E
Onomichi	23	34.25 N	133.12 E
Onslow	27	21.39 S	115.06 E
Ontario	48	44.02 N	116.58 W
Ontario ☐[4]	36	51.00 N	85.00 W
Ontario, Lake ⊜	42	43.45 N	78.00 W
Ontonagon	42	46.52 N	89.19 W
Ooldea	27	30.27 S	131.50 E
Opava	7	49.56 N	17.54 E
Opelika	44	32.39 N	85.23 W
Opelousas	44	30.32 N	92.05 W
Opole (Oppeln)	7	50.41 N	17.55 E
Opotiki	29	38.00 S	177.17 E
Opportunity	48	47.39 N	117.15 W
Opunake	29	39.27 S	173.51 E
Oradea	11	47.03 N	21.57 E
Oraibi	47	35.53 N	110.37 W
Oran	14	35.43 N	0.43 W
Orange, Austl.	27	33.17 S	149.06 E
Orange, Tex., U.S.	44	30.01 N	93.44 W
Orange (Oranje) ≏	16	28.41 S	16.28 E
Orangeburg	43	33.30 N	80.52 W
Orange Walk	32	18.06 N	88.33 W
Oranjestad	32	12.33 N	70.06 W
Ord	46	41.36 N	98.56 W
Ordway	46	38.13 N	103.46 W
Ordžonikidze	4	43.03 N	44.40 E
Örebro	6	59.17 N	15.13 E
Orechovo-Zujevo	12	55.49 N	38.59 E
Oregon ☐[3]	37	44.00 N	121.00 W
Oregon City	48	45.21 N	122.36 W
Orem	47	40.19 N	111.42 W
Orense	9	42.20 N	7.51 W
Orillia	42	44.37 N	79.25 W
Orinoco ≏	33	8.37 N	62.15 W
Orkney Islands II	5	59.00 N	3.00 W
Orlando	43	28.32 N	81.23 W
Orléanais ☐[9]	8	47.50 N	2.00 E
Orléans	8	47.55 N	1.54 E
Ormond Beach	43	29.17 N	81.02 W
Örnsköldsvik	6	63.18 N	18.43 E
Orohena, Mont ∧	30d	17.37 S	149.28 W
Or'ol	12	52.59 N	36.05 E
Oroville	39	39.31 N	121.33 W
Orsk	4	51.12 N	58.34 E
Oruro	33	17.59 S	67.09 W
Osage ≏	44	38.35 N	91.57 W
Osage City	46	38.38 N	95.50 W
Ōsaka	23	34.40 N	135.30 E
Osawatomie	46	38.31 N	94.57 W
Osborne	46	39.26 N	98.42 W
Osceola	44	35.42 N	89.58 W
Oshawa	42	43.54 N	78.51 W
Oshkosh	42	44.01 N	88.33 W
Oshogbo	14	7.47 N	4.34 E
Osijek	11	45.33 N	18.41 E
Oskaloosa	42	41.18 N	92.39 W
Oslo	6	59.55 N	10.45 E
Osnabrück	7	52.16 N	8.02 E
Osorno	34	40.34 S	73.09 W
Ossa, Mount ∧	27	41.54 S	146.01 E
Östersund	6	63.11 N	14.39 E
Ostrava	7	49.50 N	18.17 E
Ostrowiec Świętokrzyski	7	50.57 N	21.23 E
Ostrów Wielkopolski	7	51.39 N	17.49 E
Ōsumi-kaikyō ⊔	23	31.00 N	131.00 E
Oswego	38	43.27 N	76.31 W
Otaru	23a	43.13 N	141.00 E
Otranto, Strait of ≏[1]	11	40.00 N	19.00 E
Ōtsu	23	35.00 N	135.52 E
Ottawa, Ont., Can.	38	45.25 N	75.42 W
Ottawa, Ill., U.S.	42	41.21 N	88.51 W
Ottawa, Kans., U.S.	46	38.37 N	95.16 W
Ottawa ≏	36	45.20 N	73.58 W
Ottumwa	42	41.01 N	92.25 W
Ouachita Mountains ⋏	44	34.40 N	94.25 W
Ouagadougou	14	12.22 N	1.31 W
Ouahigouya	14	13.35 N	2.25 W
Ouargla	14	31.59 N	5.25 E
Oudtshoorn	16	33.35 S	22.14 E
Oujda	14	34.41 N	1.45 W
Oulu	6	65.01 N	25.28 E
Ourinhos	35	22.59 S	49.52 W
Ouro Prêto	35	20.23 S	43.30 W
Overton	39	36.33 N	114.27 W
Oviedo	9	43.22 N	5.50 W
Owensboro	44	37.46 N	87.07 W
Owens Lake ⊜	39	36.25 N	117.56 W
Owen Sound	42	44.34 N	80.56 W
Owen Stanley Range ⋏	27	9.20 S	147.55 E
Owosso	42	43.00 N	84.10 W
Owyhee ≏	48	43.46 N	117.02 W
Owyhee, Lake ⊜[1]	48	43.28 N	117.20 W
Oxford, N.S., Can.	41	45.44 N	63.52 W
Oxford, Eng., U.K.	5	51.46 N	1.15 W
Oxford, Ala., U.S.	44	33.37 N	85.50 W
Oxford, Miss., U.S.	44	34.22 N	89.32 W
Oxford, Nebr., U.S.	46	40.15 N	99.38 W
Oxford, N.C., U.S.	43	36.19 N	78.35 W
Oxnard	39	34.12 N	119.11 W
Ozark Plateau ⋏[1]	44	37.00 N	93.00 W
Ozarks, Lake of the ⊜[1]	44	38.10 N	92.50 W

P

Name	Map No.	Lat ° '	Long ° '
Paarl	16	33.45 S	18.56 E
Paauilo	39a	20.02 N	155.22 W
Pābna	21	24.00 N	89.15 E
Pachuca [de Soto]	31	20.07 N	98.44 W
Pacific	44	38.29 N	90.45 W
Pacific Islands Trust Territory ☐[2]	1	10.00 N	155.00 E
Pacific Ocean ⊤[1]	1	10.00 S	150.00 W
Padang	25	0.57 S	100.21 E
Padangsidimpuan	26	1.22 N	99.16 E
Paderborn	7	51.43 N	8.45 E
Padova	10	45.25 N	11.53 E
Padre Island I	45	27.00 N	97.15 W
Paducah	44	37.05 N	88.36 W
Paea	30d	17.41 S	149.35 W
Pago Pago	30e	14.16 S	170.42 W
Pagosa Springs	47	37.16 N	107.01 W
Pahokee	38	41.43 N	81.15 W
Painesville	38	41.43 N	81.15 W
Painted Desert ⬚[2]	47	36.00 N	111.20 W
Pakanbaru	25	0.32 N	101.27 E
Pakaraima Mountains ⋏	33	5.30 N	60.40 W
Pakistan (Pākistān) ☐[1]	19	30.00 N	70.00 E
Pakokku	26	21.20 N	95.05 E
Pakxé	26	15.07 N	105.47 E
Palana	13	59.07 N	159.58 E
Palatka	43	29.39 N	81.38 W
Palau Islands II	25	7.30 N	134.30 E
Palawan I	25	9.30 N	118.30 E
Palembang	25	2.55 S	104.45 E
Palencia	9	42.01 N	4.32 W
Palermo	10	38.07 N	13.21 E
Palestine	45	31.46 N	95.38 W
Paletwa	26	21.18 N	92.51 E
Pāli	21	25.46 N	73.20 E
Palk Strait ⊔	20	10.00 N	79.45 E
Pallier	30b	14.53 S	166.35 E
Palliser, Cape ⊁	29	41.37 S	175.17 E
Palma [de Mallorca]	9	39.34 N	2.39 E
Palmdale	39	34.35 N	118.07 W
Palmer	40	61.36 N	149.07 W
Palmerston	29	45.29 S	170.43 E
Palmerston North	29	40.21 S	175.37 E
Palmetto	43	27.31 N	82.35 W
Pamir ⋏	21	38.00 N	73.00 E
Pamlico Sound ⊔	43	35.20 N	75.55 W
Pampa	45	35.32 N	100.58 W
Pampa ⬚[1]	34	35.00 S	63.00 W
Pamplona	8	42.49 N	1.38 W
Pana	44	39.23 N	89.05 W
Panamá	32	8.58 N	79.32 W
Panama ☐[1]	32	9.00 N	80.00 W
Panama, Gulf of C	32	8.00 N	79.30 W

Name	Map No.	Lat	Long
Panamá, Istmo de ▲³	32	9.00 N	79.00 W
Panama City	44	30.10 N	85.41 W
Panay **I**	25	11.15 N	122.30 E
Pančevo	11	44.52 N	20.39 E
Pandharpur	20	17.40 N	75.20 E
Pangkalpinang	25	2.08 S	106.08 E
Panguitch	47	37.49 N	112.26 W
Panié, Mont ▲	30b	20.36 S	164.46 E
Paoli	44	38.33 N	86.28 W
Paonia	47	38.52 N	107.36 W
Papeete	30d	17.32 S	149.34 W
Papua, Gulf of **C**	25	8.30 S	145.00 E
Papua New Guinea ☐¹	1	6.00 S	143.00 E
Paracatu	35	17.13 S	46.52 W
Paradise	39	39.46 N	121.37 W
Paraguaçu Paulista	35	22.25 S	50.34 W
Paraguari	34	25.38 S	57.09 W
Paraguay ☐¹	34	23.00 S	58.00 W
Paramaribo	33	5.50 N	55.10 W
Paraná	34	31.44 S	60.32 W
Paraná ≃	34	33.43 S	59.15 W
Paranaguá	34	25.31 S	48.30 W
Paranavai	35	23.04 S	52.28 W
Pardubice	7	50.02 N	15.47 E
Parepare	25	4.01 S	119.38 E
Paris, Ont., Can.	42	43.12 N	80.23 W
Paris, Fr.	8	48.52 N	2.20 E
Paris, Tex., U.S.	45	33.40 N	95.33 W
Parker	47	34.09 N	114.17 W
Parkersburg	38	39.17 N	81.32 W
Park River	46	48.24 N	97.45 W
Parma, It.	10	44.48 N	10.20 E
Parma, Ohio, U.S.	38	41.22 N	81.43 W
Parnaíba	33	2.54 S	41.47 W
Paro	21	27.26 N	89.25 E
Parrsboro	41	45.24 N	64.20 W
Parry Sound	42	45.21 N	80.02 W
Parsons	46	37.20 N	95.16 W
Pasadena, Calif., U.S.	39	34.09 N	118.09 W
Pasadena, Tex., U.S.	45	29.42 N	95.13 W
Pascagoula	44	30.23 N	88.31 W
Pasco	48	46.14 N	119.06 W
Passau	7	48.35 N	13.28 E
Passo Fundo	34	28.15 S	52.24 W
Passos	35	20.43 S	46.37 W
Pasto	33	1.13 N	77.17 W
Patagonia ◣¹	34	44.00 S	68.00 W
Paternò	10	37.34 N	14.54 E
Paterson	38	40.55 N	74.10 W
Patna	21	25.36 N	85.07 E
Patos de Minas	35	18.35 S	46.32 W
Pátrai	11	38.15 N	21.44 E
Patrocinio	35	18.57 S	46.59 W
Patuca ≃	32	15.50 N	84.17 W
Pau	8	43.18 N	0.22 W
Paulo Afonso	33	9.21 S	38.14 W
Paungde	26	18.29 N	95.30 E
Pavia	10	45.10 N	9.10 E
Pavillion	48	43.15 N	108.42 W
Pavlodar	13	52.18 N	76.57 E
Pawnee	45	36.20 N	96.48 W
Pawnee City	46	40.07 N	96.09 W
Payette	48	44.05 N	116.56 W
Paysandú	34	32.19 S	58.05 W
Pazardžik	11	42.12 N	24.20 E
Peabody	46	38.10 N	97.07 W
Peace ≃	43	26.55 N	82.05 W
Pearl ≃	44	30.11 N	89.32 W
Pearl Harbor **C**	39a	21.22 N	157.58 W
Peć	11	42.40 N	20.19 E
Pečora ≃	13	68.13 N	54.15 E
Pecos	45	31.25 N	103.30 W
Pecos ≃	45	29.42 N	101.22 W
Pécs	7	46.05 N	18.13 E
Pee Dee ≃	43	33.21 N	79.16 W
Peekskill	38	41.17 N	73.55 W
Pegasus Bay **C**	29	43.20 S	173.00 E
Pegu	26	17.20 N	96.29 E
Peikang	24	23.34 N	120.18 E
Pekin	42	40.35 N	89.40 W
Peking			
→ Beijing	22	39.55 N	116.25 E
Pelagie, Isole **II**	10	35.40 N	12.40 E
Pelée, Montagne ▲	32	14.48 N	61.10 W
Pelee Island **I**	42	41.46 N	82.39 W
Pelly Mountains ↗	36	62.00 N	133.00 W
Pelopónnisos (Peloponnesus) ◣¹	11	37.30 N	22.00 E

Pelotas	34	31.46 S	52.20 W
Pematangsiantar	25	2.57 N	99.03 E
Pemba Island **I**	15	7.31 S	39.25 E
Pembroke	42	45.49 N	77.07 W
Penápolis	35	21.24 S	50.04 W
Pendleton	48	45.40 N	118.47 W
Pend Oreille, Lake ◉	48	48.10 N	116.11 W
Penetanguishene	42	44.47 N	79.55 W
P'enghu Liehtao **II**	24	23.30 N	119.30 E
Pennines ↗	5	54.10 N	2.05 W
Pennington Gap	43	36.41 N	83.02 W
Pennsylvania ☐³	37	40.45 N	77.30 W
Penobscot ≃	38	44.30 N	68.50 W
Pensacola	44	30.25 N	87.13 W
Penza	4	53.13 N	45.00 E
Peoria	42	40.42 N	89.36 W
Percé	41	48.31 N	64.13 W
Pereira	33	4.49 N	75.43 W
Perham	46	46.36 N	95.34 W
Périgueux	8	45.11 N	0.43 E
Perm'	4	58.00 N	56.15 E
Pernik	11	42.36 N	23.02 E
Perpignan	8	42.41 N	2.53 E
Perry	43	30.07 N	83.35 W
Perryville	40	55.54 N	159.10 W
Perth, Austl.	27	31.56 S	115.50 E
Perth, Scot., U.K.	5	56.24 N	3.28 W
Perth Amboy	38	40.31 N	74.16 W
Perth-Andover	41	46.45 N	67.42 W
Peru	44	40.45 N	86.04 W
Peru ☐¹	33	10.00 S	76.00 W
Perugia	10	43.08 N	12.22 E
Pesaro	10	43.54 N	12.55 E
Pescadores			
→ P'enghu Liehtao **II**	24	23.30 N	119.30 E
Pescara	10	42.28 N	14.13 E
Peshāwar	19	34.01 N	71.33 E
Petaluma	39	38.14 N	122.39 W
Peterborough, Austl.	27	32.58 S	138.50 E
Peterborough, Ont., Can.	42	44.18 N	78.19 W
Peterborough, Eng., U.K.	5	52.35 N	0.15 W
Petersburg, Alaska, U.S.	40	56.50 N	132.59 W
Petersburg, Va., U.S.	43	37.13 N	77.24 W
Petoskey	42	45.22 N	84.57 W
Petrified Forest National Park ♠	47	34.55 N	109.49 W
Petrolina	33	9.24 S	40.30 W
Petropavlovsk-Kamčatskij	13	53.01 N	158.39 E
Petrópolis	33	22.31 S	43.10 W
Petroşani	11	45.25 N	23.22 E
Petrovsk-Zabajkal'skij	13	51.17 N	108.50 E
Petrozavodsk	4	61.47 N	34.20 E
Pforzheim	7	48.54 N	8.42 E
Phan-rang	26	11.34 N	108.59 E
Phan-thiet	26	10.56 N	108.06 E
Phenix City	43	32.29 N	85.01 W
Phet Buri	26	13.06 N	99.57 E
Philadelphia, Miss., U.S.	44	32.46 N	89.07 W
Philadelphia, Pa., U.S.	38	39.57 N	75.07 W
Philippi	38	39.09 N	80.02 W
Philippines ☐¹	25	13.00 N	122.00 E
Philippine Sea ▼²	1	20.00 N	135.00 E
Philipsburg	38	40.53 N	78.05 W
Phillips	42	45.41 N	90.24 W
Phitsanulok	26	16.50 N	100.15 E
Phnum Pènh	26	11.33 N	104.55 E
Phoenix	47	33.27 N	112.05 W
Phôngsali	26	21.41 N	102.06 E
Phra Nakhon Si Ayutthaya	26	14.21 N	100.33 E
Phuket	26	7.53 N	98.24 E
Phumi Béng	26	13.05 N	104.18 E
Phu-quoc, Đao **I**	26	10.12 N	104.00 E
Phu-tho	26	21.24 N	105.13 E
Phu-vinh	26	9.56 N	106.20 E
Piacenza	10	45.01 N	9.40 E
Piatra-Neamţ	11	46.56 N	26.22 E
Pictured Rocks National Lakeshore ♠	42	46.35 N	86.20 W
Pidurutalagala ▲	19	7.00 N	80.46 E
Piedras Negras, Guat.	32	17.11 N	91.15 W
Piedras Negras, Méx.	31	28.42 N	100.31 W
Pierre	46	44.22 N	100.21 W
Pietermaritzburg	16	29.37 S	30.16 E
Pietersburg	16	23.54 S	29.25 E
Piet Retief	16	27.01 S	30.50 E
Pikes Peak ▲	47	38.51 N	105.03 W
Pikeville	43	37.29 N	82.31 W
Piła (Schneidemühl)	7	53.10 N	16.44 E

Name	Map No.	Lat	Long
Pinar del Río	32	22.25 N	83.42 W
Píndhos Óros ⋏	11	39.49 N	21.14 E
Pindus Mountains			
→ Píndhos Óros ⋏	11	39.49 N	21.14 E
Pine Bluff	44	34.13 N	92.01 W
Pinerolo	10	44.53 N	7.21 E
Pinetown	16	29.52 S	30.46 E
Pineville	44	31.19 N	92.26 W
P'ingtung	24	22.40 N	120.29 E
Pinsk	12	52.07 N	26.04 E
Piombino	10	42.55 N	10.32 E
Piotrków Trybunalski	7	51.25 N	19.42 E
Pipestone	46	43.58 N	96.19 W
Pipmouacane, Réservoir ⌷[1]	41	49.35 N	70.30 W
Piqua	38	40.09 N	84.15 W
Piracicaba	35	22.43 S	47.38 W
Piraiévs (Piraeus)	11	37.57 N	23.38 E
Piraju	35	23.12 S	49.23 W
Pirapora	35	17.21 S	44.56 W
Pisa	10	43.43 N	10.23 E
Pisco	33	13.42 S	76.13 W
Pittsburg	46	37.25 N	94.42 W
Pittsburgh	38	40.26 N	80.00 W
Pittsfield	38	42.27 N	73.15 W
Piura	33	5.12 S	80.38 W
Placetas	32	22.19 N	79.40 W
Plainfield	42	44.13 N	89.30 W
Plainview, Nebr., U.S.	46	42.21 N	97.47 W
Plainview, Tex., U.S.	45	34.11 N	101.43 W
Plaquemine	44	30.17 N	91.14 W
Plata, Río de la C[1]	34	35.00 S	57.00 W
Platte ≃, U.S.	37	39.16 N	94.50 W
Platte ≃, Nebr., U.S.	46	41.04 N	95.53 W
Plattsburgh	38	44.42 N	73.28 W
Plattsmouth	46	41.01 N	95.53 W
Plauen	7	50.30 N	12.08 E
Plenty, Bay of C	29	37.40 S	177.00 E
Plentywood	46	48.47 N	104.34 W
Pleven	11	43.25 N	24.37 E
Płock	7	52.33 N	19.43 E
Ploieşti	11	44.56 N	26.02 E
Plovdiv	11	42.09 N	24.45 E
Plymouth, Eng., U.K.	5	50.23 N	4.10 W
Plymouth, Mass., U.S.	38	41.58 N	70.41 W
Plymouth, N.C., U.S.	43	35.52 N	76.43 W
Plzeň	7	49.45 N	13.23 E
Po ≃	10	44.57 N	12.04 E
Pobeda, Gora ⋏	13	65.12 N	146.12 E
Pocatello	48	42.52 N	112.27 W
Poços de Caldas	35	21.48 S	46.34 W
Pointe-à-Pitre	32	16.14 N	61.32 W
Pointe-Noire	15	4.48 S	11.51 E
Point Pleasant	38	40.05 N	74.04 W
Point Reyes National Seashore ♦	39	38.00 N	122.58 W
Poland ⌷[1]	4	52.00 N	19.00 E
Polevskoj	4	56.26 N	60.11 E
Poltava	4	49.35 N	34.34 E
Polynesia II	1	4.00 S	156.00 W
Pomerania ⌷[9]	7	54.00 N	16.00 E
Pomeranian Bay C	7	54.00 N	14.15 E
Ponca City	45	36.42 N	97.05 W
Ponce	32	18.01 N	66.37 W
Ponta Grossa	34	25.05 S	50.09 W
Pontchartrain, Lake ⌷	44	30.10 N	90.10 W
Ponte Nova	35	20.24 S	42.54 W
Pontevedra	9	42.26 N	8.38 W
Pontiac, Ill., U.S.	42	40.53 N	88.38 W
Pontiac, Mich., U.S.	42	42.37 N	83.18 W
Pontianak	25	0.02 S	109.20 E
Pontotoc	44	34.15 N	89.00 W
Poopó, Lago ⌷	33	18.45 S	67.07 W
Popayán	33	2.27 N	76.36 W
Poplar	46	48.07 N	105.12 W
Poplar Bluff	44	36.45 N	90.24 W
Popocatépetl, Volcán ⋏[1]	31	19.02 N	98.38 W
Popomanaseu, Mount ⋏	27	9.42 S	160.04 E
Porbandar	21	21.38 N	69.36 E
Pordenone	10	45.57 N	12.39 E
Pori	6	61.29 N	21.47 E
Poronajsk	13	49.14 N	143.04 E
Portadown	5	54.26 N	6.27 W
Portage	42	42.12 N	85.41 W
Portageville	44	36.26 N	89.42 W
Port Alfred (Kowie)	16	33.36 S	26.55 E
Port Allegany	38	41.49 N	78.17 W
Port Angeles	48	48.07 N	123.27 W
Port Arthur	44	29.55 N	93.55 W
Port Augusta	27	32.30 S	137.46 E
Port-au-Prince	32	18.32 N	72.20 W
Port Charlotte	43	26.59 N	82.06 W
Port Clyde	41	43.56 N	69.15 W
Port Edward	16	31.02 S	30.13 E
Port Elgin	42	44.26 N	81.24 W
Port Elizabeth	16	33.58 S	25.40 E
Port Ellen	5	55.39 N	6.12 W
Porterville, Calif., U.S.	39	36.04 N	119.01 W
Port-Gentil	15	0.43 S	8.47 E
Port Gibson	44	31.58 N	90.58 W
Port Harcourt	14	4.43 N	7.05 E
Port Hedland	27	20.19 S	118.34 E
Port Huron	42	42.58 N	82.27 W
Portland, Austl.	27	38.21 S	141.36 E
Portland, Maine, U.S.	38	43.39 N	70.17 W
Portland, Oreg., U.S.	48	45.33 N	122.36 W
Port Lavaca	45	28.37 N	96.38 W
Port Lincoln	27	34.44 S	135.52 E
Port Louis	15	20.10 S	57.30 E
Port Macquarie	27	31.26 S	152.55 E
Port Moresby	27	9.30 S	147.10 E
Porto	9	41.11 N	8.36 W
Pôrto Alegre	34	30.04 S	51.11 W
Portobelo	32	9.33 N	79.39 W
Port of Spain	32	10.39 N	61.31 W
Porto-Novo	14	6.29 N	2.37 E
Port Orford	48	42.45 N	124.30 W
Pôrto Velho	33	8.46 S	63.54 W
Port Pirie	27	33.11 S	138.01 E
Port Said			
→ Būr Saʿīd	14	31.16 N	32.18 E
Port Saint Joe	43	29.49 N	85.18 W
Port Sanilac	42	43.26 N	82.33 W
Portsmouth, Eng., U.K.	5	50.48 N	1.05 W
Portsmouth, N.H., U.S.	38	43.04 N	70.46 W
Portsmouth, Ohio, U.S.	38	38.45 N	82.59 W
Portsmouth, Va., U.S.	43	36.52 N	76.24 W
Port Stanley	42	42.40 N	81.13 W
Port Sulphur	44	29.29 N	89.42 W
Portugal ⌷[1]	4	39.30 N	8.00 W
Port Washington	42	43.23 N	87.53 W
Posadas	34	27.23 S	55.53 W
Post Maurice Cortier (Bidon Cinq)	14	22.18 N	1.05 E
Potchefstroom	16	26.46 S	27.01 E
Potenza	10	40.38 N	15.49 E
Potgietersrus	16	24.15 S	28.55 E
Potholes Reservoir ⌷[1]	48	47.01 N	119.19 W
Potomac ≃	38	38.00 N	76.18 W
Potosí, Bol.	33	19.35 S	65.45 W
Potosi, Mo., U.S.	44	37.56 N	90.47 W
Potsdam	7	52.24 N	13.04 E
Poughkeepsie	38	41.42 N	73.56 W
Pouso Alegre	35	22.13 S	45.56 W
Poŭthĭsăt	26	12.32 N	103.55 E
Powder ≃	46	46.44 N	105.26 W
Powell, Lake ⌷[1]	47	37.25 N	110.45 W
Powers Lake	46	48.34 N	102.39 W
Poyanghu ⌷	24	29.00 N	116.25 E
Poza Rica de Hidalgo	31	20.33 N	97.27 W
Poznań	7	52.25 N	16.55 E
Pozzuoli	10	40.49 N	14.07 E
Prague			
→ Praha	7	50.05 N	14.26 E
Praha (Prague)	7	50.05 N	14.26 E
Prairie du Chien	42	43.03 N	91.09 W
Prattville	44	32.28 N	86.29 W
Prescott	47	34.33 N	112.28 W
Presidente Epitácio	35	21.46 S	52.06 W
Presidente Prudente	33	22.07 S	51.22 W
Prešov	7	49.00 N	21.15 E
Prespa, Lake ⌷	11	40.55 N	21.00 E
Presque Isle	41	46.41 N	68.01 W
Preston, Eng., U.K.	5	53.46 N	2.42 W
Preston, Idaho, U.S.	48	42.06 N	111.53 W
Pretoria	16	25.45 S	28.10 E
Pretty Prairie	46	37.47 N	98.01 W
Prey Vêng	26	11.29 N	105.19 E
Příbram	7	49.42 N	14.01 E
Prichard	44	30.44 N	88.07 W
Prievidza	7	48.47 N	18.37 E
Prilep	11	41.20 N	21.33 E
Primghar	46	43.05 N	95.38 W
Prince Albert	36	53.12 N	105.46 W
Prince Alfred Hamlet	16	33.18 S	19.20 E
Prince Edward Island ⌷[4]	36	46.20 N	63.20 W

Name	Map No.	Lat°′	Long°′
Prince George	36	53.55 N	122.45 W
Prince of Wales Island I, N.W. Ter., Can.	36	72.40 N	99.00 W
Prince of Wales Island I, Alaska, U.S.	40	55.47 N	132.50 W
Prince Rupert	36	54.19 N	130.19 W
Princeton	38	40.21 N	74.40 W
Prineville	48	44.18 N	120.51 W
Prinzapolca	32	13.24 N	83.34 W
Priština	11	42.39 N	21.10 E
Proctor	38	43.40 N	73.02 W
Prokopjevsk	13	53.53 N	86.45 E
Prome (Pyè)	26	18.49 N	95.13 E
Prostějov	7	49.29 N	17.07 E
Provence □[9]	8	44.00 N	6.00 E
Providence	38	41.50 N	71.25 W
Provo	47	40.14 N	111.39 W
Prudhoe Bay C	40	70.20 N	148.20 W
Pruszków	7	52.11 N	20.48 E
Prut ≃	11	45.30 N	28.12 E
Przemyśl	7	49.47 N	22.47 E
Puapua	30e	13.34 S	172.09 W
Pucallpa	33	8.23 S	74.32 W
Pudukkottai	20	10.23 N	78.49 E
Puebla [de Zaragoza]	31	19.03 N	98.12 W
Pueblo	47	38.16 N	104.37 W
Puerto Armuelles	32	8.17 N	82.52 W
Puerto Barrios	32	15.43 N	88.36 W
Puerto Berrio	33	6.29 N	74.24 W
Puerto Cabezas	32	14.02 N	83.23 W
Puerto Cortés, C.R.	32	8.58 N	83.32 W
Puerto Cortés, Hond.	32	15.48 N	87.56 W
Puerto la Cruz	33	10.13 N	64.38 W
Puertollano	9	38.41 N	4.07 W
Puerto Maldonado	33	12.36 S	69.11 W
Puerto Montt	34	41.28 S	72.57 W
Puerto Rico □[2]	32	18.15 N	66.30 W
Puerto Vallarta	31	20.37 N	105.15 W
Puget Sound ʯ	48	47.50 N	122.30 W
Pula	10	44.52 N	13.50 E
Pulaski	44	35.12 N	87.02 W
Puław̧y	7	51.25 N	21.57 E
Pune (Poona)	20	18.32 N	73.52 E
Puno	33	15.50 S	70.02 W
Puntarenas	32	9.58 N	84.50 W
Punto Fijo	33	11.42 N	70.13 W
Purcell Mountains ⩘	48	49.00 N	115.40 W
Puri	21	19.48 N	85.51 E
Purnea	21	25.47 N	87.31 E
Purūlia	21	23.20 N	86.22 E
Pusan	22	35.06 N	129.03 E
Putian	24	25.28 N	119.02 E
Puto	30a	5.41 S	154.43 E
Puyallup	48	47.11 N	122.18 W
Pyinmana	26	19.44 N	96.13 E
P'yŏngyang	22	39.01 N	125.45 E
Pyramid Lake ⊜	39	40.00 N	119.35 W
Pyrenees ⩘	9	42.40 N	1.00 E
Pyu	26	18.29 N	96.26 E

Q

Qandahār	19	31.32 N	65.30 E
Qatar □[1]	17	25.00 N	51.10 E
Qingdao (Tsingtao)	22	36.06 N	120.19 E
Qinhuangdao	22	39.56 N	119.36 E
Qiqihaer (Tsitsihar)	22	47.19 N	123.55 E
Qom	17	34.39 N	50.54 E
Quanzhou	24	24.54 N	118.35 E
Québec	41	46.49 N	71.14 W
Quebec (Québec) □[4]	36	52.00 N	72.00 W
Quedlinburg	7	51.48 N	11.09 E
Queen Charlotte Islands II	36	53.00 N	132.00 W
Queen Charlotte Sound ʯ	36	51.30 N	129.30 W
Queen Maud Land ◢[1]	3	72.30 S	12.00 E
Queenstown, N.Z.	29	45.02 S	168.40 E
Queenstown, S. Afr.	16	31.52 S	26.52 E
Quelimane	15	17.53 S	36.51 E
Quemoy → Chinmen Tao I	24	24.27 N	118.23 E
Que Que	15	18.55 S	29.49 E
Querétaro	31	20.36 N	100.23 W
Quetta	19	30.12 N	67.00 E
Quezon City	25	14.38 N	121.00 E
Quibdó	33	5.42 N	76.40 W
Quilpie	27	26.37 S	144.15 E

Quimper	8	48.00 N	4.06 W
Quincy, III., U.S.	44	39.56 N	91.23 W
Quincy, Mich., U.S.	42	41.57 N	84.53 W
Qui-nhon	26	13.46 N	109.14 E
Quitman	44	32.03 N	88.43 W
Quito	33	0.13 S	78.30 W
Qumbu	16	31.10 S	28.48 E

R

Rabat, Magreb	14	34.02 N	6.51 W
Rabat (Victoria), Malta	10	36.02 N	14.14 E
Rach-gia	26	10.01 N	105.05 E
Racibórz (Ratibor)	7	50.06 N	18.13 E
Racine	42	42.43 N	87.48 W
Radford	43	37.08 N	80.34 W
Radom	7	51.25 N	21.10 E
Radomsko	7	51.05 N	19.25 E
Raeford	43	34.59 N	79.14 W
Raetihi	29	39.26 S	175.17 E
Rafaela	34	31.16 S	61.29 W
Rafah	18	31.18 N	34.15 E
Ragusa	10	36.55 N	14.44 E
Rahīmyār Khān	21	28.25 N	70.18 E
Rāichūr	20	16.12 N	77.22 E
Raigarh	21	21.54 N	83.24 E
Rainier, Mount ⋀	48	46.52 N	121.46 W
Raipur	21	21.14 N	81.38 E
Rājahmundry	20	16.59 N	81.47 E
Rajang ≃	25	2.04 N	111.12 E
Rājapālaiyam	20	9.27 N	77.34 E
Rajcichinsk	13	49.46 N	129.25 E
Rājkot	21	22.18 N	70.47 E
Raleigh	43	35.47 N	78.39 W
Ramm, Jabal ⋀	17	29.35 N	35.24 E
Ramona	45	36.32 N	95.55 W
Rāmpur	21	28.49 N	79.02 E
Rancagua	34	34.10 S	70.45 W
Rānchī	21	23.21 N	85.20 E
Randers	6	56.28 N	10.03 E
Randfontein	16	26.11 S	27.42 E
Randolph	47	41.40 N	111.11 W
Rangeley	38	44.58 N	70.39 W
Rangoon	26	16.47 N	96.10 E
Rankin Inlet	36	62.45 N	92.10 W
Rann of Kutch ⊵	21	24.00 N	70.00 E
Rantauprapat	26	2.06 N	99.50 E
Rantoul	44	40.19 N	88.09 W
Rapid City	46	44.05 N	103.14 W
Rapid River	42	45.56 N	86.58 W
Ras Dashen ⋀	17	13.10 N	38.26 E
Rathbun Lake ⊜[1]	42	40.54 N	93.05 W
Rat Islands II	40	52.00 N	178.00 E
Ratlām	21	23.19 N	75.04 E
Raton	45	36.54 N	104.24 W
Rauma	6	61.08 N	21.30 E
Raurkela	21	22.13 N	84.53 E
Ravenna	10	44.25 N	12.12 E
Ravensburg	7	47.47 N	9.37 E
Ravenshoe	27	17.37 S	145.29 E
Ravensthorpe	27	33.35 S	120.02 E
Rāwalpindi	19	33.36 N	73.04 E
Rawlins	48	41.47 N	107.14 W
Raymondville	45	26.29 N	97.47 W
R'azan'	12	54.38 N	39.44 E
Razgrad	11	43.32 N	26.31 E
Reading, Eng., U.K.	5	51.28 N	0.59 W
Reading, Pa., U.S.	38	40.20 N	75.56 W
Readstown	42	43.27 N	90.45 W
Real, Cordillera ⩘	33	19.00 S	66.30 W
Recife	33	8.03 S	34.54 W
Recklinghausen	7	51.36 N	7.13 E
Red (Hong-ha) (Yuanjiang) ≃, As.	26	20.17 N	106.34 E
Red ≃, U.S.	37	31.00 N	91.40 W
Red Bay	44	34.27 N	88.09 W
Red Bluff Reservoir ⊜[1]	45	31.57 N	103.56 W
Red Deer	36	52.16 N	113.48 W
Reddersburg	16	29.38 S	26.07 E
Redding	39	40.35 N	122.24 W
Redfield	46	44.53 N	98.31 W
Red Lodge	48	45.11 N	109.15 W
Redmond	48	44.17 N	121.11 W
Red Oak	46	41.01 N	95.14 W
Red Sea ⲷ[2]	17	20.00 N	38.00 E
Red Wing	42	44.34 N	92.31 W
Redwood Falls	46	44.32 N	95.07 W

Name	Map No.	Lat ° '	Long ° '
Redwood National Park ♦	48	41.30 N	124.05 W
Reefton	29	42.07 S	171.52 E
Regensburg	7	49.01 N	12.06 E
Reggio di Calabria	10	38.07 N	15.39 E
Reggio nell'Emilia	10	44.43 N	10.36 E
Regina	36	50.25 N	104.39 W
Rehovot	18	31.54 N	34.49 E
Reims	8	49.15 N	4.02 E
Rendsburg	7	54.18 N	9.40 E
Renfrew	42	45.28 N	76.41 W
Rennes	8	48.05 N	1.41 W
Reno	39	39.31 N	119.48 W
Rensselaer	44	40.57 N	87.09 W
Republic	48	48.39 N	118.44 W
Republican ≃	46	39.03 N	96.48 W
Resistencia	34	27.27 S	58.59 W
Reşiţa	11	45.17 N	21.53 E
Réthimnon	11	35.22 N	24.29 E
Reunion (Réunion) □²	15	21.06 S	55.36 E
Reus	9	41.09 N	1.07 E
Reutlingen	7	48.29 N	9.11 E
Revelstoke	36	50.59 N	118.12 W
Revillagigedo, Islas II	31	19.00 N	111.30 W
Rewa	21	24.32 N	81.18 E
Rewāri	21	28.11 N	76.37 E
Rexburg	48	43.49 N	111.47 W
Rey, Isla del I	32	8.22 N	78.55 W
Reykjavik	4	64.09 N	21.51 W
Reynosa	31	26.07 N	98.18 W
Rhaetian Alps ⋌	8	46.30 N	10.00 E
Rheine	7	52.17 N	7.26 E
Rhine (Rhein) (Rhin) ≃	7	51.52 N	6.02 E
Rhinelander	42	45.38 N	89.25 W
Rhode Island □³	37	41.40 N	71.30 W
Rhode Island Sound ⋃	38	41.25 N	71.25 W
Rhodes			
→ Ródhos I	11	36.10 N	28.00 E
Rhodope Mountains ⋌	11	41.30 N	24.30 E
Rhône ≃	8	43.20 N	4.50 E
Riau, Kepulauan II	26	1.00 N	104.30 E
Ribeirão Prêto	33	21.10 S	47.48 W
Richardson	45	32.57 N	96.44 W
Richfield	47	38.46 N	112.05 W
Richland	48	46.17 N	119.18 W
Richmond, Ind., U.S.	44	39.50 N	84.54 W
Richmond, Ky., U.S.	38	37.45 N	84.18 W
Richmond, Va., U.S.	43	37.30 N	77.28 W
Ridgetown	42	42.26 N	81.54 W
Riesa	7	51.18 N	13.17 E
Rieti	10	42.24 N	12.51 E
Rif ⋌	9	35.00 N	4.00 W
Rift Valley ⋁	15	3.00 S	29.00 E
Rīga	12	56.57 N	24.06 E
Riga, Gulf of			
→ Rižskij Zaliv ⊂	12	57.30 N	23.35 E
Rīgestān ⋅¹	19	31.00 N	65.00 E
Rijeka	10	45.20 N	14.27 E
Riley	46	39.18 N	96.50 W
Rimini	10	44.04 N	12.34 E
Rimouski	41	48.26 N	68.33 W
Riobamba	33	1.40 S	78.38 W
Rio Branco	33	9.58 S	67.48 W
Rio Cuarto	34	33.08 S	64.21 W
Rio de Janeiro	33	22.54 S	43.14 W
Rio Gallegos	34	51.38 S	69.13 W
Rio Grande	34	32.02 S	52.05 W
Riohacha	33	11.33 N	72.55 W
Rio Verde	35	17.43 S	50.56 W
Ripley	38	38.49 N	81.43 W
Ripon	42	43.51 N	88.50 W
Ritter, Mount ⋀	39	37.42 N	119.12 W
Rivera	34	30.54 S	55.31 W
Riverhead	38	40.55 N	72.40 W
Riverina ⋅¹	28	35.30 S	145.30 E
Riverside	33	33.59 N	117.22 W
Riverton Heights	48	47.28 N	122.17 W
Rivière-du-Loup	41	47.50 N	69.32 W
Riyadh			
→ Ar-Riyāḍ	17	24.38 N	46.43 E
Rižskij Zaliv (Rīgas Jūras Līcis)			
(Gulf of Riga) ⊂	12	57.30 N	23.35 E
Roanne	8	46.02 N	4.04 E
Roanoke	43	37.16 N	79.57 W
Roanoke (Staunton) ≃	43	35.56 N	76.43 W
Roanoke Island I	43	35.53 N	75.39 W
Roanoke Rapids	43	36.28 N	77.40 W
Roberval	36	48.31 N	72.13 W
Robinson	44	39.00 N	87.44 W
Rocha	34	34.29 S	54.20 W
Rochefort	8	45.57 N	0.58 W
Rochester, Minn., U.S.	42	44.02 N	92.29 W
Rochester, N.H., U.S.	38	43.18 N	70.59 W
Rochester, N.Y., U.S.	38	43.10 N	77.36 W
Rock Falls	42	41.47 N	89.41 W
Rockford	42	42.17 N	89.06 W
Rockhampton	27	23.23 S	150.31 E
Rock Hill	43	34.56 N	81.01 W
Rockingham	43	34.56 N	79.46 W
Rock Island	42	41.30 N	90.34 W
Rockland	38	44.06 N	69.06 W
Rock Springs	48	41.35 N	109.13 W
Rockville	38	39.05 N	77.09 W
Rockwood	43	35.52 N	84.41 W
Rocky Mount, N.C., U.S.	43	35.56 N	77.48 W
Rocky Mount, Va., U.S.	43	37.00 N	79.54 W
Rocky Mountain National Park ♦	47	40.19 N	105.42 W
Rocky Mountains ⋌	1	48.00 N	116.00 W
Rodez	8	44.21 N	2.35 E
Ródhos (Rhodes)	11	36.26 N	28.13 E
Ródhos I	11	36.10 N	28.00 E
Roebourne	27	20.47 S	117.09 E
Roeselare	7	50.57 N	3.08 E
Rogers, Mount ⋀	43	36.39 N	81.33 W
Rogue ≃	39	42.26 N	124.25 W
Rohtak	21	28.54 N	76.34 E
Rolla, Mo., U.S.	44	37.57 N	91.46 W
Rolla, N. Dak., U.S.	46	48.52 N	99.37 W
Roma (Rome)	10	41.54 N	12.29 E
Roman	11	46.55 N	26.56 E
Romania (România) □¹	4	46.00 N	25.30 E
Romans[-sur-Isère]	8	45.03 N	5.03 E
Rome			
→ Roma, It.	10	41.54 N	12.29 E
Rome, Ga., U.S.	43	34.16 N	85.11 W
Rome, N.Y., U.S.	38	43.13 N	75.27 W
Romeo	42	42.48 N	83.01 W
Roraima, Mount ⋀	33	5.12 N	60.44 W
Rosario, Arg.	34	32.57 S	60.40 W
Roseau	32	15.18 N	61.24 W
Roseburg	48	43.13 N	123.20 W
Rosenberg	45	29.33 N	95.48 W
Roseville	42	45.01 N	93.09 W
Ross Ice Shelf ⊠	3	81.30 S	175.00 W
Ross Sea ⊤²	3	76.00 S	175.00 W
Rostock	7	54.05 N	12.07 E
Rostov-na-Donu	4	47.14 N	39.42 E
Roswell	45	33.24 N	104.32 W
Rotorua	29	38.09 S	176.15 E
Rotterdam	7	51.55 N	4.28 E
Roubaix	8	50.42 N	3.10 E
Rouen	8	49.26 N	1.05 E
Roundup	48	46.27 N	108.33 W
Rouyn	42	48.15 N	79.01 W
Rovaniemi	6	66.34 N	25.48 E
Rovigo	10	45.04 N	11.47 E
Roy	47	41.10 N	112.02 W
Royale, Isle I	42	48.00 N	89.00 W
Ruapehu ⋀	29	39.17 S	175.34 E
Rubcovsk	13	51.33 N	81.10 E
Ruby	40	64.44 N	155.30 W
Ruby Lake ☷	39	40.10 N	115.30 W
Rudolf, Lake ◎	17	3.30 N	36.00 E
Rudong	24	32.19 N	121.12 E
Rugby	46	48.22 N	100.00 W
Rügen I	7	54.25 N	13.24 E
Ruian	27	27.49 N	120.38 E
Ruidoso	47	33.20 N	105.40 W
Rukwa, Lake ◎	15	8.00 S	32.25 E
Rupert	48	42.37 N	113.41 W
Ruse	11	43.50 N	25.57 E
Russellville, Ala., U.S.	44	34.30 N	87.44 W
Russellville, Ark., U.S. ♣	45	35.17 N	93.08 W
Ruston	44	32.32 N	92.38 W
Rutherfordton	43	35.22 N	81.57 W
Rutland	38	43.36 N	72.59 W
Rwanda □¹	15	2.30 S	30.00 E
Rybinsk	12	58.03 N	38.52 E
Rybinskoje Vodochraniliśče ◎¹	12	58.30 N	38.25 E
Rysy ⋀	7	49.12 N	20.04 E
Ryukyu Islands			
→ Nansei-shotō II	22	26.30 N	128.00 E
Rzeszów	7	50.03 N	22.00 E

Name	Map No.	Lat ° '	Long ° '

S

Name	Map No.	Lat	Long
Saarbrücken	7	49.14 N	6.59 E
Saaremaa I	12	58.25 N	22.30 E
Sab, Tônlé ◙	26	13.00 N	104.00 E
Sabhah	14	27.03 N	14.26 E
Sabinas Hidalgo	31	26.30 N	100.10 W
Sabine ≃	31	30.00 N	93.45 W
Sabine Lake ◙	44	29.50 N	93.50 W
Sable, Cape ≻, N.S., Can.	41	43.25 N	65.35 W
Sable, Cape ≻, Fla., U.S.	43	25.12 N	81.05 W
Sac City	46	42.25 N	95.00 W
Sachalin, Ostrov (Sakhalin) I	13	51.00 N	143.00 E
Sachty	4	47.42 N	40.13 E
Sacramento	39	38.03 N	121.56 W
Sacramento ≃	39	38.03 N	121.56 W
Sacramento Valley v	39	39.15 N	122.00 W
Sado I	23	38.00 N	138.25 E
Safford	47	32.50 N	109.43 W
Saga	23	33.15 N	130.18 E
Sagami-nada C	23	35.00 N	139.30 E
Sāgar	21	23.50 N	78.45 E
Saginaw	42	43.25 N	83.58 W
Saginaw Bay C	42	43.50 N	83.40 W
Sagua de Tánamo	32	20.35 N	75.14 W
Sagua la Grande	32	22.49 N	80.05 W
Saguaro National Monument ♠	47	32.12 N	110.38 W
Saguenay ≃	41	48.08 N	69.44 W
Sagunto	9	39.41 N	0.16 W
Sahara ♠2	14	26.00 N	13.00 E
Sahāranpur	21	29.58 N	77.33 E
Saidpur	21	25.47 N	88.54 E
Sai-gon → Thanh-pho Ho Chi Minh	26	10.45 N	106.40 E
Saint Anthony, Newf., Can.	36	51.22 N	55.35 W
Saint Anthony, Idaho, U.S.	48	43.58 N	111.41 W
Saint Augustine	43	29.54 N	81.19 W
Saint-Brieuc	8	48.31 N	2.47 W
Saint Catharines	42	43.10 N	79.15 W
Saint Charles	44	38.47 N	90.29 W
Saint Christopher (Saint Kitts) I	32	17.20 N	62.45 W
Saint Clair	42	42.49 N	82.30 W
Saint Cloud	42	45.33 N	94.10 W
Saint Croix I	32	17.45 N	64.45 W
Saint Croix ≃	41	45.10 N	67.10 W
Saint-Denis, Fr.	8	48.56 N	2.22 E
Saint-Denis, Réu.	15	20.52 S	55.28 E
Saint Eleanor's	41	46.25 N	63.49 W
Saint Élias, Mount ∧	40	60.18 N	140.55 W
Saint-Étienne	8	45.26 N	4.24 E
Sainte-Foy	41	46.47 N	71.17 W
Saint George	27	28.02 S	148.35 E
Saint George's	32	12.03 N	61.45 W
Saint George's Channel 𝕌	5	52.00 N	6.00 W
Saint Helens	48	45.52 N	122.48 W
Saint Helens, Mount ∧	48	46.12 N	122.11 W
Saint Helier	8	49.12 N	2.37 W
Saint-Hyacinthe	38	45.38 N	72.57 W
Saint James, Mich., U.S.	42	45.45 N	85.31 W
Saint James, Minn., U.S.	46	43.59 N	94.38 W
Saint-Jean	38	45.19 N	73.16 W
Saint-Jérôme	38	45.46 N	74.00 W
Saint John	41	45.16 N	66.03 W
Saint John's	36	47.34 N	52.43 W
Saint Johns ≃	43	30.24 N	81.24 W
Saint Johnsbury	38	44.25 N	72.01 W
Saint Joseph	44	39.46 N	94.51 W
Saint-Joseph-de-Beauce	41	46.18 N	70.53 W
Saint Joseph Island I	42	46.13 N	83.57 W
Saint-Jovite	38	46.07 N	74.36 W
Saint Kitts → Saint Christopher I	32	17.20 N	62.45 W
Saint Kitts-Nevis □2	32	17.20 N	62.45 W
Saint Lawrence ≃	36	49.30 N	67.00 W
Saint Lawrence, Gulf of C	36	48.00 N	62.00 W
Saint Lawrence Island I	40	63.30 N	170.30 W
Saint-Lô	8	49.07 N	1.05 W
Saint-Louis, Sén.	14	16.02 N	16.30 W
Saint Louis, Mo., U.S.	44	38.38 N	90.11 W
Saint Lucia □1	32	13.53 N	60.58 W
Saint Lucia, Lake ◙	16	28.05 S	32.26 E
Saint-Malo	8	48.39 N	2.01 W
Saint-Malo, Golfe de C	8	48.45 N	2.00 W
Sainte-Marie, Cap ≻	15	25.36 S	45.08 E
Saint Marys	38	41.26 N	78.34 W
Saint Matthews	43	33.40 N	80.46 W
Saint-Nazaire	8	47.17 N	2.12 W
Saint Paul	42	44.58 N	93.07 W
Saint Peter Port	8	49.27 N	2.32 W
Saint Petersburg	43	27.46 N	82.38 W
Saint Pierre and Miquelon □2	36	46.55 N	56.10 W
Saint-Quentin	8	49.51 N	3.17 E
Saintes	8	45.45 N	0.52 W
Saint Thomas	42	42.47 N	81.12 W
Saint Vincent □1	32	13.15 N	61.12 W
Saint Vincent, Gulf C	28	35.00 S	138.05 E
Saipan I	25	15.12 N	145.45 E
Sajama, Nevado ∧	33	18.06 S	68.54 W
Sakai	23	34.35 N	135.28 E
Sakakawea, Lake ◙1	46	47.50 N	102.20 W
Sakata	23	38.55 N	139.50 E
Sakau	30b	16.49 S	168.24 E
Sakhalin → Sachalin, Ostrov I	13	51.00 N	143.00 E
Sakrivier	16	30.54 S	20.28 E
Salamanca	9	40.58 N	5.39 W
Saldanha	16	33.00 S	17.56 E
Salem, Bhārat	20	11.39 N	78.10 E
Salem, Ill., U.S.	44	38.38 N	88.57 W
Salem, Mass., U.S.	38	42.31 N	70.55 W
Salem, Mo., U.S.	44	37.39 N	91.32 W
Salem, Ohio, U.S.	38	40.54 N	80.52 W
Salem, Oreg., U.S.	36	44.57 N	123.01 W
Salem, S. Dak., U.S.	46	43.44 N	97.23 W
Salem, Va., U.S.	43	37.17 N	80.03 W
Salerno	10	40.41 N	14.47 E
Salgótarján	7	48.07 N	19.48 E
Salihli	11	38.29 N	28.09 E
Salina, Kans., U.S.	46	38.50 N	97.37 W
Salina, Utah, U.S.	47	38.58 N	111.51 W
Salinas	39	36.40 N	121.39 W
Salinas ≃	39	36.45 N	121.48 W
Salisbury, Eng., U.K.	5	51.05 N	1.48 W
Salisbury, Md., U.S.	38	38.22 N	75.36 W
Salisbury, Zimb.	15	17.50 S	31.03 E
Salmon	48	45.11 N	113.54 W
Salmon ≃	48	45.51 N	116.46 W
Salmon River Mountains ∧	48	44.45 N	115.30 W
Salta	34	24.47 S	65.25 W
Saltillo	31	25.25 N	101.00 W
Salt Lake City	47	40.46 N	111.53 W
Salto	34	31.23 S	57.58 W
Salton Sea ◙	39	33.19 N	115.50 W
Salvador	33	12.59 S	38.31 W
Salween (Nujiang) ≃	26	16.31 N	97.37 E
Salyersville	43	37.45 N	83.04 W
Salzgitter	7	52.10 N	10.25 E
Samar I	25	12.00 N	125.00 E
Samarinda	25	0.30 S	117.09 E
Sambalpur	21	21.27 N	83.58 E
Samoa Islands II	30e	14.00 S	171.00 W
Sámos I	11	37.48 N	26.44 E
Samothrace → Samothráki I	11	40.30 N	25.32 E
Samothráki I	11	40.30 N	25.32 E
Sampit	25	2.32 S	112.57 E
Sam Rayburn Reservoir ◙1	44	31.27 N	94.37 W
Samut Prakan	26	13.36 N	100.36 E
Șan'ā'	17	15.23 N	44.12 E
San Andrés, Isla de I	32	12.32 N	81.42 W
San Angelo	45	31.28 N	100.26 W
San Antonio	45	29.28 N	98.31 W
San Antonio, Cabo ≻	32	21.52 N	84.57 W
San Benito	32	16.55 N	89.54 W
San Bernardino	39	34.06 N	117.17 W
San Bernardino Mountains ∧	39	34.10 N	117.00 W
San Blas, Cape ≻	37	29.40 N	85.22 W
San Carlos de Bariloche	34	41.09 S	71.18 W
San Clemente	39	33.26 N	117.37 W
San Clemente Island I	39	32.54 N	118.29 W
San Cristóbal	33	7.46 N	72.14 W
San Cristóbal I	30a	10.36 S	161.45 E
Sancti-Spiritus	32	21.56 N	79.27 W
Sand Hills ∧2	46	42.00 N	101.00 W
San Diego	39	32.43 N	117.09 W
Sandnes	6	58.51 N	5.44 E
Sandoway	26	18.28 N	94.22 E
Sandpoint	48	48.16 N	116.33 W
Sandusky	38	41.27 N	82.42 W
Sandviken	6	60.37 N	16.46 E
Sandy Springs	43	33.55 N	84.23 W
San Fernando, Esp.	9	36.28 N	6.12 W

Name	Map No.	Lat	Long
Séguédine	14	20.12 N	12.59 E
Seguin	45	29.34 N	97.58 W
Sekondi-Takoradi	14	4.59 N	1.43 W
Selawik	40	66.37 N	160.03 W
Selçuk	11	37.56 N	27.22 E
Seldovia	40	59.27 N	151.43 W
Selichova, Zaliv ⊂	13	60.00 N	158.00 E
Selkirk Mountains ⋏	48	51.00 N	117.40 W
Selma	44	32.25 N	87.01 W
Selvas ➜³	33	5.00 S	68.00 W
Selwyn Mountains ⋏	36	63.10 N	130.20 W
Semara	14	26.44 N	14.41 W
Semarang	25	6.58 S	110.25 E
Seminole	45	35.14 N	96.41 W
Semipalatinsk	13	50.28 N	80.13 E
Sendai, Nihon	22		
	23	38.15 N	140.53 E
Seneca Lake ⊜	38	42.40 N	76.57 W
Senegal (Sénégal) □¹	14	14.00 N	14.00 W
Senja ∎	6	69.20 N	17.30 E
Senmonorom	26	12.27 N	107.12 E
Senneterre	42	48.23 N	77.15 W
Sentinel	45	35.09 N	99.10 W
Seoul			
→ Soŭl	22	37.33 N	126.58 E
Sepi	30a	8.33 S	159.50 E
Sept-Îles (Seven Islands)	41	50.12 N	66.23 W
Sequim	48	48.05 N	123.06 W
Sequoia National Park ♦	39	36.30 N	118.30 W
Seram (Ceram) ∎	25	3.00 S	129.00 E
Seram, Laut (Ceram Sea) ₸²	25	2.30 S	128.00 E
Seremban	26	2.43 N	101.56 E
Serengeti Plain ≌	15	2.50 S	35.00 E
Serowe	15	22.25 S	26.44 E
Sérrai	11	41.05 N	23.32 E
Sète	8	43.24 N	3.41 E
Sete Lagoas	33	19.27 S	44.14 W
Seto-naikai ₸²	23	34.20 N	133.30 E
Sevastopol'	4	44.36 N	33.32 E
Severn ≃	5	51.35 N	2.40 W
Severnaja Dvina ≃	4	64.32 N	40.30 E
Severnaja Zeml'a ∎∎	13	79.30 N	98.00 E
Severodvinsk	4	64.34 N	39.50 E
Severo-Kuril'sk	13	50.40 N	156.08 E
Sevier Lake ⊜	47	38.55 N	113.09 W
Sevilla	9	37.23 N	5.59 W
Seward, Alaska, U.S.	40	60.06 N	149.26 W
Seward, Nebr., U.S.	46	40.55 N	97.06 W
Seward Peninsula ≻¹	40	65.00 N	164.00 W
Seychelles □¹	15	4.35 S	55.40 E
Sfax	14	34.44 N	10.46 E
's-Gravenhage (The Hague)	7	52.06 N	4.18 E
Shāhjahānpur	21	27.53 N	79.55 E
Shām, Jabal ash- ⋏	17	23.13 N	57.16 E
Shamattawa	36	55.52 N	92.05 W
Shamokin	38	40.47 N	76.34 W
Shandī	14	16.42 N	33.26 E
Shanghai	22	31.14 N	121.28 E
Shangqiu	24	34.27 N	115.42 E
Shangrao	24	28.26 N	117.58 E
Shannon ≃	5	52.36 N	9.41 W
Shantou (Swatow)	24	23.23 N	116.41 E
Shaoguan	24	24.50 N	113.37 E
Shaoyang	22	27.06 N	111.25 E
Sharon	38	41.14 N	80.31 W
Shasta, Mount ⋏¹	39	41.20 N	122.20 W
Shasta Lake ⊜¹	39	40.50 N	122.25 W
Shattuck	45	36.16 N	99.53 W
Shaw	44	33.36 N	90.46 W
Shawano	42	44.47 N	88.36 W
Shawnee	45	35.20 N	96.55 W
Shaykh, Jabal ash- ⋏	18	33.26 N	35.51 E
Shebele (Shebelle) ≃	17	0.50 N	43.10 E
Sheberghān	21	36.41 N	65.45 E
Sheboygan	42	43.46 N	87.36 W
Sheffield, N.Z.	29	43.23 S	172.01 E
Sheffield, Eng., U.K.	5	53.23 N	1.30 W
Sheffield, Tex., U.S.	45	30.41 N	101.49 W
Shelburne, N.S., Can.	41	43.46 N	65.19 W
Shelburne, Ont., Can.	42	44.04 N	80.12 W
Shelby, Mont., U.S.	48	48.30 N	111.51 W
Shelby, N.C., U.S.	43	35.17 N	81.32 W
Shelbyville, Ind., U.S.	44	39.31 N	85.47 W
Shelbyville, Ky., U.S.	44	38.13 N	85.14 W
Shenandoah National Park ♦	38	38.48 N	78.12 W
Shenyang (Mukden)	22	41.48 N	123.27 E
Sherbrooke	38	45.25 N	71.54 W
Sheridan	48	44.48 N	106.58 W
Sherman	45	33.38 N	96.36 W
Sherman Station	41	45.54 N	68.26 W
Sherwood	41	46.17 N	63.08 W
Shetland Islands ∎∎	5	60.30 N	1.30 W
Shibīn al-Kawm	14	30.33 N	31.01 E
Shijiazhuang	22	38.03 N	114.28 E
Shikārpur	19	27.57 N	68.38 E
Shikoku ∎	23	33.45 N	133.30 E
Shillong	21	25.34 N	91.53 E
Shimoga	20	13.55 N	75.34 E
Shimonoseki	23	33.57 N	130.57 E
Shīrāz	17	29.36 N	52.32 E
Shizuoka	23	34.58 N	138.23 E
Shkodër	11	42.05 N	19.30 E
Sholāpur	20	17.41 N	75.55 E
Shreveport	44	32.30 N	93.45 W
Shwebo	26	22.34 N	95.42 E
Siālkot	21	32.30 N	74.31 E
Sian			
→ Xi'an	22	34.15 N	108.52 E
Sibasa	16	22.53 S	30.33 E
Šibenik	10	43.44 N	15.54 E
Siberia			
→ Sibir' ➜¹	13	65.00 N	110.00 E
Sibi	21	29.33 N	67.53 E
Sibir' (Siberia) ➜¹	13	65.00 N	110.00 E
Sibiu	11	45.48 N	24.09 E
Sibolga	26	1.45 N	98.48 E
Sichote-Alin' ⋏	13	48.00 N	138.00 E
Sicilia (Sicily) ∎	10	37.30 N	14.00 E
Sicily			
→ Sicilia ∎	10	37.30 N	14.00 E
Sidi bel Abbès	4	35.13 N	0.10 W
Siegen	7	50.52 N	8.02 E
Siěmréab	26	13.22 N	103.51 E
Siena	10	43.19 N	11.21 E
Sierra Blanca Peak ⋏	47	33.23 N	105.48 W
Sierra Leone □¹	14	8.30 N	11.30 W
Sighetul Marmaţiei	11	47.56 N	23.54 E
Sighişoara	11	46.13 N	24.48 E
Sigourney	42	41.20 N	92.12 W
Sīkar	21	27.37 N	75.09 E
Sikasso	14	11.19 N	5.40 W
Sikeston	44	36.53 N	89.35 W
Silchar	21	24.49 N	92.48 E
Silesia □⁹	7	51.00 N	16.45 E
Silĩguri	21	26.42 N	88.26 E
Silistra	11	44.07 N	27.16 E
Silver Bay	42	47.17 N	91.16 W
Silver Bow Park	48	46.01 N	112.28 W
Silver City	47	32.46 N	108.17 W
Simanovsk	13	52.00 N	127.42 E
Simcoe	42	42.50 N	80.18 W
Simcoe, Lake ⊜	42	44.20 N	79.20 W
Simeulue, Pulau ∎	26	2.35 N	96.00 E
Simferopol'	4	44.57 N	34.06 E
Simla	21	31.06 N	77.10 E
Simplon Pass)(	8	46.15 N	8.02 E
Sīnā', Shibh Jazīrat (Sinai Peninsula) ≻¹	17	29.30 N	34.00 E
Sinai Peninsula			
→ Sīnā', Shibh Jazīrat ≻¹	17	29.30 N	34.00 E
Singapore	26	1.17 N	103.51 E
Singapore □¹	25	1.22 N	103.48 E
Sinŭiju	22	40.05 N	124.24 E
Sioux City	46	42.30 N	96.23 W
Sioux Falls	46	43.32 N	96.44 W
Sioux Lookout	36	50.06 N	91.55 W
Siracusa	10	37.04 N	15.17 E
Sirājganj	21	24.27 N	89.43 E
Sisak	10	45.29 N	16.23 E
Siskiyou Pass)(	48	42.03 N	122.36 W
Sisseton	46	45.40 N	97.03 W
Sitka	40	57.03 N	135.14 W
Sittwe (Akyab)	26	20.09 N	92.54 E
Skagerrak ⋃	6	57.45 N	9.00 E
Skagway	40	59.28 N	135.19 W
Skarżysko-Kamienna	7	51.08 N	20.53 E
Skelleftea	6	64.46 N	20.57 E
Skellefteälven ≃	6	64.42 N	21.06 E
Skien	6	59.12 N	9.36 E
Skíros ∎	11	38.53 N	24.32 E
Skokie	42	42.02 N	87.46 W
Skopje	11	41.59 N	21.26 E
Skye, Island of ∎	5	57.15 N	6.10 W
Slavgorod	13	53.00 N	78.40 E

Name	Map No.	Lat ° '	Long ° '
Slavonija ➤¹	10	45.00 N	18.00 E
Slavonski Brod	11	45.10 N	18.01 E
Sleepy Eye	46	44.18 N	94.43 W
Slidell	44	30.17 N	89.47 W
Sligo	5	54.17 N	8.28 W
Sliven	11	42.40 N	26.19 E
Słupsk (Stolp)	7	54.28 N	17.01 E
Smederevo	11	44.40 N	20.56 E
Smiths Falls	42	44.54 N	76.01 W
Smithton	27	40.51 S	145.07 E
Smoky Hill ≃	46	39.03 N	96.48 W
Smolensk	12	54.47 N	32.03 E
Snake ≃	48	46.12 N	119.02 W
Snyder	45	32.44 N	100.55 W
Sobat ≃	17	9.22 N	31.33 E
Sobral	33	3.42 S	40.21 W
Soči	4	43.35 N	39.45 E
Société, Îles de la (Society Islands)			
II	30d	17.00 S	150.00 W
Socorro	47	34.04 N	106.54 W
Soda Springs	48	42.39 N	111.36 W
Soekmekaar	16	23.28 S	29.58 E
Sofia			
→ Sofija	11	42.41 N	23.19 E
Sofija (Sofia)	11	42.41 N	23.19 E
Sognafjorden ⊂²	6	61.06 N	5.10 E
Soissons	8	49.22 N	3.20 E
Söke	11	37.45 N	27.24 E
Şokoto	14	13.04 N	5.16 E
Sologoncy	13	66.13 N	114.14 E
Solomon Islands □¹	1	8.00 S	159.00 E
Solomon Sea ▼²	27	8.00 S	155.00 E
Somalia □¹	17	10.00 N	49.00 E
Sombor	11	45.46 N	19.07 E
Somerset	43	37.05 N	84.36 W
Somerset East	16	32.42 S	25.35 E
Somerset Island I	36	73.15 N	93.30 W
Somosomo	30c	16.46 S	179.58 W
Songkhla	26	7.12 N	100.36 E
Sorel	38	46.02 N	73.07 W
Sorocaba	35	23.29 S	47.27 W
Soroti	15	1.43 N	33.37 E
Sosnovo-Oz'orskoje	13	52.31 N	111.30 E
Sos'va	13	63.40 N	62.06 E
Sŏul (Seoul)	22	37.33 N	126.58 E
South Africa □¹	15	30.00 S	26.00 E
South America ▲¹	1	15.00 S	60.00 W
Southampton	5	50.55 N	1.25 W
Southampton Island I	36	64.20 N	84.40 W
South Bend	44	41.41 N	86.15 W
Southbridge	29	43.49 S	172.15 E
South Carolina □³	37	34.00 N	81.00 W
South China Sea ▼²	22	19.00 N	115.00 E
South Dakota □³	37	44.15 N	100.00 W
Southend-on-Sea	5	51.33 N	0.43 E
Southern Alps ⋏	29	43.30 S	170.30 E
Southern Cross	27	31.13 S	119.19 E
South Georgia I	34	54.15 S	36.45 W
South Haven	42	42.24 N	86.16 W
South Indian Lake	36	56.46 N	98.57 W
South Island I	29	43.00 S	171.00 E
South Orkney Islands II	3	60.35 S	45.30 W
South Pass)(	48	42.22 N	108.55 W
South Platte ≃	37	41.07 N	100.42 W
South Point ⋟	28	39.00 S	146.20 E
South Pole ➤	3	90.00 S	0.00
South Porcupine	42	48.28 N	81.13 W
Southport	5	53.39 N	3.01 W
South Sandwich Islands II	3	57.45 S	26.30 W
South Shetland Islands II	3	62.00 S	58.00 W
South Superior	48	41.46 N	108.58 W
Sovetskaja Gavan'	13	48.58 N	140.18 E
Spain □¹	4	40.00 N	4.00 W
Spanish Fork	47	40.07 N	111.39 W
Spanish North Africa □²	9	35.53 N	5.19 W
Spanish Town	32	17.59 N	76.57 W
Sparks	39	39.32 N	119.45 W
Sparta, Tenn., U.S.	44	35.56 N	85.29 W
Sparta, Wis., U.S.	42	43.57 N	90.47 W
Spartanburg	43	34.57 N	81.55 W
Spárti (Sparta)	11	37.05 N	22.27 E
Spassk-Dal'nij	13	44.37 N	132.48 E
Spencer	46	43.09 N	95.09 W
Spencer Gulf ⊂	28	34.00 S	137.00 E
Split	10	43.31 N	16.27 E
Spokane	48	47.40 N	117.23 W
Spokane ≃	48	47.44 N	118.20 W
Spoleto	10	42.44 N	12.44 E
Spornoje	13	62.20 N	151.03 E
Springbok	16	29.43 S	17.55 E
Springdale, Newf., Can.	36	49.30 N	56.04 W
Springdale, Ark., U.S.	44	36.11 N	94.08 W
Spring Dale, W. Va., U.S.	43	37.53 N	80.48 W
Springer	45	36.22 N	104.36 W
Springfield, Ill., U.S.	44	39.47 N	89.40 W
Springfield, Mass., U.S.	38	42.07 N	72.36 W
Springfield, Mo., U.S.	44	37.14 N	93.17 W
Springfield, Ohio, U.S.	38	39.56 N	83.49 W
Springfield, Oreg., U.S.	44	44.03 N	123.01 W
Springfield, Tenn., U.S.	44	36.31 N	86.52 W
Springfontein	16	30.19 S	25.36 E
Springhill	41	45.39 N	64.03 W
Springs	16	26.13 S	28.25 E
Spruce Knob ⋏	38	38.42 N	79.32 W
Srednekolymsk	13	67.27 N	153.41 E
Sri Gangānagar	21	29.55 N	73.53 E
Sri Lanka □¹	19	7.00 N	81.00 E
Srīnagar	21	34.05 N	74.49 E
Stade	7	53.36 N	9.28 E
Stafford	5	52.48 N	2.07 W
Stalingrad			
→ Volgograd	4	48.44 N	44.25 E
Stamford	38	41.03 N	73.32 W
Standerton	16	26.58 S	29.07 E
Standish	42	43.59 N	83.57 W
Stanger	16	29.27 S	31.14 E
Stanke Dimitrov	11	42.16 N	23.07 E
Stanley Falls ↳	15	0.15 N	25.30 E
Stanovoje Nagorje (Stanovoy Mountains) ⋏	13	56.00 N	114.00 E
Stanovoy Mountains			
→ Stanovoje Nagorje ⋏	13	56.00 N	114.00 E
Starachowice	7	51.03 N	21.04 E
Stara Planina (Balkan Mountains) ⋏	11	43.15 N	25.00 E
Stara Zagora	11	42.25 N	25.38 E
Starke	43	29.57 N	82.07 W
Starogard Gdański	7	53.59 N	18.33 E
State College, Miss., U.S.	43	33.26 N	88.47 W
State College, Pa., U.S.	38	40.48 N	77.52 W
Statesboro	43	32.27 N	81.47 W
Statesville	43	35.47 N	80.53 W
Staunton	38	38.09 N	79.04 W
Stavanger	6	58.58 N	5.45 E
Stavropol'	4	45.02 N	41.59 E
Steamboat Springs	47	40.29 N	106.50 W
Steinkjer	6	64.01 N	11.30 E
Steinkopf	16	29.18 S	17.43 E
Stella	16	26.38 S	24.48 E
Stendal	7	52.36 N	11.51 E
Stepanakert	4	39.49 N	46.44 E
Sterkstroom	16	31.32 S	26.32 E
Sterling, Colo., U.S.	46	40.37 N	103.13 W
Sterling, Ill., U.S.	42	41.48 N	89.42 W
Sterlitamak	4	53.37 N	55.58 E
Steubenville	38	40.22 N	80.37 W
Stevens Pass)(	48	47.45 N	121.04 W
Stevens Point	42	44.31 N	89.34 W
Stewart	36	55.56 N	129.59 W
Stewart Island I	29	47.00 S	167.50 E
Steyr	7	48.03 N	14.25 E
Stillwater	45	36.07 N	97.04 W
Stockholm	6	59.20 N	18.03 E
Stockton	39	37.57 N	121.17 W
Stœng Trèng	26	13.31 N	105.58 E
Stoke-on-Trent	5	53.00 N	2.10 W
Stowe	38	44.28 N	72.41 W
Stralsund	7	54.19 N	13.05 E
Strand	16	34.06 S	18.50 E
Strasbourg	8	48.35 N	7.45 E
Stratford	42	43.22 N	80.57 W
Straubing	7	48.53 N	12.34 E
Streator	42	41.07 N	88.50 W
Stretensk	13	52.15 N	117.43 E
Sturgis	46	44.25 N	103.31 W
Stutterheim	16	32.33 S	27.28 E
Stuttgart, B.R.D.	7	48.46 N	9.11 E
Stuttgart, Ark., U.S.	44	34.30 N	91.33 W
Subotica	11	46.06 N	19.39 E
Suceava	11	47.39 N	26.19 E
Suchana	13	68.45 N	118.00 E
Süchbaatar	22	50.15 N	106.12 E
Suchumi	4	43.01 N	41.02 E
Sucre	33	19.02 S	65.17 W

Name	Map No.	Lat ° '	Long ° '
Sudan □¹	17	15.00 N	30.00 E
Sudbury	42	46.30 N	81.00 W
Sukkur	19	27.42 N	68.52 E
Sula, Kepulauan ‖	25	1.52 S	125.22 E
Sulaimān Range ⋀	21	30.30 N	70.10 E
Sulawesi (Celebes) ▮	25	2.00 S	121.00 E
Sullana	33	4.53 S	80.41 W
Sullivan	44	38.13 N	91.10 W
Sulmona	10	42.03 N	13.55 E
Sulu Archipelago ‖	25	6.00 N	121.00 E
Sulu Sea ▼²	25	8.00 N	120.00 E
Sumatera (Sumatra) ▮	25	0.05 S	102.00 E
Sumatra → Sumatera ▮	25	0.05 S	102.00 E
Sumba ▮	25	10.00 S	120.00 E
Şumbawa ▮	25	8.40 S	118.00 E
Šumen	11	43.16 N	26.55 E
Summerville	43	33.01 N	80.11 W
Summit Lake	36	54.17 N	122.38 W
Sumter	43	33.55 N	80.20 W
Sunbury	38	40.52 N	76.47 W
Sunderland	5	54.55 N	1.23 W
Sundsvall	6	62.23 N	17.18 E
Sunnyvale	39	37.23 N	122.01 W
Suoche (Yarkand)	22	38.25 N	77.16 E
Suordach	13	66.43 N	132.04 E
Superior, Ariz., U.S.	47	33.18 N	111.06 W
Superior, Mont., U.S.	48	47.12 N	114.53 W
Superior, Nebr., U.S.	46	40.01 N	98.04 W
Superior, Wis., U.S.	42	46.44 N	92.05 W
Superior, Lake ⊜	42	48.00 N	88.00 W
Suquṭrā (Socotra) ▮	17	12.30 N	54.00 E
Şūr (Tyre)	18	33.16 N	35.11 E
Surabaya	25	7.15 S	112.45 E
Surakarta	25	7.35 S	110.50 E
Surat	21	21.10 N	72.50 E
Surat Thani (Ban Don)	26	9.08 N	99.19 E
Surendranagar	21	22.42 N	71.41 E
Surgut	13	61.14 N	73.20 E
Surigao	25	9.45 N	125.30 E
Suriname □¹	33	4.00 N	56.00 W
Şurt, Khalīj ⊂	14	31.30 N	18.00 E
Šuryškary	13	65.54 N	65.22 E
Susquehanna ≈	38	39.33 N	76.05 W
Susurluk	11	39.54 N	28.10 E
Sutlej (Satluj) (Langchuhe) ≈	21	29.23 N	71.02 E
Suva	30c	18.08 S	178.25 E
Suwa	23	36.02 N	138.08 E
Suwannee ≈	43	29.18 N	83.09 W
Suways, Qanāt as- (Suez Canal) ⤢	18	29.55 N	32.33 E
Suzhou (Soochow)	24	31.18 N	120.37 E
Svobodnyj	13	51.24 N	128.08 E
Swainsboro	43	32.36 N	82.20 W
Swakop ≈	16	22.38 S	14.36 E
Swan River	36	52.06 N	101.16 W
Swansboro	43	34.36 N	77.07 W
Swansea	5	51.38 N	3.57 W
Swaziland □¹	15	26.30 S	31.30 E
Sweden □¹	4	62.00 N	15.00 E
Sweetwater	45	32.28 N	100.25 W
Świdnica (Schweidnitz)	7	50.51 N	16.29 E
Świnoujście (Swinemünde)	7	53.53 N	14.14 E
Switzerland □¹	4	47.00 N	8.00 E
Syalach	13	66.12 N	124.00 E
Sydney	27	33.52 S	151.13 E
Syktyvkar	4	61.40 N	50.46 E
Sylacauga	44	33.10 N	86.15 W
Sylhet	21	24.54 N	91.52 E
Syracuse	38	43.03 N	76.09 W
Syria □¹	18	35.00 N	38.00 E
Syzran'	4	53.09 N	48.27 E
Szczecin (Stettin)	7	53.24 N	14.32 E
Szczecinek (Neustettin)	7	53.43 N	16.42 E
Szeged	7	46.15 N	20.09 E
Székesfehérvár	7	47.12 N	18.25 E
T			
Tabor	13	71.16 N	150.12 E
Tabora	15	5.01 S	32.48 E
Tacna	33	18.01 S	70.15 W
Tacoma	48	47.15 N	122.27 W
Tadinou	30b	21.33 S	167.52 E
Taegu	22	35.52 N	128.35 E
Taga	30e	13.46 S	172.28 W
Tagus (Tejo) (Tajo) ≈	9	38.40 N	9.24 W
Tahat ⋀	14	23.18 N	5.47 E
Tahlequah	45	35.55 N	94.58 W
Tahoe, Lake ⊜	39	38.58 N	120.00 W
Tahoua	14	14.54 N	5.16 E
Taihape	29	39.40 S	175.48 E
Taihu ⊜	24	31.15 N	120.10 E
T'ainan	24	23.00 N	120.12 E
T'aipei	24	25.03 N	121.30 E
Taiping	26	4.51 N	100.44 E
Taiwan (T'aiwan) □¹	22	23.30 N	121.00 E
Taiyuan	22	37.55 N	112.30 E
Taizhou	24	32.30 N	119.58 E
Tajmyr, Poluostrov ⊁¹	13	76.00 N	104.00 E
Tajšet	13	55.57 N	98.00 E
Tajumulco, Volcán ⋀¹	32	15.02 N	91.55 W
Takaka	29	40.51 S	172.48 E
Takamatsu	23	34.20 N	134.03 E
Takaoka	23	36.45 N	137.01 E
Takapuna	29	36.47 S	174.47 E
Takasaki	23	36.20 N	139.01 E
Takatsuki	23	34.51 N	135.37 E
Takefu	23	35.54 N	136.10 E
Takêv	26	10.59 N	104.47 E
Takla Makan → Talimupendi ⤹²	22	39.00 N	83.00 E
Talara	33	4.34 S	81.17 W
Talaud, Kepulauan ‖	25	4.20 N	126.50 E
Talca	34	35.26 S	71.40 W
Talcahuano	34	36.43 S	73.07 W
Talimupendi (Takla Makan) ⤹²	22	39.00 N	83.00 E
Talladega	44	33.26 N	86.06 W
Tallahassee	43	30.25 N	84.16 W
Tallassee	44	32.27 N	85.54 W
Tallinn	12	59.25 N	24.45 E
Tamale	14	9.25 N	0.50 W
Tamatave	15	18.10 S	49.23 E
Tambej	13	71.30 N	71.50 E
Tambov	12	52.43 N	41.25 E
Tampa	43	27.57 N	82.27 W
Tampa Bay ⊂	43	27.45 N	82.35 W
Tampere	6	61.30 N	23.45 E
Tampico	31	22.13 N	97.51 W
Tamworth	27	31.05 S	150.55 E
Tana, Lake ⊜	17	12.00 N	37.20 E
Tanabe	23	33.44 N	135.22 E
Tananarive → Antananarivo	15	18.55 S	47.31 E
Tandil	34	37.19 S	59.09 W
Tando Ādam	21	25.46 N	68.40 E
Tanega-shima ▮	23b	30.40 N	131.00 E
Tanga	15	5.04 S	39.06 E
Tanganyika, Lake ⊜	15	6.00 S	29.30 E
Tanger (Tangier)	14	35.48 N	5.45 W
Tangshan	22	39.38 N	118.11 E
Tanimbar, Kepulauan ‖	25	7.30 S	131.30 E
Tanjungbalai	26	2.58 N	99.48 E
Tanjungpinang	26	0.55 N	104.27 E
Tanoriki	30b	14.59 S	168.09 E
Tanţā	14	30.47 N	31.00 E
Tanzania □¹	15	6.00 S	35.00 E
Tapachula	31	14.54 N	92.17 W
Tapajós ≈	33	2.24 S	54.41 W
Tāpi ≈	20	21.06 N	72.41 E
Tara	13	56.54 N	74.22 E
Ţarābulus (Tripoli), Lībīya	14	32.54 N	13.11 E
Ţarābulus (Tripoli), Lubnān	18	34.26 N	35.51 E
Ţarābulus (Tripolitania) ⤹¹	14	31.00 N	15.00 E
Taranto	10	40.28 N	17.15 E
Taranto, Golfo di ⊂	10	40.10 N	17.20 E
Tarboro	43	35.54 N	77.32 W
Tareja	13	73.20 N	90.37 E
Târgovişte	11	43.15 N	26.34 E
Tarkio	44	40.27 N	95.23 W
Tarko-Sale	13	64.55 N	77.49 E
Tarkwa	14	5.19 N	1.59 W
Tarnów	7	50.01 N	21.00 E
Tarragona	9	41.07 N	1.15 E
Tarrasa	9	41.34 N	2.01 E
Tarutung	26	2.01 N	98.58 E
Tashi Gang Dzong	21	27.19 N	91.34 E
Tasikmalaya	25	7.20 S	108.12 E
Tasman Bay ⊂	29	41.00 S	173.20 E
Tasmania ▮	28	42.00 S	147.00 E
Tasman Sea ▼²	27	30.00 S	157.00 E
Taštagol	13	52.47 N	87.53 E
Tatarsk	13	55.13 N	75.58 E

Name	Map No.	Lat °′	Long °′
Tatum	45	33.16 N	103.19 W
Taumarunui	29	38.52 S	175.17 E
Taum Sauk Mountain ∧	44	37.34 N	90.44 W
Taunggyi	26	20.47 N	97.02 E
Taupo	29	38.41 S	176.05 E
Taupo, Lake ◎	29	38.49 S	175.55 E
Tauranga	29	37.42 S	176.10 E
Tautira	30d	17.44 S	149.09 W
Tavoy	26	14.05 N	98.12 E
Tavşanlı	11	39.33 N	29.30 E
Tawas City	42	44.16 N	83.31 W
Tawkar	14	18.26 N	37.44 E
Tazewell	43	37.07 N	81.31 W
Tazovskij	13	67.28 N	78.42 E
Te Anau	29	45.25 S	167.43 E
Te Anau, Lake ◎	29	45.12 S	167.48 E
Tecuci	11	45.50 N	27.26 E
Tecumseh	45	35.15 N	96.56 W
Tegucigalpa	32	14.06 N	87.13 W
Tehrān	4	35.40 N	51.26 E
Tehuacán	31	18.27 N	97.23 W
Tehuantepec	31	16.20 N	95.14 W
Tehuantepec, Golfo de ⊂	31	16.00 N	94.50 W
Tehuantepec, Istmo de •³	31	17.00 N	95.00 W
Tekamah	46	41.47 N	96.13 W
Tekirdağ	11	40.59 N	27.31 E
Tekoa	48	47.14 N	117.04 W
Te Kuiti	29	38.20 S	175.10 E
Tel Aviv-Yafo	18	32.04 N	34.46 E
Telescope Peak ∧	39	36.10 N	117.05 W
Teli	13	51.07 N	90.14 E
Tellicherry	20	11.45 N	75.32 E
Telok Anson	26	4.02 N	101.01 E
Témiscaming	42	46.43 N	79.06 W
Temple	45	31.06 N	97.21 W
Temuco	34	38.44 S	72.36 W
Tenāli	20	16.15 N	80.35 E
Ténéré •²	14	19.00 N	10.30 E
Tennant Creek	27	19.40 S	134.10 E
Tennessee □³	37	35.50 N	85.30 W
Tennessee ≃	44	37.04 N	88.33 W
Tenterfield	27	29.03 S	152.01 E
Teófilo Otoni	35	17.51 S	41.30 W
Tepic	31	21.30 N	104.54 W
Teramo	10	42.39 N	13.42 E
Teresina	33	5.05 S	42.49 W
Ternej	13	45.03 N	136.37 E
Terre Haute	44	39.28 N	87.24 W
Terrell	45	32.44 N	96.17 W
Tete	15	16.13 S	33.35 E
Tetovo	11	42.01 N	20.58 E
Tevere (Tiber) ≃	8	41.44 N	12.14 E
Texarkana, Ark., U.S.	44	33.26 N	94.02 W
Texarkana, Tex., U.S.	44	33.26 N	94.03 W
Texas □³	37	31.30 N	99.00 W
Texas City	45	29.23 N	94.54 W
Thabazimbi	16	24.41 S	27.21 E
Thailand □¹	25	15.00 N	100.00 E
Thailand, Gulf of ⊂	26	10.00 N	101.00 E
Thai-nguyen	26	21.36 N	105.50 E
Thames	29	37.08 S	175.33 E
Thames ≃	5	51.28 N	0.43 E
Thāna	20	19.12 N	72.58 E
Thanh-hoa	26	19.48 N	105.46 E
Thanh-pho Ho Chi Minh (Sai-gon)	26	10.45 N	106.40 E
Thásos ∣	11	40.41 N	24.47 E
Thaton	26	16.55 N	97.22 E
Thayetmyo	26	19.19 N	95.11 E
The Dalles	48	45.36 N	121.10 W
The Everglades ≅	43	26.00 N	80.40 W
The Hague			
→ 's-Gravenhage	7	52.06 N	4.18 E
Theodore	27	24.57 S	150.05 E
Theodore Roosevelt Lake ◎¹	47	33.42 N	111.07 W
Thermopolis	48	43.39 N	108.13 W
The Slot ⊔	30a	8.00 S	158.10 E
Thessalía +¹	11	39.30 N	22.00 E
Thessaloníki (Salonika)	11	40.38 N	22.56 E
Thetford Mines	38	46.05 N	71.18 W
Thibodaux	44	29.48 N	90.49 W
Thief River Falls	46	48.07 N	96.10 W
Thielsen, Mount ∧	48	43.09 N	122.04 W
Thimbu	21	27.28 N	89.39 E
Thionville	8	49.22 N	6.10 E
Thíra ∣	11	36.24 N	25.29 E
Thomasville	43	30.50 N	83.59 W
Thompson Falls	48	47.36 N	115.21 W
Thomson	43	33.28 N	82.30 W
Thongwa	26	16.46 N	96.32 E
Thonze	26	17.38 N	95.47 E
Three Forks	48	45.54 N	111.33 W
Thunder Bay	42	48.23 N	89.15 W
Thüringer Wald ⋏	8	50.30 N	10.30 E
Tianjin (Tientsin)	22	39.08 N	117.12 E
Tibesti ⋏	14	21.30 N	17.30 E
Tibet □⁹	22	31.00 N	88.00 E
Tiburón, Isla ∣	31	29.00 N	112.23 W
Tien Shan ⋏	22	42.00 N	80.00 E
Tientsin			
→ Tianjin	22	39.08 N	117.12 E
Tierra del Fuego, Isla Grande de ∣	34	54.00 S	69.00 W
Tifton	43	31.27 N	83.31 W
Tigil'	13	57.48 N	158.40 E
Tigris (Dijlah) ≃	17	31.00 N	47.25 E
Tijuana	31	32.32 N	117.01 W
Tillabéry	14	14.13 N	1.27 E
Tillsonburg	42	42.51 N	80.44 W
Timaru	29	44.24 S	171.15 E
Timbuktu			
→ Tombouctou	14	16.46 N	3.01 W
Timișoara	11	45.45 N	21.13 E
Timmins	42	48.28 N	81.20 W
Timms Hill ∧²	42	45.27 N	90.11 W
Timor ∣	25	9.00 S	125.00 E
Timor Sea ⊤²	27	11.00 S	128.00 E
Tinian ∣	25	15.00 N	145.38 E
Tinsukia	21	27.30 N	95.22 E
Tioga	46	48.24 N	102.56 W
Tipperary	5	52.29 N	8.10 W
Tiquisate	32	14.17 N	91.22 W
Tiranë	11	41.20 N	19.50 E
Tire	11	38.04 N	27.45 E
Tîrgovişte	11	44.56 N	25.27 E
Tîrgu-Jiu	11	45.02 N	23.17 E
Tîrgu Mureş	11	46.33 N	24.33 E
Tîrgu-Ocna	11	46.15 N	26.37 E
Tiruchchirāppalli	20	10.49 N	78.41 E
Tirunelveli	20	8.44 N	77.42 E
Tiruppur	20	11.06 N	77.21 E
Tiruvannāmalai	20	12.13 N	79.04 E
Tisza (Tisa) ≃	11	45.15 N	20.17 E
Titicaca, Lago ◎	33	15.50 S	69.20 W
Titograd	11	42.26 N	19.14 E
Titovo Užice	11	43.51 N	19.51 E
Titusville	43	28.37 N	80.49 W
Tivoli	10	41.58 N	12.48 E
Tlemcen	14	34.52 N	1.15 W
Toba, Danau ◎	26	2.35 N	98.50 E
Tobago ∣	32	11.15 N	60.40 W
Tocantins ≃	33	1.45 S	49.10 W
Toccoa	43	34.35 N	83.19 W
Togo □¹	14	8.00 N	1.10 E
Toiyabe Range ⋏	39	39.10 N	117.10 W
Tokushima	23	34.04 N	134.34 E
Tokuyama	23	34.03 N	131.49 E
Tōkyō	23	35.42 N	139.46 E
Tolbuhin	11	43.34 N	27.50 E
Toledo, Esp.	9	39.52 N	4.01 W
Toledo, Ohio, U.S.	38	41.39 N	83.32 W
Toledo Bend Reservoir ◎¹	44	31.30 N	93.45 W
Toljatti	4	53.31 N	49.26 E
Tomah	42	43.59 N	90.30 W
Tomakomai	23a	42.38 N	141.36 E
Tomaniivi, Mount ∧	30c	17.37 S	178.01 E
Tomaszów Mazowiecki	7	51.32 N	20.01 E
Tombigbee ≃, U.S.	44	31.04 N	87.58 W
Tombigbee ≃, Ala., U.S.	44	31.04 N	87.58 W
Tombouctou (Timbuktu)	14	16.46 N	3.01 W
Tomini, Teluk ⊂	25	0.20 S	121.00 E
Tompkinsville	44	36.42 N	85.41 W
Tomsk	13	56.30 N	84.58 E
Tone ≃	23	35.44 N	140.51 E
Tonga □¹	1	20.00 S	175.00 W
Tongue ≃	48	46.24 N	105.52 W
Tonkin, Gulf of ⊂	26	20.00 N	108.00 E
Tonopah	39	38.04 N	117.14 W
Tønsberg	6	59.17 N	10.25 E
Toowoomba	27	27.33 S	151.57 E
Topeka	46	39.03 N	95.41 W
Torino (Turin)	10	45.03 N	7.40 E
Torokina	30a	6.14 S	155.03 E
Toronto	42	43.39 N	79.23 W
Toros Dağları ⋏	18	37.00 N	33.00 E

Name	Map No.	Lat ° '	Long ° '
Torrens, Lake ⌒	27	31.00 S	137.50 E
Torreón	31	25.33 N	103.26 W
Torres Strait ⊔	27	10.25 S	142.10 E
Torrington	38	41.48 N	73.08 W
Tortona	10	44.54 N	8.52 E
Toruń	7	53.02 N	18.35 E
Tottori	23	35.30 N	134.14 E
Toubkal, Jbel ∧	14	31.05 N	7.55 W
Touggourt	14	33.10 N	6.00 E
Toulon	8	43.07 N	5.56 E
Toulouse	8	43.36 N	1.26 E
Toungoo	26	18.56 N	96.26 E
Tours	8	47.23 N	0.41 E
Townsend	48	46.19 N	111.31 W
Townsville	27	19.16 S	146.48 E
Toyama	23	36.41 N	137.13 E
Toyohashi	23	34.46 N	137.23 E
Toyota	23	35.05 N	137.09 E
Tracy, Calif., U.S.	39	37.44 N	121.25 W
Tracy, Minn., U.S.	46	44.14 N	95.37 W
Tralee	5	52.16 N	9.42 W
Transkei □[9]	15	31.20 S	29.00 E
Transylvania □[9]	11	46.30 N	24.00 E
Transylvanian Alps			
→ Carpaţii Meridionali ⋏	11	45.30 N	24.15 E
Trapani	10	38.01 N	12.31 E
Traverse City	42	44.46 N	85.37 W
Treinta y Tres	34	33.14 S	54.23 W
Trelew	34	43.15 S	65.18 W
Tremblant, Mont ∧	38	46.16 N	74.35 W
Tremonton	47	41.43 N	112.10 W
Trenčín	7	48.54 N	18.04 E
Trento	10	46.04 N	11.08 E
Trenton, Ont., Can.	42	44.06 N	77.35 W
Trenton, N.J., U.S.	38	40.13 N	74.45 W
Tres Arroyos	34	38.23 S	60.17 W
Três Corações	35	21.42 S	45.16 W
Três Lagoas	35	20.48 S	51.43 W
Três Pontas	35	21.22 S	45.31 W
Treviso	10	45.40 N	12.15 E
Trichūr	20	10.31 N	76.13 E
Trier	7	49.45 N	6.38 E
Trieste	10	45.40 N	13.46 E
Triglav ∧	10	46.23 N	13.50 E
Trikala	11	39.34 N	21.46 E
Trincomalee	20	8.34 N	81.14 E
Trinidad	46	37.10 N	104.31 W
Trinidad **I**	32	10.30 N	61.15 W
Trinidad and Tobago □[1]	32	11.00 N	61.00 W
Trinity ⌒	45	29.47 N	94.42 W
Tripoli			
→ Ṭarābulus	14	32.54 N	13.11 E
Trípolis	11	37.31 N	22.21 E
Trivandrum	20	8.29 N	76.55 E
Trnava	7	48.23 N	17.35 E
Troick	4	54.06 N	61.35 E
Trois-Rivières	38	46.21 N	72.33 W
Trompsburg	16	30.01 S	25.46 E
Tromsø	6	69.40 N	18.58 E
Trondheim	6	63.25 N	10.25 E
Troutville	43	37.25 N	79.53 W
Troy, Ala., U.S.	44	31.48 N	85.58 W
Troy, N.Y., U.S.	38	42.43 N	73.40 W
Troy, Ohio, U.S.	38	40.02 N	84.13 W
Troyes	8	48.18 N	4.05 E
Truckee ⌒	39	39.51 N	119.24 W
Trujillo	33	8.07 S	79.02 W
Truro	41	45.22 N	63.16 W
Truth or Consequences (Hot			
Springs)	47	33.08 N	107.15 W
Tryon	43	35.13 N	82.14 W
Tshidilamolomo	16	25.50 S	24.41 E
Tsu	23	34.43 N	136.31 E
Tsuchiura	23	36.05 N	140.12 E
Tsugaru-kaikyō ⊔	23	41.35 N	141.00 E
Tsumeb	15	19.13 S	17.42 E
Tsuruoka	23	38.44 N	139.50 E
Tsuyama	23	35.03 N	134.00 E
Tual	25	5.40 S	132.45 E
Tubarão	34	28.30 S	49.01 W
Tucson	47	32.13 N	110.58 W
Tucumcari	45	35.10 N	103.44 W
Tuktoyaktuk	36	69.27 N	133.02 W
Tula	12	54.12 N	37.37 E
Tulagi	30a	9.06 S	160.09 E
Tulancingo	31	20.05 N	98.22 W
Tulare	39	36.13 N	119:21 W
Tularosa	47	33.04 N	106.01 W
Tulcán	33	0.48 N	77.43 W
Tulcea	11	45.11 N	28.48 E
Tuléar	15	23.21 S	43.40 E
Tullahoma	44	35.22 N	86.11 W
Tulsa	45	36.09 N	95.58 W
Tulun	13	54.35 N	100.33 E
Tumaco	33	1.49 N	78.46 W
Tumany	13	60.56 N	155.56 E
Tumbes	33	3.34 S	80.28 W
T'umen'	13	57.09 N	65.32 E
Tumkūr	20	13.21 N	77.05 E
Tunis	14	36.48 N	10.11 E
Tunisia □[1]	14	34.00 N	9.00 E
Tunja	33	5.31 N	73.22 W
Tuobuja	13	62.00 N	122.02 E
Tuolumne ⌒	39	37.36 N	121.10 W
Tupã	35	21.56 S	50.30 W
Tupaciguara	35	18.35 S	48.42 W
Tupelo	44	34.16 N	88.43 W
Turda	11	46.34 N	23.47 E
Turgutlu	11	38.30 N	27.43 E
Turin			
→ Torino	10	45.03 N	7.40 E
Turkey □[1], As., Eur.	4	39.00 N	35.00 E
Turks and Caicos Islands □[2]	32	21.45 N	71.35 W
Turks Islands **II**	32	21.24 N	71.07 W
Turku (Åbo)	6	60.27 N	22.17 E
Turquino, Pico ∧	32	19.59 N	76.50 W
Turuchansk	13	65.49 N	87.59 E
Tuscaloosa	44	33.13 N	87.33 W
Tuticorin	20	8.47 N	78.08 E
Tutuila **I**	30e	14.18 S	170.42 W
Tuxpan de Rodríguez Cano	31	20.57 N	97.24 W
Tuxtla Gutiérrez	31	16.45 N	93.07 W
Tweed	42	44.29 N	77.19 W
Tweeling	16	27.38 S	28.31 E
Twin Falls	48	42.34 N	114.28 W
Two Rivers	42	44.09 N	87.34 W
Tyler	45	32.21 N	95.18 W
Tyndall	46	42.59 N	97.52 W
Tyndinskij	13	55.10 N	124.43 E
Tyrrhenian Sea (Mare Tirreno) ⌄[2]	10	40.00 N	12.00 E

U

Name	Map No.	Lat ° '	Long ° '
Ubá	35	21.07 S	42.56 W
Ube	23	33.56 N	131.15 E
Uberaba	33	19.45 S	47.55 W
Uberlândia	33	18.56 S	48.18 W
Ubon Ratchathani	26	15.14 N	104.54 E
Ucayali ⌒	33	4.30 S	73.27 W
Udaipur	21	24.35 N	73.43 E
Uddevalla	6	58.21 N	11.55 E
Udine	10	46.03 N	13.14 E
Udon Thani	26	17.26 N	102.46 E
Udża	13	71.14 N	117.10 E
Ueda	23	36.24 N	138.16 E
Ufa	4	54.44 N	55.56 E
Uganda □[1]	15	1.00 N	32.00 E
Ugie	16	31.10 S	28.13 E
Uinta Mountains ⋏	47	40.45 N	110.05 W
Uitenhage	16	33.40 S	25.28 E
Ujiji	15	4.55 S	29.41 E
Ujjain	21	23.11 N	75.46 E
Ujung Pandang (Makasar)	25	5.07 S	119.24 E
Ukiah	39	39.09 N	123.13 W
Ulaan Baatar	22	47.55 N	106.53 E
Ulan Bator			
→ Ulaan Baatar	22	47.55 N	106.53 E
Ulan-Ude	13	51.50 N	107.37 E
Uljanovsk	4	54.20 N	48.24 E
Ulm	7	48.24 N	10.00 E
Ulysses	46	37.35 N	101.22 W
Umeå	6	63.50 N	20.15 E
Umm Durmān (Omdurman)	14	15.38 N	32.30 E
Umnak Island **I**	40	53.25 N	168.10 W
Umpqua ⌒	48	43.42 N	124.03 W
Umtali	15	18.58 S	32.40 E
Umtata	16	31.35 S	28.47 E
Umzinto	16	30.22 S	30.33 E
Unalakleet	40	63.53 N	160.47 W
Unalaska Island **I**	40	53.45 N	166.45 W
'Unayzah	17	26.06 N	43.56 E
Uncompahgre Peak ∧	47	38.04 N	107.28 W
Underberg	16	29.50 S	29.22 E

Name	Map No.	Lat ° '	Long ° '
Ungava, Péninsule d' ⊱¹	36	60.00 N	74.00 W
Ungava Bay ⊂	36	59.30 N	67.30 W
Unimak Island I	40	54.50 N	164.00 W
Union, Mo., U.S.	44	38.27 N	91.00 W
Union, S.C., U.S.	43	34.43 N	81.37 W
Union, W. Va., U.S.	43	37.36 N	80.33 W
Union City	44	36.26 N	89.03 W
Union of Soviet Socialist Republics □¹, As., Eur.	1	60.00 N	80.00 E
Uniontown	38	39.54 N	79.44 W
United Arab Emirates □¹	17	24.00 N	54.00 E
United Kingdom □¹	4	54.00 N	2.00 W
United States □¹	37	38.00 N	97.00 W
University City	44	38.39 N	90.19 W
Upington	16	28.25 S	21.15 E
Upolu I	30e	13.55 S	171.45 W
Upper Arlington	38	40.00 N	83.03 W
Upper Klamath Lake ⊜	48	42.23 N	122.55 W
Upper Red Lake ⊜	46	48.10 N	94.40 W
Upper Volta □¹	14	13.00 N	2.00 W
Uppsala	6	59.52 N	17.38 E
Ural ≃	4	47.00 N	51.48 E
Ural Mountains → Ural'skije Gory ⋏	13	66.00 N	63.00 E
Ural'skije Gory ⋏	13	66.00 N	63.00 E
Urbana, Ill., U.S.	44	40.07 N	88.12 W
Urbana, Ohio, U.S.	38	40.07 N	83.45 W
Urla	11	38.18 N	26.46 E
Uruapan [del Progreso]	31	19.25 N	102.04 W
Uruguaiana	34	29.45 S	57.05 W
Uruguay □¹	33	33.00 S	56.00 W
Uruguay (Uruguai) ≃	34	34.12 S	58.18 W
Uşak	11	38.41 N	29.25 E
Ussurijsk	13	43.48 N	131.59 E
Ust'-Belaja	13	65.30 N	173.20 E
Ust'-Čaun	13	68.47 N	170.30 E
Ústí nad Labem	7	50.40 N	14.02 E
Ust'-Išim	13	57.42 N	71.10 E
Ust'-Kamčatsk	13	56.15 N	162.30 E
Ust'-Kamenogorsk	13	49.58 N	82.38 E
Ust'-Kut	13	56.46 N	105.40 E
Ust'-Maja	13	60.25 N	134.32 E
Usumacinta ≃	31	18.24 N	92.38 W
Utah □³	37	39.30 N	111.30 W
Utah Lake ⊜	47	40.13 N	111.49 W
Utica	38	43.05 N	75.14 W
Utrecht, Ned.	7	52.05 N	5.08 E
Utrecht, S. Afr.	16	27.38 S	30.20 E
Utsunomiya	23	36.33 N	139.52 E
Uvalde	45	29.13 N	99.47 W
Uvat	13	59.09 N	68.54 E
Uvongo Beach	16	30.51 S	30.23 E
Uwajima	23	33.13 N	132.34 E
Uxbridge	42	44.06 N	79.07 W
Uzunköprü	11	41.16 N	26.41 E
V			
Vaal ≃	16	27.40 S	26.09 E
Vaalwater	16	24.20 S	28.03 E
Vaasa (Vasa)	6	63.06 N	21.36 E
Vadsø	6	70.05 N	29.46 E
Vaduz	8	47.09 N	9.31 E
Vaileka	30c	17.23 S	178.09 E
Vākhān ≃	21	37.00 N	72.40 E
Valdez	40	61.07 N	146.16 W
Valdivia	34	39.48 S	73.14 W
Val-d'Or	42	48.07 N	77.47 W
Valdosta	43	30.50 N	83.17 W
Valença	35	13.22 S	39.05 W
Valence	8	44.56 N	4.54 E
Valencia, Esp.	9	39.28 N	0.22 W
Valencia, Ven.	33	10.11 N	68.00 W
Valencia □⁹	9	39.30 N	0.40 W
Valenciennes	8	50.21 N	3.32 E
Valera	33	9.19 N	70.37 W
Valladolid	9	41.39 N	4.43 W
Vallejo	39	38.07 N	122.14 W
Valletta	10	35.54 N	14.31 E
Valley City	46	46.55 N	97.59 W
Valleyfield	38	45.15 N	74.08 W
Valley Station	44	38.06 N	85.52 W
Valparaíso, Chile	34	33.02 S	71.38 W
Valparaiso, Ind., U.S.	44	41.28 N	87.03 W
Vanavara	13	60.22 N	102.16 E
Van Buren	44	35.26 N	94.21 W

Name	Map No.	Lat ° '	Long ° '
Vancouver, B.C., Can.	36	49.16 N	123.07 W
Vancouver, Wash., U.S.	48	45.39 N	122.40 W
Vancouver Island I	36	49.45 N	126.00 W
Vandalia	44	38.58 N	89.06 W
Vanderbijlpark	16	26.42 S	27.54 E
Vandergrift	38	40.36 N	79.34 W
Vänern ⊜	6	58.55 N	13.30 E
Van Reenen	16	28.22 S	29.24 E
Vanrhynsdorp	16	31.36 S	18.44 E
Vanua Levu I	30c	16.33 S	179.15 E
Vanuatu □¹	30b	16.00 S	167.00 E
Vanwyksvlei	16	30.18 S	21.49 E
Vārānasi (Benares)	21	25.20 N	83.00 E
Varangerfjorden ⊂²	6	70.00 N	30.00 E
Vardø	6	70.21 N	31.02 E
Varese	10	45.48 N	8.48 E
Varkaus	6	62.19 N	27.55 E
Varna	11	43.13 N	27.55 E
Vassar	42	43.22 N	83.35 W
Västerås	6	59.37 N	16.33 E
Vatican City (Città del Vaticano) □¹	10	41.54 N	12.27 E
Vatnajökull ⊓	4	64.25 N	16.50 W
Vättern ⊜	6	58.24 N	14.36 E
Växjö	6	56.52 N	14.49 E
Velika Morava ≃	11	44.43 N	21.03 E
Veliko Tǎrnovo	11	43.04 N	25.39 E
Vellore	20	12.56 N	79.08 E
Velva	46	48.04 N	100.56 W
Venado Tuerto	34	33.45 S	61.58 W
Venezia (Venice)	10	45.27 N	12.21 E
Venezuela □¹	33	8.00 N	66.00 W
Venezuela, Golfo de ⊂	33	11.30 N	71.00 W
Venice → Venezia	10	45.27 N	12.21 E
Venterstad	16	30.47 S	25.48 E
Ventura	39	34.17 N	119.18 W
Veracruz [Llave]	31	19.12 N	96.08 W
Verāval	21	20.54 N	70.22 E
Verchneimbatskoje	13	63.11 N	87.58 E
Verchojansk	13	67.35 N	133.27 E
Verchojanskij Chrebet ⋏	13	67.00 N	129.00 E
Verdun, Qué., Can.	38	45.27 N	73.34 W
Verdun, Fr.	8	49.10 N	5.23 E
Vereeniging	16	26.38 S	27.57 E
Vermillion	46	42.47 N	96.56 W
Vermont □³	37	43.50 N	72.45 W
Vernal	47	40.27 N	109.32 W
Vernon	38	41.52 N	72.27 W
Vero Beach	43	27.38 N	80.24 W
Véroia	11	40.31 N	22.12 E
Verona	10	45.27 N	11.00 E
Versailles, Fr.	8	48.48 N	2.08 E
Versailles, Ky., U.S.	44	38.03 N	84.44 W
Verviers	7	50.35 N	5.52 E
Verwoerd Reservoir ⊜¹	16	30.40 S	25.40 E
Vestfjorden ⊂²	6	68.08 N	15.00 E
Vesuvio ⋏¹	10	40.49 N	14.26 E
Viangchan (Vientiane)	26	17.58 N	102.36 E
Viareggio	10	43.52 N	10.14 E
Vicenza	10	45.33 N	11.33 E
Vichy	8	46.08 N	3.26 E
Vicksburg	44	32.14 N	90.56 W
Victoria, B.C., Can.	36	48.25 N	123.22 W
Victoria (Xianggang), H.K.	24	22.17 N	114.09 E
Victoria, Sey.	15	4.38 S	55.27 E
Victoria, Tex., U.S.	45	28.48 N	97.00 W
Victoria, Lake ⊜	15	1.00 S	33.00 E
Victoria Island I	36	71.00 N	114.00 W
Victoria Peak ⋏	32	16.48 N	88.37 W
Victoriaville	38	46.03 N	71.57 W
Victoria West	16	31.25 S	23.04 E
Victorville	39	34.32 N	117.18 W
Vidalia	43	32.13 N	82.25 W
Vidin	11	43.59 N	22.52 E
Vienna → Wien	7	48.13 N	16.20 E
Vierfontein	16	27.03 S	26.46 E
Vietnam □¹	25	16.00 N	108.00 E
Vigo	9	42.14 N	8.43 W
Vijayawāda	20	16.31 N	80.37 E
Vila	30b	17.44 S	168.19 E
Vila Nova de Gaia	9	41.08 N	8.37 W
Vila Velha	35	20.20 S	40.17 W
Vilhelmina	6	64.37 N	16.39 E
Villach	7	46.36 N	13.50 E
Villa Hayes	34	25.06 S	57.34 W

Name	Map No.	Lat ° '	Long ° '
Villahermosa	31	17.59 N	92.55 W
Villa María	34	32.25 S	63.15 W
Villavicencio	33	4.09 N	73.37 W
Ville-Saint-Georges	41	46.07 N	70.40 W
Villeurbanne	8	45.46 N	4.53 E
Vilnius	12	54.41 N	25.19 E
Vincennes	44	38.41 N	87.32 W
Vindhya Range ⚹	21	23.00 N	77.00 E
Vineland	38	39.29 N	75.02 W
Vinh	26	18.40 N	105.40 E
Vinh-long	26	10.15 N	105.58 E
Vinnica	4	49.14 N	28.29 E
Vinson Massif ⯅	3	78.35 S	85.25 W
Virden	36	49.51 N	100.55 W
Virginia, S. Afr.	16	28.12 S	26.49 E
Virginia, Minn., U.S.	42	47.31 N	92.32 W
Virginia □[3]	37	37.30 N	78.45 W
Virginia Beach	43	36.51 N	75.58 W
Virgin Islands □[2]	32	18.20 N	64.50 W
Viroqua	42	43.34 N	90.53 W
Virudunagar	20	9.36 N	77.58 E
Visalia	39	36.20 N	119.18 W
Viscount Melville Sound ☋	36	74.10 N	113.00 W
Vishākhapatnam	20	17.42 N	83.18 E
Visnagar	21	23.42 N	72.33 E
Vista	39	33.12 N	117.15 W
Viti Levu ▮	30c	18.00 S	178.00 E
Vitim ≊	13	59.26 N	112.34 E
Vitória, Bra.	33	20.19 S	40.21 W
Vitoria, Esp.	9	42.51 N	2.40 W
Vitória da Conquista	33	14.51 S	40.51 W
Vittoria	10	36.57 N	14.32 E
Vizianagaram	20	18.07 N	83.25 E
Vladimir	12	56.10 N	40.25 E
Vladivostok	13	43.10 N	131.56 E
Vlorë	11	40.27 N	19.30 E
Vltava ≊	7	50.21 N	14.30 E
Volga ≊	4	45.55 N	47.52 E
Volgograd (Stalingrad)	4	48.44 N	44.25 E
Volgogradskoje Vodochranilišče ⬠[1]	4	49.20 N	45.00 E
Voločanka	13	71.00 N	94.28 E
Vólos	11	39.21 N	22.56 E
Volta, Lake ⬠[1]	14	7.30 N	0.15 E
Volta Redonda	33	22.32 S	44.07 W
Voronež	4	51.40 N	39.10 E
Vorošilovgrad	4	48.34 N	39.20 E
Vosges ⚹	8	48.30 N	7.10 E
Vostočno-Sibirskoje More (East Siberian Sea) ⫶[2]	13	74.00 N	166.00 E
Votuporanga	35	20.24 S	49.59 W
Vraca	11	43.12 N	23.33 E
Vrangel'a, Ostrov ▮	13	71.00 N	179.30 W
Vrede	16	27.30 S	29.06 E
Vryheid	16	29.39 S	30.18 E
Vunisea	30c	19.03 S	178.09 E
W			
Wabash ≊	44	37.46 N	88.02 W
Wabowden	36	54.55 N	98.38 W
Waco	45	31.55 N	97.08 W
Waddeneilanden ▮▮	7	53.26 N	5.30 E
Waddenzee ⫶[2]	7	53.15 N	5.15 E
Waddington, Mount ⯅	37	51.23 N	125.15 W
Wadena	46	46.26 N	95.08 W
Wādī Halfā'	14	21.56 N	31.20 E
Wad Madanī	14	13.25 N	33.28 E
Wagga Wagga	27	35.07 S	147.22 E
Wagoner	45	35.58 N	95.22 W
Wah	21	33.48 N	72.42 E
Wahiawa	39a	21.30 N	158.01 W
Wahpeton	46	46.16 N	96.36 W
Waiau	29	42.39 S	173.03 E
Waihi	29	37.24 S	175.51 E
Waipara	29	43.04 S	172.45 E
Waipukurau	29	40.00 S	176.34 E
Wairoa	29	39.02 S	177.25 E
Wakayama	23	34.13 N	135.11 E
Wa Keeney	46	39.01 N	99.53 W
Wakunai	30a	5.52 S	155.13 E
Wałbrzych (Waldenburg)	7	50.46 N	16.17 E
Wales □[8]	5	52.30 N	3.30 W
Walgett	27	30.01 S	148.07 E
Walhalla	43	34.46 N	83.04 W
Walker ≊	39	38.54 N	118.47 W
Walker Lake ⬠	39	38.44 N	118.43 W
Walkerton	42	44.07 N	81.09 W
Wallaceburg	42	42.36 N	82.23 W
Wallachia □[9]	11	44.00 N	25.00 E
Walla Walla	48	46.08 N	118.20 W
Walsenburg	47	37.37 N	104.47 W
Walterboro	43	32.55 N	80.39 W
Walters	45	34.22 N	98.19 W
Walvisbaai (Walvis Bay)	16	22.59 S	14.31 E
Walvis Bay → Walvisbaai	16	22.59 S	14.31 E
Wanaka	29	44.42 S	169.09 E
Wanganui	29	39.56 S	175.03 E
Wankie	15	18.22 S	26.29 E
Wanxian	22	30.52 N	108.22 E
Wapato	48	46.27 N	120.25 W
Wapello	42	41.11 N	91.11 W
War	43	37.18 N	81.41 W
Warangal	20	18.00 N	79.35 E
Warden	16	27.56 S	29.00 E
Warner Robins	43	32.37 N	83.36 W
Warren, Ark., U.S.	44	33.37 N	92.04 W
Warren, Mich., U.S.	42	42.28 N	83.01 W
Warren, Ohio, U.S.	38	41.14 N	80.52 W
Warren, Pa., U.S.	38	41.51 N	79.08 W
Warrensburg	44	38.46 N	93.44 W
Warrnambool	27	38.23 S	142.29 E
Warsaw → Warszawa, Pol.	7	52.15 N	21.00 E
Warsaw, Ind., U.S.	44	41.14 N	85.51 W
Warsaw, N.C., U.S.	43	35.00 N	78.05 W
Warsaw, Va., U.S.	43	37.57 N	76.46 W
Warszawa (Warsaw)	7	52.15 N	21.00 E
Wasatch Range ⚹	47	41.15 N	111.30 W
Washington, D.C., U.S.	38	38.54 N	77.01 W
Washington, Ga., U.S.	43	33.44 N	82.44 W
Washington, Pa., U.S.	38	40.10 N	80.15 W
Washington □[3]	37	47.30 N	120.30 W
Washington, Mount ⯅	38	44.15 N	71.15 W
Washington Court House	38	39.32 N	83.26 W
Waterbury	38	41.33 N	73.02 W
Waterford	5	52.15 N	7.06 W
Waterloo, Ont., Can.	42	43.28 N	80.31 W
Waterloo, Iowa, U.S.	42	42.30 N	92.20 W
Watertown, N.Y., U.S.	38	43.59 N	75.55 W
Watertown, S. Dak., U.S.	46	44.54 N	97.07 W
Waterville	38	44.33 N	69.38 W
Watonga	45	35.51 N	98.25 W
Watrous	36	51.40 N	105.28 W
Watson Lake	36	60.07 N	128.48 W
Waukegan	42	42.22 N	87.50 W
Waukesha	42	43.01 N	88.14 W
Wausau	42	44.59 N	89.39 W
Waxahachie	45	32.24 N	96.51 W
Waycross	43	31.13 N	82.21 W
Waynesboro, Ga., U.S.	43	33.06 N	82.01 W
Waynesboro, Pa., U.S.	38	39.45 N	77.35 W
Waynesboro, Va., U.S.	43	38.04 N	78.53 W
Waynesville	43	35.29 N	83.00 W
Weatherford	45	32.46 N	97.48 W
Webster	46	45.20 N	97.31 W
Webster Springs	38	38.29 N	80.25 W
Weddell Sea ⫶[2]	3	72.00 S	45.00 W
Weenen	16	28.57 S	30.03 E
Weifang	22	36.42 N	19.04 E
Weirton	38	40.25 N	80.35 W
Weiser	48	44.15 N	116.58 W
Welch	43	37.25 N	81.31 W
Weleetka	45	35.20 N	96.08 W
Welkom	16	27.59 S	26.45 E
Wellington	29	41.18 S	174.47 E
Wells	39	41.07 N	114.58 W
Wellsford	29	36.17 S	174.31 E
Wellston	38	39.07 N	82.32 W
Wels	7	48.10 N	14.02 E
Wenatchee	48	47.25 N	120.19 W
Wendover	47	40.44 N	114.02 W
Wenzhou	24	28.01 N	120.39 E
Weslaco	45	26.09 N	97.59 W
Wessington Springs	46	44.05 N	98.34 W
West Branch	42	44.17 N	84.14 W
West Des Moines	42	41.35 N	93.43 W
Westerly	38	41.22 N	71.50 W
Western Ghāts ⚹	20	14.00 N	75.00 E
Western Sahara □[2]	14	24.30 N	13.00 W
Western Samoa □[1]	30e	13.55 S	172.00 W
Westerville	38	40.08 N	82.56 W